Wilsonian Maritime Diplomacy
1913–1921

Wilsonian Maritime Diplomacy
1913–1921

Jeffrey J. Safford

RUTGERS UNIVERSITY PRESS
New Brunswick, New Jersey

Library of Congress Cataloging in Publication Data

Safford, Jeffrey J   1934–
Wilsonian maritime diplomacy, 1913–1921.

Bibliography: p.   Includes index.
1. United States—Foreign relations—1913–1921.
2. Merchant marine—United States—History.
3. Wilson, Woodrow, Pres. U.S., 1856–1924. I. Title.
E768.S23   387.5′0973   77-13293
ISBN 0-8135-0850-9

For June, Hugh,
Meredith, Alexander, and Brooke

Contents

Preface

Since man initially created them, merchant fleets have been utilized to serve as agents of national interest. The maritime exploits of ancient Phoenicia heralded a steady progression of successful state-supported seaborne pursuits through Venice, Holland, Portugal, and Spain to the massive British Empire. The twentieth century reaffirms this nautical course of history. Today, nations intent upon extending their sovereign concerns abroad take keen interest in the maintenance and operation of their merchant marines. Governments monitor their fleets closely, encourage their growth, furnish them with subsidies, clothe them with protective policies, help them locate trade and cargoes, employ them in national defense, and in numerous and increasing cases vigorously and jealously direct their affairs. Few alternatives appear available—nations determined to achieve a competitive global position have been forced to employ these methods, willingly or not. In this age of extraordinary internationalism, a major consequence has been that world shipping, while essentially a commercial operation, has inevitably been conducted on highly political terms.

Maritime developments in the present decade substantiate this. In an environment where the overseas merchant marine of the United States has fallen behind that of the Soviet Union in tonnage and stands embarrassingly compromised and threatened in international councils by the numerical clout and mercantile aspirations of the Third World, it was predictable that the Merchant Marine Act of 1970 would reemphasize America's avowed determination "to control its own independent, commercial fleet." For maritime growth is not only recognized as necessary to conduct the commercial policy of the world's largest trading nation, but is viewed simultaneously as a vital expression and instrument of United States foreign policy in a world increasingly influenced by hostile political and military rivalries and by economic-philosophic assumptions markedly alien to those underlying American policy. Helen Delich Bentley, former chairman of the Federal Maritime Commission, noted that even Russia comprehended the lessons of history—it could not hope to achieve or maintain greatness without also acquiring major maritime power. Consequently, the Soviet Union's determination to employ its ships "as an inherent instrument of national policy," obligated the United States to utilize its own in the interests of the Free World.

Such concepts, of course, have a long record in the American past; the nation's colonial and early national shipping industry, for example, has received due recognition as a force of international importance. During those salubrious times for the American merchant marine, the fleet was considered a vital commercial resource and object of national pride. Following the Civil War, however, a drastic decline shook the nation's merchant fleet, and the United States fell to all-time lows in global maritime involvement and prestige. All efforts to rectify the situation failed; on the eve of World War I, America's oceangoing merchant fleet constituted only a skeletal 2 percent of the world's deep-sea mercantile marine.

Then followed an amazing renaissance. Within the rationalizing context of the European war, a geometrically enlarged American merchant fleet emerged in record-shattering time. While the unprecedented growth of the fleet was significant in the first instance as a war expedient, the United States government also considered it as a means by which to challenge Great Britain's commercial supremacy on the seas, thereby hoping to influence the conduct of international affairs. Most particularly, the new American fleet was designed to serve as a powerful bargaining agent in the creation of a liberal and pro-American postwar peace. It is the purpose of this book to demonstrate how the administration of Woodrow Wilson, the first modern American administration to reemphasize shipping as an agent in diplomacy, overcame half a century's accumulated handicaps to create and then employ the warborn American merchant marine as a major resource of international political significance.

Acknowledgments

To acknowledge the invaluable assistance I received in the course of this study is without doubt one of my most pleasing tasks. It will be clear at once that I have profited from the work of a number of scholars in the diplomacy of the Wilson period, an indebtedness that I cannot document adequately in my footnotes. Most of the research for this study was done at the Library of Congress; the National Archives; the Hoover Institution on War, Revolution, and Peace; and the Montana State, Notre Dame, Rutgers, and Yale University libraries. I want to thank their staffs for the exceedingly helpful assistance they gave me. I am especially grateful to Kenneth T. Hall, archivist of the United States Shipping Board Papers at the National Archives. The history department at Rutgers University, always a source of cordial assistance and scholarly stimulation, supported this study when it was in a much abbreviated and somewhat differently focused form. Subsequently, my research was facilitated by an American Philosophical Society grant (Penrose Fund) and several Montana State University faculty research grants, these latter through the courtesy of Roy E. Huffman, vice president for research and a special friend of the humanities.

I am inexpressibly indebted to the following friends for ideas, stimulation, encouragement, and constructive criticism: Robert Greenhalgh Albion of Harvard University (emeritus), Robert D. Cuff of York University, George M. Curtis, III, of the John Marshall Papers, Larry R. Gerlach of the University of Utah, Jerry Israel of Illinois Wesleyan University, Burton I. Kaufman of Kansas State University, Benjamin W. Labaree of Williams College, Noel Pugach of New Mexico State University, Hans Schmidt of the University of Zambia, Warren I. Susman of Rutgers University, Charles J. Tull of the University of Indiana at South Bend, David Budlong Tyler of Wagner College (emeritus), and William Appleman Williams of Oregon State University. I am also warmly obliged to colleagues in the history department at Montana State University, particularly Michael P. Malone, Pierce C. Mullen, Richard B. Roeder, and Thomas R. Wessel.

In addition, the editors of the *Pacific Historical Review* and *The Historian* have graciously allowed me the use of materials from articles of mine they have published. Also, thanks are due to Wesleyan University Press for permission to quote from a previously published essay.*

But the greatest of my obligations are to Lloyd C. Gardner of Rutgers University, who as friend and mentor will never fully comprehend the service he rendered by steering me out of administrative work and back into the classroom; to my parents, Hildegard and Raymond M. Safford, for an incalculable list of supports and encouragements; and to my lovely wife, June Billings Safford, whose buoyant spirit and unselfish devotion to this project made everything possible.

* "The American Merchant Marine as an Expression of Foreign Policy: Woodrow Wilson and the Genesis of Modern Maritime Diplomacy," in *The Atlantic World of Robert G. Albion,* ed. Benjamin W. Labaree. Copyright © 1975 by Wesleyan University. Reprinted by permission of Wesleyan University Press.

Chapter I
Prologue

The end of the Civil War signaled the beginning of what has appropriately been called the dark age for the American merchant marine in foreign trade. Whereas American shipping registered in overseas commerce before the war was 2.5 million tons, by 1865 it had declined to 1.5 million tons. Amid the clipper ship boom in 1855, United States shipyards launched over 2,000 new vessels, and Americans spoke optimistically of threatening Great Britain's maritime supremacy. By the cessation of hostilities ten years later, however, such hopes had become mere dreams. In 1860, over 70 percent of all tonnage entering American ports from foreign countries was carried in American bottoms, but by 1866 this had fallen to 44 percent, and three years later to 39 percent. The decline continued at a precipitous rate; by the end of the century, American vessels carried less than 10 percent of all American foreign commerce.[1]

Southern commerce raiders were the most direct cause of the depression in American shipping. With a very small but highly effective fleet of armed cruisers, the Confederacy destroyed 100,000 tons of Northern ships, caused prohibitive war-risk insurance rates, and discouraged foreign shippers from using American vessels during the war. As a result, many owners whose vessels escaped actual damage sought refuge under foreign registry.

1. Robert G. Albion, William A. Baker, and Benjamin W. Labaree, *New England and the Sea*, p. 161; Samuel A. Lawrence, *United States Merchant Shipping Policies and Politics*, pp. 32–33; U.S., Congress, House, Committee on Merchant Marine and Fisheries, *Causes of the Reduction of American Tonnage and the Decline of Navigation Interests*, 41st Cong., 2d sess., Appendix, p. 259 (hereafter cited as *Causes of the Reduction*).

By the war's close, nearly one-third of the entire American deep-sea fleet had been sold or transferred to foreign flags, most notably to the archcompetitor, Great Britain. Moreover, many shipowners proved reluctant to return their vessels to American registry, having found working conditions both infinitely better and less costly under different flags. An irate but shortsighted postwar Congress compounded difficulties by refusing to readmit any of those vessels to the American flag fleet.[2]

The Civil War also presented Great Britain with a golden opportunity to disrupt American foreign trade routes and services. Prior to the war, American shippers turned substantial profits in the carriage of freight and first-class and steerage passengers; after the conflict this work was in the hands of British and other foreign interests. That the English sought to use the war to hamper the activities of the American merchant marine was made abundantly clear when London did not prevent British shipwrights from constructing the *Alabama* and the *Florida,* two of the infamous cruisers the Confederacy commissioned to prey on Union shipping.[3]

Yet, while the Civil War brought about a serious decline, the American merchant marine actually had begun to atrophy at least a decade earlier. The collapse in the late 1850's of the fabulous but seriously overextended clipper ship business, and the failure of the prestigious and subsidized American Collins Line caused largely by mismanagement, sectional politics, and the panic of 1857, marked a visible beginning of the end. In addition, shipbuilding costs had begun to rise rapidly and skilled labor decreased in supply. Although the predominantly wooden American merchant fleet was more cheaply constructed, its value depreciated and repair costs rose at rates double those of foreign iron ships. American stockholders also demanded profits far in excess of those considered just abroad, and the nation's major ports did not provide facilities and services commensurate with the charges they imposed upon American shippers and shipowners.[4] Besides, commer-

2. Albion, Baker, and Labaree, *New England and the Sea,* p. 162; Robert G. Albion and Jennie Barnes Pope, *Sea Lanes in Wartime,* pp. 170–71.

3. Albion, Baker, and Labaree, *New England and the Sea,* pp. 156–58, 163.

4. David Budlong Tyler, *Steam Conquers the Atlantic,* Chapters 15, 22. An excellent analysis of the shipping industry from the Civil War to World War I is John G. B. Hutchins, *The American Maritime Industries and Public Policy, 1789–1914.* For reference in this work to the technical transition in shipping and its effect on the American merchant marine see pp. 432–40, 470–75. Two older but highly informative analyses of the maritime

cial investors had begun to abandon their maritime interests for the more lucrative profits of interior economic development. A House commerce committee subsequently noted: Lacking "sufficient capital of our own to improve our soil, develop our mines and manufactures, build our railroads, carry our government bonds, and own ships for our ocean-carrying trades, all at the same time, capital has sought those investments that would yield the largest returns." Shipping was not among the big gainers and suffered accordingly.[5] To complicate matters, American industrialists girded their businesses with high protective tariffs. Vital materials required for ship construction—cable, anchors, copper, zinc, iron, lead, tin, paints, rope, and canvas—all were placed on the protected lists. In 1870, both the House Committee on Merchant Marine and Fisheries and the chief of tonnage, Joseph Nimmo, recommended duty-free privileges for many of these materials; but save for token reductions the century would wind down with prohibitive tariff walls still standing.[6]

With commercial attention diverted from the sea by internal improvements, high tariffs, and skyrocketing costs, the American merchant marine lost its competitive vitality, falling far astern in the technological revolution that swept the seas at midcentury. Practicing a basic financial conservatism in maritime affairs, Americans still used wooden hulls, paddle wheels, and sails long after their seagoing competitors discarded them for iron, propeller, and steam. Thus while the United States possessed vast industrial strengths, its shipbuilding industries increasingly lost their ability to compete with Great Britain and Germany in the construction of economical and efficient oceangoing vessels. Some claimed that the United States fell behind because its foreign competitors were provided with government subsidies

---

demise are David A. Wells, *The Question of Ships*, Part I, "The Decay of our Ocean Mercantile Marine—Its Cause and Cure"; and Winthrop L. Marvin, *The American Merchant Marine*. A good but strongly free ships oriented study of the politics of shipping is contained in Paul Maxwell Zeis, *American Shipping Policy*.

5. U.S., Congress, House, Committee on Merchant Marine and Fisheries, *Causes of the Decadence of the Merchant Marine*, 46th Cong., 3rd sess., p. 3 (hereafter cited as *Causes of the Decadence*).

6. Tyler, *Steam Conquers the Atlantic*, p. 356; U.S., Congress, House, Committee on Merchant Marine and Fisheries, *Foreign Commerce and Decadence of American Shipping*, 41st Cong., 2d sess., Doc. 111; idem, *Causes of the Reduction*, 41st Cong., 2d sess., Doc. 111, Appendix, p. 259.

to modernize and support their merchant fleets. But the United States had experimented with subsidies in the prewar period with unsatisfactory results. When some lines subsequently appeared capable of turning a profit without government aid, all subsidies to American shipping were discontinued in the early 1870's. Numerous congressional committees and shipbuilding lobbies urged the readoption of a government bounty to be granted to American vessels engaged in foreign trade, but the public had been soured. Instead, the post–Civil War Congress chose the alternatives of supporting tariff barriers and banning foreign-built vessels from registry under the American flag. In addition, Congress punitively denied reentry to American ships transferred during the war. For four decades, high tariffs and restricted registry were the fundamental ingredients of American maritime policy.[7]

At no time did the policy of protection function free from opposition. Throughout this period, there was an incessant struggle between those who sought to retain and strengthen protection and those who sought to abolish it. On the one hand, the shipbuilding industries, represented largely by the Republican party, championed restricted registry, high tariffs, and a reintroduction of government subsidies. These were the only ways, they argued, to compete with foreign ship construction and the only logical approach to the reconstitution of what had been formerly the most extensive enterprise in American business. On the other hand, shipowners and operators, found mainly in the Democratic camp, sought relief from the prohibitively priced American shipbuilding industry by obtaining repeal of the new navigation laws. They maintained that costs would be decreased substantially and the American merchant fleet made more competitive and useful if cheaply built and operated foreign vessels were allowed to carry the nation's foreign trade. Of all the world's maritime states, only the United States failed to employ a free ships policy.

Politics, however, prohibited either policy from wholly materializing. When President Ulysses S. Grant recommended a subsidy as a desirable way to enlarge the merchant marine, his opponents defeated the plan, supporting free ships and arguing that subsidies smacked of Eastern preference to an industry that had long been favored by the G.O.P. The

7. Tyler, *Steam Conquers the Atlantic*, Chapters 15, 21.

debate over the measure was typical of the type of argument that would prevail right up to World War I—an irresolvable conflict over the means to an end. Neither lobby enjoyed any meaningful degree of success. The shipbuilders received protection but were unable to get a clear congressional commitment to subsidy, while the shipowners and operators completely failed to break down the high wall of tariff and restriction. Consequently, both builders and operators suffered, but ultimately the main victims were the producers of exports and the managers of export and import trade.

Many carried the debate another step and argued that the real loss was above all to the whole fabric of national existence—political and social, as well as economic. Chroniclers have done well in describing the awesome growth of the American economy in the post–Civil War era. Huge sums of money and vast amounts of energy were expended in the process of development, and the result was constant agrarian and industrial surplus. The domestic market soon found itself unable fully to absorb the fruits of the nation's productivity. The results were falling prices, unemployment, and a periodically depressed economy, the more serious ramifications of which were most often exhibited in unprecedented labor and agrarian upheaval. Constant employment and remunerative markets appealed to many as logical and desirable alternatives to social disorder; and if local markets had apparently demonstrated an inability to absorb the national glut, foreign markets and efficient and competitive means of access to them would have to be developed.[8]

Both political parties were deeply concerned with this state of affairs. For example, in 1881 only one-sixth of America's exports and imports were transported in American vessels. "Free traders" and protectionists alike scored the situation as an unbecoming and most serious circumstance. John Kasson, an influential diplomat and inveterate proponent of reciprocity, thus demanded new oceanic services, maintaining that unless markets and ships were obtained the nation's eyes would "soon look inward upon discontent."[9] An eminent free ships advocate and nationally renowned econ-

8. See, for example, Ray Ginger, *Age of Excess;* Samuel P. Hays, *The Response to Industrialism, 1885–1914;* Walter LaFeber, *The New Empire;* Thomas J. McCormick, *China Market;* Milton Plesur, *America's Outward Thrust;* William A. Williams, *The Roots of the Modern American Empire.*

9. John A. Kasson, "The Monroe Doctrine in 1881."

our own grease."[10] Republicans readily agreed: President Chester A. Arthur omist, David Aimes Wells, remarked, "We are certain to be smothered in expressed extreme dissatisfaction with the decline, and the Republican-dominated House Committee on Commerce warned that unless new markets were established and the merchant marine revived there would be no way "to prevent an overstocked market, and a consequent depression of business."[11] John Roach, one of the nation's largest shipbuilders and a prominent lobbyist for subsidy and protection, argued that, "block up the road to markets for a year through foreign complications, and widespread bankruptcy and ruin would result." The only way to avoid such complications was "to control the carrying of our products by owning and being able to build ships."[12]

Roach's concern for "foreign complications" underscored yet an additional issue of importance to the merchant marine movement. The need for American ships to expedite overseas commerce was serious enough: Add an oceanic war to that and the problem could be disastrously compounded. A special joint congressional committee elaborated in 1882: As the American merchant marine declined, American shippers had become increasingly beholden to British transports, but a war between Great Britain and any other power capable of putting warships to sea would make an already ruinous situation infinitely worse, for American exports and imports in British bottoms would be "liable to capture and confiscation." American ships under British registry, or any other registry involved in war, would suffer a similar fate.[13] Such reasoning strengthened the overall drive for a permanent merchant marine under American flag.

The issue also helped prompt bipartisan support for the modernization and expansion of the United States Navy, one of the newer and more influential voices to join the maritime debate. No one better epitomized the relationship between naval expansion and commercial growth than Admiral

10. Quoted in David M. Pletcher, *The Awkward Years*, p. 143.
11. James D. Richardson, ed., *A Compilation of the Messages and Papers of the Presidents, 1787–1897*, 8:63; U.S., Congress, House, Committee on Merchant Marine and Fisheries, *Causes of the Decadence*, 46th Cong., 3d sess., pp. 2, 14.
12. John Roach, "Shall Americans Build Ships?" Milton Plesur discusses maritime policy in the 1880's in *America's Outward Thrust*, pp. 93–98.
13. U.S., Congress, House, Committee on Merchant Marine and Fisheries, *American Shipping*, 47th Cong., 2d sess., H. Rept. 1827, p. 13.

Alfred Thayer Mahan. Mahan's literary talent and military position brought him national and international fame, and he played an important role in generating maritime interest. Mahan believed that America's surplus production had created a situation guaranteeing the eventuality of a worldwide struggle for control of the international marketplace, a struggle for national solvency in which the navy was destined to play a determining role. Accordingly, Mahan's plan for external expansion called for foreign markets, a merchant marine to service them, and a navy—equipped with a mercantile auxiliary—to protect both.[14] Under President Benjamin Harrison's aegis, all aspects of Mahan's plan received unprecedented encouragement. The result in terms of a mercantile fleet was the passage of the Merchant Marine Act of 1891, the first serious effort to develop a system of steamship lines under American contract. But the act proved ineffective because its provisions for subsidy payments were too inflexible and because only American-built ships, an increasing rarity, were eligible for federal aid.

The antiprotection lobby received considerable support from agrarian circles. Combining new scientific knowledge with technological advances and improved marketing techniques, the post–Civil War farmer produced enormous surpluses in a diminishing domestic marketplace. As a result, few segments of the late nineteenth-century economy clamored more for foreign outlets than agriculture and its representatives; and the more the farmer utilized the new business methods the more he found himself dependent upon other spokes in the economic wheel. Of paramount importance to him was efficient and cheap transportation. Central to the farmer's concern were the national railways and internal waterway systems. Consequently, he lobbied for nondiscriminatory and predictable rates that did not fluctuate wildly according to season and the money supply centered in the Northeast. The historic refusal of Wall Street and the railroads to yield to that de-

14. Alfred Thayer Mahan, *The Interest of America in Sea Power*, pp. 3–27; idem, *The Influence of Seapower upon History, 1660–1783*, p. 26; LaFeber, *New Empire*, pp. 85–94. Peter Karsten questions LaFeber's interpretation of Mahan, arguing that Mahan was primarily a strong navy advocate who used commercial arguments to gather popular support. See Karsten, *The Naval Aristocracy*, pp. 338–39. Nevertheless, Mahan's works stressed the need for commercial expansion. Even though Mahan was persuaded later in the 1890's that foreign merchant vessels could serve the navy's needs satisfactorily, his initial insistence upon expanded transportational services had an important positive effect upon the campaign for an American merchant marine.

mand and the agrarian's consequent assault on their position shaped much of late nineteenth-century American history. But the restrictions on his business the farmer faced involved more than internal transportation; he realized early that his access to the international marketplace was adversely affected by high tariffs and the direct influence of protection on the demise of American shipping in foreign trade. In this respect, even the railroads and the farmer's other traditional enemies, the millers and meat processors, agreed—the monopoly of Great Britain and Germany over oceanic shipping and overseas freight rates severely handicapped all. Consequently, together they pushed for improved American shipping services, even though they might have clashed over preferable ways to implement their expansion.[15]

It was no coincidence that the phenomenon of populism, the political front for the farmers' economic grievances in the 1880's and 1890's, paralleled the antisubsidy movement. Rural America argued that subsidy and protection posed serious threats to the integrity of laissez-faire capitalism. Espousing the arguments of free enterprise, the farmer viewed the shipping industries as just one more segment of the national economy. On the same basis that he could advocate government regulation of the railroads, the farmer could argue that the shipping industries needed to be stripped of their protection; both measures would serve to democratize the economy. In short, the agriculturalist demanded that government abandon subsidy, rescind the registration laws, and adopt a free ships policy. The House minority report to the Merchant Marine Act of 1891 clearly stated these fundamental concerns.

> At this time no industry is suffering such depression as that of agriculture. From every section of the United States petitions have been flowing into Congress from organized farmers' associations depicting the deplorable condition of their business and asking Congress for legislation that will relieve them of the burden of excessive taxation and unjust laws. The attempt is made to convert the farmers to the support of this measure [the Merchant Marine Act] by the alluring statement that it will furnish a new market for the products of the farm. The farmer has been beguiled with the alleged advantages of the "home market" until his farm is mortgaged and he has become debt-ridden, discouraged, and disgusted with the whole

15. See, for instance, Williams, *Roots of American Empire;* Howard R. Schonberger, *Transportation to the Seaboard.*

policy of protection which creates a privileged class of the few at the expense of the many. That it is the object of the promoters of this scheme to restore our merchant marine to the seas and to thereby create a better market for our products may well be doubted. Both of these objects, in the opinion of the minority of this committee, may better be attained by means which will not create additional burdens upon the people, but will lighten those burdens, and that is the repeal of all laws in restraint of trade.

The farming industry, and all other industries as well, would have the same right to be subsidized, and if subsidies are to be granted upon the ground that the business of navigating ships does not pay without Government aid, the farmer has as much right to demand that the Government pay him a subsidy upon the products of his farm that his business may become profitable. The subsidized ship would be useless to the American commerce without farm products to be transported to foreign markets, and the ships are as much dependent upon the farm products as the farmer is upon the ships in getting his products to market.[16]

Serious financial disorder and crisis as the result of the panic of 1893 served to augment the farmer's anguish, but he could not get the upper hand. The conflict between free ships and nondiscrimination on the one hand, and subsidy and high tariffs on the other, maintained its intensity—so much so that even the nationalizing effect of the Spanish-American War and President William McKinley's extraordinary appeal for nonpartisanship were unable to resolve the impasse.

McKinley's ascendancy seemed destined to rule out such an outcome. Under his administration, business was vigorous, confident, and continuously prosperous. Agriculture produced healthy crop dividends, the defeat of "free silver" fostered confidence, and American iron and steel became dominant in the international market. In addition, investment capital increased geometrically, and United States foreign trade balances attained such volume that the European financial press began to warn of the "American invasion" and even of the "American peril."[17] Much of this energy

16. U.S., Congress, House, *American Merchant Marine in the Foreign Trade,* 51st Cong., 1st sess., H. Rept. 1210, pp. xxxix, xli.

17. Alexander D. Noyes, *Forty Years of American Finance,* Chapter 7. The standard accounts of the "invasion" are found in Christopher Furness, *The American Invasion;* and William T. Stead, *The Americanization of the World.* Two good accounts by Americans closely related to the expanding economy are Frank A. Vanderlip, *The American Commercial Invasion of Europe;* and Carroll D. Wright, "The Commercial Ascendancy of the United States."

was released because McKinley's appeal for nonpartisanship removed business from the political arena. Thus, George J. Baldwin, a prominent southern Democrat and traction and utilities magnate, could remark that "the country demands McKinley and the Republican principles because of their sound business views." In Baldwin's opinion, the time had passed for sentimental opposition to the G.O.P.[18] Correspondingly, the time appeared propitious for breaking the political deadlock over maritime matters.

A major demonstration of this came in 1899–1900 during the hearings of the Industrial Commission, a partly congressional, partly public panel created by Congress to investigate combinations in restraint of trade on a nonpartisan basis. The commission demonstrated a strong concern with the economic crises of the 1890's and the narrowing domestic marketplace. For these reasons, it favored the development of a merchant marine.[19] Witness after witness, agrarian and industrial alike, testified to the inadequacy of existing transportation facilities for foreign trade. In fact, the evidence presented in the nineteen-volume report constitutes one of the most impressive testments on record to national agreement on behalf of a merchant marine. The commission concluded that "the great increase in domestic production in the United States, providing a surplus for foreign exportation, [required] more and better means of transportation," and specifically an ocean steamship network unilaterally controlled by American ownership.[20]

The outcome of the Spanish-American conflict provided additional cause for the development of a merchant marine. Islands acquired as a result of the war supplied not only new markets but also the modus operandi for exploiting even newer markets, especially those of the Orient. In addition, the responsibility of protecting the new island outposts fostered a national defense argument that added weight to the case of those who sought a naval auxiliary. Even the antiimperialists argued the commercial necessity for a merchant marine as the result of America's new world position.

18. Baldwin to Peter O. Knight, November 12, 1900, George J. Baldwin Papers.

19. See S. N. D. North, "The Industrial Commission"; Daniel A. Tompkins, *American Commerce, Its Expansion,* Preface; idem, "Markets for American Cotton Goods," an address before the New England Cotton Manufacturers' Association, Washington, D.C., October 19, 1900, Daniel Augustus Tompkins Papers, Southern Historical Collection (hereafter cited as SHC).

20. U.S., Industrial Commission, 1899–1902, *Final Report,* 19:576–79.

The outbreak of war in South Africa added still another stimulus for a national fleet. The Boer War (1899–1902) prompted Great Britain to withdraw a substantial number of its merchant vessels from foreign trade in order to support the British military forces in the South Atlantic. The resulting impact on freight rates and service was so severe, especially in 1900 on the northeast coast of the United States, that a congressional committee subsequently claimed that the Boer War had been paid for by American exporters.[21] These two international events spurred Capitol Hill shipping advocates to propose several new subsidy bills, all of which pointed to the surplus problem and the need to eliminate once and for all American dependence upon foreign vessels.

Wall Street's investments in oceanic shipping seemed to support congressional sentiments. In 1901, J. Pierpont Morgan astonished the world by purchasing the British Leyland Line, which had an aggregate tonnage that alone equaled the tonnage of all American steel screw steamers employed in foreign trade the previous year. Many American businessmen rejoiced, even though Morgan retained the fleet under British registry. Paul Reinsch, a noted economist and later Woodrow Wilson's minister to China, epitomized the reception: "The time of the industrial merchant adventurer is over, in these days of general consolidation there is no activity more favorable . . . than the merchant marine."[22] The business-conscious United States commissioner of navigation, E. T. Chamberlain, added that Morgan's purchase "refuted the theory that it is a matter of national indifference whether foreign interests or American interests control our ocean transportational facilities for exports."[23]

McKinley himself was convinced that the stage was set for the creation of a national merchant fleet. His reelection in 1900 enhanced his hopes for enlightened colonial policies, reciprocal trade agreements, and, in particular, extended maritime service—about which McKinley repeatedly emphasized his conviction that the external absorption of American surpluses was dependent on a solution to the maritime problem. Perhaps his most forceful

---

21. Lawrence, *Merchant Shipping Policies*, pp. 33–34.
22. Paul S. Reinsch, "The Merchant Marine of the World."
23. U.S., Commerce Department, *Annual Report of the Commissioner of Navigation for the Fiscal Year Ended June 30, 1901*, p. 33.

statement on this point was delivered in Buffalo on September 5, 1901, the very day he was mortally wounded by an anarchist.

> Our capacity to produce has developed so enormously and our products have so multiplied that the problem of more markets requires our urgent and immediate attention. . . . One of the needs of the times is to direct commercial lines from our vast fields of production to the fields of consumption that we have but barely touched. Next in advantage to having the thing to sell is to have the convenience to carry it to the buyer. We must encourage our merchant marine. We must have ships. They must be under the American flag, built and manned and owned by Americans.[24]

But nothing came of it. Despite the overwhelming support for the establishment of a merchant marine, no satisfactory shipping policy could be achieved. With McKinley's death, the Republican majority fell back on its theory that costs prohibited the economical construction and operation of American ships and that high tariffs and subsidization were the only feasible policy. This was a narrow and largely political and sectional view, a position impassioned less with national concern than with the localized needs of the shipbuilding industry. On the other hand, most Democrats and other low-tariff advocates took a broader view, arguing for a merchant marine in consideration of its functions not as one industry but as an instrument of foreign trade. Above all, they maintained, was the whole issue of tariffs. One could not expect to dispose of the nation's surpluses without accepting the premise central to those advocating reciprocal trade: the need to buy as well as to sell. But high tariffs fostered retaliation, not cooperative trade agreements. The cost factor could also be solved, they suggested, by repealing the navigation laws, the backbone of maritime protection and special interest. For instance, when a subsidy bill came before a congressional committee in 1902, the Democratic minority argued successfully that it represented class legislation—favoring specific moneyed interests without recourse to the public welfare: "The industrial mechanic, the frugal farmer, the busy merchant, and the toiling laborer are entitled to as much consideration at the hands of the Government as the shipowners."[25] A similar fate

---

24. James D. Richardson, ed., *A Supplement to a Compilation of the Messages and Papers of the Presidents,* pp. 292–96.
25. U.S., Congress, Senate, *Minority Report,* 57th Cong., 1st sess., Rept. 201.

befell the recommendations of the Merchant Marine Commission of 1904–1905 which made the basic blunder of ignoring the agriculturalists and artisans and confining its hearings almost exclusively to the testimony of the carriers and shipbuilders.[26]

More important, President Theodore Roosevelt's own tariff policy did nothing to break the deadlock. In fact, with the maritime problem tied unalterably to the policy of protection, Roosevelt shunted the shipping question off to the side, reasoning that any confrontation with the problem of tariffs and reciprocity would throw his administration on the rocks. House majority whip, Joe Cannon, remarked, "we know from long experience that no matter how great an improvement the new tariff may be it almost always results in the party in power losing the following election."[27] Consequently, Roosevelt branded protection a hot issue and neatly closeted the question. As a result, by 1906 tariff inflexibility was one of the major concerns of the American exporter. Among other difficulties, Japan had joined a growing list of nations engaged in subsidy, and serious troubles appeared imminent in German tariff reprisals. The latter shaped up as a first-class obstacle to American export interests. Reciprocity gained new allies, and Roosevelt's reluctance to acknowledge the problem drew considerable criticism. "To delay now," a prominent grain exporter impatiently remarked, "when we have the opportunity to win our share of foreign commerce by granting simply a 'quid pro quo,' may entail great loss in the future."[28] The chairman of the Reciprocal Tariff League, A. H. Sanders, observed that while American grain and beef industries strained at the seams with surpluses, the German consumer couldn't buy their products because the Congress and the Reichstag stood between him and the American supply. "If Congress delays," he argued, "the opportunity will be virtually lost. . . . Still, we are told to wait."[29]

But Roosevelt could not be persuaded to alter his tariff strategy. Arguing for patience late in 1907, he told commercial interests that he intended to postpone tariff matters for the duration of his term, remarking that the

26. U.S., Merchant Marine Commission, *Report of the Merchant Marine Commission.*
27. Quoted in William Henry Harbaugh, *The Life and Times of Theodore Roosevelt,* p. 230.
28. Louis Muller, "Our Tariff in its Relations to the Grain Trade."
29. Alvin H. Sanders, "Reciprocity with Continental Europe."

tariff "can not with wisdom be dealt with in a year preceding a Presidential election, because . . . experience has conclusively shown that at such a time it is impossible to get men to treat it from the standpoint of the public good." As he saw it, the most sensible time to deal with the issue would be immediately after such an election.[30] That meant that not only tariff but maritime matters as well would have to wait for more than a year, or more probably until March 1909 when a new administration took office.

President William Howard Taft's handling of the tariff proved out Roosevelt's and Cannon's warnings. The Payne–Aldrich tariff of 1909 that Taft naively termed "a good bill and real downward revision,"[31] turned out to be nothing more than another protectionist horse trade deceivingly disguised by the rhetoric of technicality. Upon close examination, the measure actually displayed a scheme of high rates unsuitable to serve as an active agent in the acquisition of foreign markets. The country soon perceived that it had been hoodwinked again by the protectionists. As a powerful weapon in the hands of disgruntled Progressives, the tariff issue was projected into the congressional campaign of 1910. On this rock they had placed in their own path the keel of the Republicans' ship of state was broken. The trouncing administered the G.O.P. in the election of 1910 by Democrats and Progressives sounded the death knell for subsidy and paved the way for a policy of free ships and discrimination.

Significantly, big business took a position in line with Democratic and Progressive sentiment. In 1907, the National Association of Manufacturers argued strongly for subsidy; by 1910 it was giving strong consideration to a free ships position.[32] In the same year, the Merchant Marine League, established by Republican national chairman Mark Hanna and supported entirely by corporate industry, believed "that our foreign-going merchant marine will never be restored by any method of direct protection." The Merchant Marine League proposed a discriminatory measure instead.[33] The National Marine League adopted a similar policy. On the basis of such thinking, a free ships provision was nearly written into the Republican

---

30. United States, Department of State, *Papers Relating to the Foreign Relations of the United States, 1907*, pp. xx–xxi (hereafter cited as *FR* plus year).

31. Quoted in Harbaugh, *Life of Theodore Roosevelt*, p. 365.

32. Winthrop L. Marvin to Daniel Augustus Tompkins, January 14, 1910, Tompkins Papers, SHC.

33. John A. Penton to Tompkins, May 9, 1910, Tompkins Papers, SHC.

party's last subsidy measure in 1911. In the following session, Democrats introduced a limited free ships bill that would have cancelled those measures of the navigation laws restricting the registry of foreign vessels in American overseas trade. After much debate, the measure was attached to the more important bipartisan Panama Canal bill which was already predicated on reserving toll-free use of the Isthmian short cut for the American coastwise trade.

The Panama Canal bill was the product of two closely related concerns. The first was long lived and related to the opportunities American exporters and importers believed were available to them in the burgeoning Latin American market. The second argued the need to develop an overseas merchant marine in order to maximize American participation in Latin American trade, which became increasingly likely with the imminent opening of the new canal. Agitation for these concerns began under the Maine statesman, James G. Blaine, in the 1880's and 1890's and was accentuated by a series of Pan-American conferences and the labors of Elihu Root, Roosevelt's secretary of state. With the commencement of actual work on the canal in 1904, appetites for both Latin American trade and augmented shipping services reached voracious levels.

Taft hammered away at the issue throughout his administration. The relationship between the lack of American shipping and the canal was recognized as a major problem. As a veteran diplomat, Henry White, put it, "There is but one way—and one way only—by which that intercourse can be placed on a proper footing, and that is by ships of our own."[34] The National Association of Manufacturers termed the situation incongruous and a terrible indictment—the United States appeared to be building the canal at a cost of $300 million solely to benefit the foreign trade networks and merchant marines of Germany and England.[35] Congressional opinion was summarized vividly by one fiery Progressive who argued that the only way to remedy the maritime and Latin American trade problem was to "obliterate the obstacles [and] tear down the barriers."[36]

The maritime provisions of the Panama Canal bill were structured to do

34. Henry White, "The Fourth International Conference of the American States."
35. National Association of Manufacturers, "Report of the Committee on the Merchant Marine," 1909, Tompkins Papers, Library of Congress (hereafter cited as LC).
36. Remarks of William Sulzer (House, N.Y.), *Congressional Record*, House, 61st Cong., 1st sess., July 8, 1909, p. 4318.

that precisely. The bill's central features extended a rebate on tolls to American vessels in the coastwide trade, in addition to containing a free ships provision that allowed foreign ships not under five years of age to register under the American flag for use in overseas trade. That trade expansionists were fixed on discrimination was indicated by the lengths to which they were prepared to go to remedy the shipping problem, for the tolls rebate clause was construed in clear violation of the Hay–Pauncefote Treaty of 1901. The dispute turned on a clause in the treaty which stated that

> the Canal shall be free and open to the vessels of commerce and of war of all nations . . . on terms of entire equality, so that there shall be no discrimination against any such nation, or its citizens or subjects, in respect of the conditions or charges of traffic, or otherwise. Such conditions and charges of traffic shall be just and equitable.[37]

The meaning of this clause had been clear in 1901. Great Britain secured it as compensation for voiding the old Clayton–Bulwer Treaty of 1850 which stipulated that the two powers would cooperate in constructing an Isthmian canal. But now that the canal was nearing completion after the expenditure of vast sums of American money and physical energy, American expansionists took a common position that the nation could interpret the equal terms clause as meaning equality for all nations except the United States. Lewis Nixon, a member of the United States delegation to the Fourth Pan-American Conference and also a leading shipbuilder, held for the majority that "we cannot regain our rightful share of our own carriage without displeasing others who now think they are in possession of vested rights in our commerce."[38] Taft insisted, despite strenuous British objection, on signing the discriminatory measure, and Progressives and Democrats backed him wholeheartedly. Congress passed the bill with comfortable margins on August 21, 1912. But the act was not applicable until the canal was completed sometime in 1914. When President Taft refused to refer the matter to international arbitration on the realistic grounds that the United States would probably lose, it became clear that he had bequethed a hornet's nest to his successor in the White House.[39]

37. Ruhl J. Bartlett, ed., *The Record of American Diplomacy*, p. 398.
38. Lewis Nixon, "Panama Canal Tolls."
39. Henry F. Pringle, *The Life and Times of William Howard Taft*, 2:650–51.

Chapter II

The Wilsonians Come to Power

Few could have come to office better prepared to unravel the tangled affairs of the Taft administration than Woodrow Wilson. The new president's tasks were facilitated by a favorable set of political circumstances. Foremost, the worst impediments to progress under Taft had been eradicated—bossism and a split Congress. In 1910, midwestern progressives had challenged and successfully shorn Joe Cannon of his almost dictatorial control over the House. A partial Democratic control of Congress achieved that year was broadened to large majorities in both houses in 1912. Furthermore, good numbers on the losing side, namely La Follette Progressives and Roosevelt Bull Moosers, sympathized with Wilson on the need for reform legislation. Indeed, save for the conservative remnant of the G.O.P., the vast majority of the electorate sought reform, especially in currency and protection matters. Republican and Democratic progressives shared one in common, above all the others—together they demanded foreign trade expansion as the sine qua non of the nation's economic welfare. Lowered tariffs, reciprocal trade, a big navy, and an expanded merchant marine were high on their list of priorities.[1] By virtue of these circumstances, it simply required that Wilson advance a strong leadership capable of synthesizing congressional and public attitudes. This the new president did admirably.[2]

1. Robert Seager, II, "The Progressives and American Foreign Policy, 1898–1917," pp. 198–99; Arthur S. Link, *The Road to the White House*, Chapter 14.
2. The best account of the political circumstances upon Wilson's ascension to the White House and the manner in which he capitalized on them is contained in Arthur S. Link, "Woodrow Wilson: The Philosophy, Methods, and Impact of Leadership," in *Woodrow Wilson and the World of Today*, ed. Arthur P. Dudden, pp. 1–21.

From the outset, Woodrow Wilson determined to employ the government as a positive force in the nation's economy in order to protect and strengthen the free enterprise system. For he believed that the profit motive directed through private enterprise was a manifestation of natural law as it related to the political economy. The success of private, competitive enterprise would be the crucial determinant of the vitality of the republican state—its freedoms, institutions, and prosperity. Consequently, Wilson labored to strengthen America's economic growth and expansion. To accomplish this, he set out through government to establish an unimpeded flow of trade and eliminate artificial barriers to it. These assumptions were as basic to Wilson's foreign policy as they were in their application at home.[3]

The primary themes of Wilson's foreign policy concepts can be outlined briefly. Wilson supported American expansion into the foreign marketplace as early as the turn of the century. His last scholarly works are replete with arguments that the United States had, by necessity, to crack the shell of isolation for active participation in world affairs. America's access to the markets of the globe was mandatory—to which "diplomacy, and if need power, must make an open way. Sharp struggles" could be expected in the combat for that trade.[4] Wilson's adherence to Frederick Jackson Turner's frontier thesis added emphasis to these arguments. No sooner had Americans faced the realities of a closing continental frontier, Wilson observed, than they made "new frontiers" for themselves beyond the surrounding seas. Wilson viewed the Spanish-American War as a dynamic and natural extension of that frontier thrust, as an outlet for the nation's industrial energies, and as a safety valve for its social dislocations. As a candidate for the Democratic presidential nomination early in 1912, Wilson hit the circuit hard in elaboration of these beliefs. "America turns upon herself her seething millions and the cauldron grows hotter and hotter," he maintained before the General Assembly of Virginia. The nation's "great irresistable energy . . . is doing more than it can keep within its own shops and limits, and therefore has got to be released for the commercial conquest of the

3. Martin J. Sklar, "Woodrow Wilson and the Political Economy of Modern United States Liberalism"; William Diamond, *The Economic Thought of Woodrow Wilson*, p. 29.
4. Woodrow Wilson, *A History of the American People*, 5:292, 294–96; Harley Notter, *The Origins of the Foreign Policy of Woodrow Wilson*, p. 144.

world. Say what you will . . . you have got to legislate for the release of the energies of America."[5]

When Wilson spoke of America's "irresistable energy," he was referring directly to the nation's remarkable commercial growth after the turn of the century. Since 1900, American foreign trade had increased almost beyond imagination—exports had grown by over 75 percent, grossing nearly $2.5 billion in Wilson's initial year in office, and the favorable balance of trade (exports over imports) had reached $653 million, an alltime national high. Even adjusting for inflated commodity prices, between 1900 and 1913 United States foreign trade increased by a true 80 percent. Cotton, pursued closely by iron and steel products, provided the major proportion of export trade. The new president was determined to do everything in his capacity to maintain, protect, and increase these lucrative sources of national income.[6]

An equally vital source of Wilson's outward look was his extended hope for the creation of a world community of nations based on liberal, capitalistic ideals. Thus Wilson's marketplace materialism became identified inextricably with concepts of a moral mission. As one historian has put it, Wilson sincerely believed "that the United States could secure the markets of the world and at the same time reform the world without losing its soul." Another has observed that Wilson's world view considered "the extension of American trade around the world [as] inseparable from the export of American liberalism." These positions hold that Wilson argued firmly for the necessity and propriety of an American universal mission aimed at achieving a lasting moral and constitutional world peace based on the principles and achieved through the power of an expanding American political economy.[7]

5. Woodrow Wilson, "Democracy and Efficiency," pp. 289–99; idem, "The Ideals of America," pp. 721–34; idem, *Selected Literary and Political Papers and Addresses of Woodrow Wilson*, 1:378–79. See also William Appleman Williams, "The Frontier Thesis and American Foreign Policy"; Diamond, *Economic Thought of Wilson*, pp. 131–34.

6. Burton I. Kaufman, *Efficiency and Expansion*, pp. 3–4.

7. The primary integrators have been William A. Williams and N. Gordon Levin, Jr. Williams' views are best expressed in *The Tragedy of American Diplomacy;* the quotation is taken from Williams, "Rise of an American World Power Complex," in *Struggle against History*, ed. Neil D. Houghton, pp. 1–19, see p. 14; Levin's major contribution is *Woodrow Wilson and World Politics*, see p. 18; see also Sidney Bell, *Righteous Conquest*, Chapter 1.

To this picture Wilson added a third dimension. The technological, industrial, communications, and work-force factors which propelled America's economy to the forefront in world trade had already been experienced in the nations of Western Europe. Faced on all fronts by rival European trade interests with similar foreign policy commitments, the United States found itself at a disadvantage because it was comparatively new on the commercial and diplomatic scene and did not possess the organization and experience in foreign trade enjoyed by its primary competitors, notably Great Britain and Germany. Consequently, Wilson endeavored to eliminate these weaknesses by championing the gospel of efficiency and by actively advancing the federal government as a coordinating and integrating force. In important ways, Wilson's foreign policy served as an extension of the domestic reform movement—efficiency, centralization, and the search for order translated into international terms.[8]

In order to achieve these ends, Wilson insisted upon removing the impediments to greater American success in world commerce. This he proposed to do by reforming the domestic economy in three major ways. First, he emphasized the necessity for lower tariffs as central to the release of American surpluses. Taking the position of the reciprocal trade advocates, Wilson maintained that liberalized trade relations would require worldwide lowering of tariffs, with America serving as the example. "We have bound ourselves hand and foot in a smug domestic helplessness by this jacket of a tariff we have wound around us," he declared in his 1912 campaign. "We are going to change it because the conditions of America are going to burst through it." On another occasion, he said, "Every manufacturer is waking up to the fact that if we do not let anybody climb over our tariff wall to get in, he has got to climb to get out."[9]

Second, Wilson was determined to democratize the domestic economy, to break down the inelastic and self-centered power of Wall Street's money and banking trusts in order to redistribute and utilize their credit facilities to greater advantage in domestic and foreign trade. The legal right for

8. An important work is Kaufman, *Efficiency and Expansion;* for an excellent summary of works covering relationships between the domestic reform movement and foreign policy during the progressive era, see the introduction to Jerry Israel, *Progressivism and the Open Door.*

9. Wilson, *Selected Literary and Political Papers,* 1:382; address delivered at Boston, January 27, 1912, *Congressional Record,* 62d Cong., 2d sess., Appendix, pp. 494–97.

American banks to establish foreign branches was an undebated goal. Noting in 1912 that national banks were not permitted to engage in foreign banking, Wilson expressed his objection "to the idea of a great commercial nation turning all its processes in on itself and not taking advantage of the economic energy which it has not yet released."[10]

Finally, Wilson reproached what he considered a deliberate neglect of the "arms of commerce," the maritime services that would transport the goods released through tariff and financial reforms. It was foolhardy, if not self-destructive, he maintained, to expect efficiency and profits in foreign trade if one depended upon his competitors to deliver his produce. Wilson had statistical evidence on hand. Between 1870 and 1910, the national wealth had increased 600 percent, railroad mileage 400 percent, Lake Superior iron ore production 600 percent, and coal production 1,000 percent, but the foreign trade fleet of the United States had *decreased* 50 percent. Whereas in 1870 American vessels carried 37.6 percent of the nation's export trade, in 1910 they hauled but 8.7 percent.[11] Americans, Wilson asserted, had "more to fear . . . because of the multitude of English, French and German carriers upon the seas" than they had to fear from the "ingenuity of the English manufacturers or the enterprise of the German merchants."[12] With its home markets completely saturated, America had to sweep the seas for commercial outlets. To that end, a merchant marine was "absolutely indispensable" if the pulse of the country was to "beat in the corners of the globe."[13] Moreover, "Without a great merchant marine, we cannot take our rightful place in the commerce of the world."[14]

Chosen president that November by an electorate highly supportive of planks such as these, Wilson firmed up his platform by appointing men as

10. Woodrow Wilson, *A Cross Roads of Freedom*, p. 114.

11. U.S., Commerce Department, *Shipping and Shipbuilding Subsidies*, p. 18. The actual size of the total United States fleet increased in tonnage, but the profits and sanctuary of the domestic trade were such that the greater part of the increase entered coastwise and Great Lakes trade rather than foreign trade. This report was prepard by Jesse E. Saugstad and is hereafter cited as Saugstad, *Shipping and Shipbuilding Subsidies*. See also idem, *Report of the Commissioner of Navigation*, 1910, pp. 7, 12.

12. Wilson, *Selected Literary and Political Papers*, 1:381.

13. Wilson, *A Cross Roads of Freedom*, p. 115.

14. Ibid., pp. 33–34.

convinced as he of the necessity to increase American foreign trade through government initiatives. At the start, one new cabinet member stood out in his effort to improve the nation's foreign trade position. The first secretary of commerce following the reorganization of the Department of Commerce and Labor into two separate agencies was William C. Redfield, an industrialist from Brooklyn. Redfield had spent a lifetime in the manufacture of iron and steel products. He had also become involved in investment banking, and from 1905 to 1913 was a director of the Equitable Life Insurance Company. Redfield was convinced that new markets were required for the enormous production resulting from industrial innovation and efficiency. "Our foreign trade is . . . a safety valve that relieves the pressure of over-production at home," he remarked in his book, *The New Industrial Day,* "we must stay there or shut down our shops." In 1910, the American Manufacturers' Export Association elected him president. In the same year, Redfield was elected to the House of Representatives, but he declined to seek reelection in 1912 to work for the Wilson campaign as its tariff expert. Over the first fifteen months of Wilson's initial term, no one played a more active role than Redfield in promoting foreign trade. This was most apparent in his strengthening and expansion of the foreign trade activities of the Bureau of Foreign and Domestic Commerce and in his creation of a permanent system of commercial attachés assigned to those nations with which the United States conducted considerable trade. Throughout his tour of duty, Redfield also supported maritime expansion, although never so forcefully as did the new secretary of the treasury, William G. McAdoo.[15]

William Gibbs McAdoo has been described appropriately as the "most ambitious, aggressive, and domineering member of Wilson's circle." An advanced progressive with strong agrarian and populist identifications, McAdoo was an embryonic welfare stater who eventually moved easily into the New Deal. Transplanted from Georgia, McAdoo had succeeded as a promoter and businessman in New York—for example, he organized a syndicate that built the Hudson River subway tubes. Although he was conversant with and respected by the nation's financial moguls, McAdoo's

15. William C. Redfield, *The New Industrial Day,* pp. 46–47; Kaufman, *Efficiency and Expansion,* pp. 68–70.

maverick support of social justice and antitrust causes estranged him somewhat from Wall Street's leaders. His driving goal was to establish public
control through the Treasury Department over the nation's money markets.
While he did not participate actively in foreign trade matters in the fifteen
months before the war, concentrating on banking reform legislation and
fiscal aid programs for farmers, the foundations for such involvement were
intrinsic in his character and outlook. "A man of action and tenacity, [who]
liked change, especially when he could take a hand in engineering it,"
McAdoo would become, after the outbreak of war, the administration's
foremost lobbyist for Pan-Americanism and a government merchant marine
and would in many ways replace Redfield as the cabinet's most active promoter of foreign trade. Of all his advisers, Wilson trusted and listened to
McAdoo the most. When McAdoo married the president's youngest daugh-
ter in May 1914, these bonds were considerably strengthened.[16]

Another cabinet member who would play a strong supportive role in the
Wilson quest for oceanic access to markets was Josephus Daniels, secretary
of the navy. An editor from North Carolina, Daniels had made the *Raleigh
News and Observer* one of the South's most strident advocates of progressive reform. As secretary of the navy, he was prepared to nationalize
virtually every industry that provided the navy with equipment, supplies,
or services. Once the world war broke out, he would become an outspoken
proponent of a government merchant marine as a naval auxiliary and
carrier of American goods. To him, the navy and a strong federally operated mercantile marine were complimentary and desirable national goals.[17]

Three other initial appointees played roles of importance. The secretary
of state, William Jennings Bryan, held office through June 1915. In those
two years, Bryan strongly encouraged American foreign branch banking and
the expansion of trade into Latin America, despite his reputation as an
antiimperialist. Since one of the primary impediments to improved Latin
American trade relations was the absence of adequate shipping service,
Bryan's efforts to strengthen hemispheric commercial ties were helpful to
the merchant marine cause. The new secretary of labor, William B. Wilson,

16. Arthur S. Link, *The New Freedom*, pp. 114–16; *Encyclopedia of American Biography*, s.v. "McAdoo, William Gibbs."

17. Harold and Margaret Sprout, *The Rise of American Naval Power, 1776–1918*, p. 309.

also became a party to maritime growth. A former official of the United Mine Workers Union and congressman from Pennsylvania, William Wilson's long commitment to improved working conditions for American seamen became an important means by which the administration sought to equalize commercial conditions between the United States and its maritime rivals. Another who shared the president's interest in expanded foreign trade was Colonel Edward M. House, his intimate adviser in diplomatic affairs. House's fervant desire to create a Pan-American union to serve as a model for an European peace strengthened the efforts of Bryan and McAdoo to augment hemispheric commerce and the means to transport it. House's concern over British wartime commercial activity also bolstered America's preparation for postwar competition. In various ways, House would relate to American maritime policy to the end of the peace conference following the war.[18]

Finally, although he did not join the administration permanently until late in 1914, Edward N. Hurley became one of Wilson's most respected foreign trade advisers. Like Redfield, Hurley bridged practically all of the reforms Wilson sought to achieve for the expansion of American foreign commerce—advocating maritime growth, scientific tariff reform, and new and liberalized laws governing American overseas banking. A machine tool and electrical home appliance manufacturer from Chicago, Hurley was an officer of the Illinois Manufacturers' Association and a leader in the industrial efficiency and national trade association movements. In 1910, he played a role of prominence in the Democratic party's decision to push Wilson for the New Jersey governorship. Following Wilson's presidential victory in 1912, Hurley was persuaded by Redfield to tour South America for the purpose of gauging trade possibilities. Shortly thereafter, Hurley played a major role in organizing the National Foreign Trade Council (NFTC), the first successful attempt to unite the nation's major business interests and leaders in a common effort to promote foreign trade. Late in 1914, Wilson appointed Hurley vice chairman of the newly created Federal

18. Sklar, "Wilson and the Political Economy of Liberalism." Virtually no attention has been given to this aspect of William B. Wilson's career. A number of authors have treated House's commercial views within their examinations of the Wilson era. See, for example, Bell, *Righteous Conquest*, Chapter 5; Levin, *Wilson and World Politics*, pp. 20–25.

Trade Commission (FTC), which functioned for business much as the Department of Agriculture functioned for farmers. Under Hurley's impetus, the FTC soon became one of the administration's most vigorous and effective agents for the development of overseas commerce, organizing its own commercial attaché system, conducting broad trade investigations to encourage industrial efficiency, and working to break down the Clayton Anti-Trust Act's restrictions on combinations in foreign commerce. When America's involvement in the war in 1917 brought about an emergency need for a massive shipbuilding program and the concomitant rationalization for a major postwar commercial fleet, Wilson turned naturally to Hurley for leadership.[19]

One of Woodrow Wilson's initial statements as a presidential candidate in 1912 had been to declare his support for the Panama Canal bill as a benefit to American shipping.[20] Soon after being elected, however, Wilson reversed himself and prepared to repudiate his former position on the basis of political and diplomatic reasoning. From a technical standpoint, the basic legality of the tolls rebate clause was unimpeachable. The measure had been construed to benefit the coastwise trade only, and no one contested America's right to do so, even the British. But granting discriminations violated the provisions of the Hay–Pauncefote Treaty. As long as the Anglo-American pact remained in effect, the United States could not honorably enforce the Panama Canal Tolls Act. Walter Hines Page, American ambassador to Great Britain, spoke to this difficulty when he noted from London: "We made a bargain—a solemn compact—and we have broken it. Whether it were a good bargain or a bad one, a silly one or a wise one; that's far from the point." North Dakota Senator Porter J. McCumber put it more bluntly:

19. Hurley is beginning to receive due historical attention. There is a brief precis by Gabriel Kolko of Hurley's position with the Federal Trade Commission. In *The Triumph of Conservatism*, Kolko aptly describes Hurley's government role as foreign trade oriented and totally identified with business. See pp. 270, 272–77. Kaufman, *Efficiency and Expansion*, emphasizes the relationships between Hurley's interests in foreign trade and the efficiency movement. Hurley's personal views before the war are presented in his own study, *Awakening of Business*.

20. Wilson, *A Cross Roads of Freedom*, p. 43.

"We are too big in national power to be too little in national integrity."[21] Yet, while many—including Elihu Root and Theodore Roosevelt—took similar positions, self-interest rather than morality governed congressional sentiment at this time. The issues promised to produce a donnybrook of monumental proportions.

Other issues, more important than honor, were at stake. At that particular stage in his yearling administration, Wilson stood on two major accounts to lose much more than he could possibly gain by enforcing the tolls provision. First, his economic platform stressed tariff and currency reform in addition to maritime legislation. Protectionism and financial inflexibility had long been scored as major impediments to the facilitation of American foreign trade. The essence of trade was reciprocity. Oscar W. Underwood, representative from Alabama and author of the administration's tariff bill, expressed it thus: "We cannot expect to dispose of our surplus products in foreign markets if we maintain in this country a tariff wall so high that other nations are unable to trade with us on reasonable terms. . . . We cannot expect foreign nations to invite us to their market when we exclude them from ours."[22] Wilson's desire to burst the tariff "straight-jacket," as he constantly referred to it, was also determined by his conviction that an open world market based on reciprocal trade would release the extraordinary power of American technological efficiency and expertise and that given a fair field and no favoritism "the skill of American workmen would dominate the markets of all the globe."[23]

Legislation aimed at democratizing banking and money procedures was also given top priority and was in many respects tailored with a clear eye to the needs of the nation's foreign commerce and investment. Secretary of the Treasury McAdoo voiced Wilson's arguments that a centralized banking authority assured the federal government a leading role in its implementation of domestic and foreign commercial policy, that the branch banking clause in the proposed federal reserve bill would break down foreign credit discrimination against American exporters and importers abroad, and that an elastic and geographically dispersed currency would

21. Page to Wilson, September 10, 1913, in Burton J. Hendrick, *The Life and Letters of Walter H. Page*, 1:249; McCumber's remarks in ibid., p. 257.

22. Underwood, "High Tariff and American Trade Abroad," pp. 22–24.

23. Wilson, *A Cross Roads of Freedom*, p. 119.

serve as an invaluable aid to trade interests, especially farmers, who needed ready cash and credit for the seasonal transportation of their crops to domestic and foreign markets. McAdoo would maintain that the Federal Reserve Act of 1913 "put this country in position to become the dominant financial power of the world."[24]

Given the enormous significance of these two undertakings, Wilson deduced that a volatile public discussion of the Panama Canal Act might precipitate a disastrous congressional debate and impede reform legislation in any or all of the desired areas—tariff, finance, or maritime. In the early stages of debate, this was especially true for the tariff. As Josephus Daniels noted, Wilson decided within weeks after taking office to avoid the maritime issue for fear it "would divide his party in the midst of [the] great tariff struggle."[25] When Great Britain sought explanation of Wilson's Panama tolls position, William Jennings Bryan instructed the British ambassador, James Bryce, that Wilson was postponing a decision for fear of its negative effect on party solidarity in relation to the congressional tariff reform effort.[26]

The second issue on which Wilson stood to lose by favoring tolls discrimination involved the administration's imbroglio with Mexico. Wilson's inaugural had come almost simultaneously with the revolutionary ascendancy of Victoriano Huerta, whose bandito-like method of governing and questionable concern for American proprietary interests in Mexico proved personally despicable to the new president. Initial American efforts at arbitration failed, and United States relations with Huerta reached a complete deadlock by the fall of 1913. Wilson's distress with the Mexican impasse was compounded by his belief that Japanese and British commercial interests were not only taking advantage of the turbulent situation to entrench themselves in Mexico but also were clandestinely providing Huerta with his main source of income. Thus piqued, on October 27 Wilson threatened forceably to eject foreign concessionaires from Latin America. But the president knew full well that since British support of his Mexican policy was imperative, concessions would have to come from the United States. Wilson said as much within days of his outburst, assuring the British

24. McAdoo to George W. Norris, August 27, 1915, William Gibbs McAdoo Papers.
25. Josephus Daniels, *The Cabinet Diaries of Josephus Daniels, 1913–1920*, p. 44.
26. Arthur S. Link, *Woodrow Wilson and the Progressive Era, 1910–1917*, p. 91.

Embassy that as soon as feasible, meaning directly following the enactment of his major reforms in tariff and currency, the United States would honor its treaty obligations, "both in the letter and in the spirit."[27]

Unrecognized by most, Wilson had already demonstrated that he disfavored discriminatory measures impinging upon the nation's foreign treaties. When the Underwood Tariff was passed into law on October second, a discriminatory rider attached to it gave American importers a 5 percent preferential rate cut for employing vessels of American registry. The nation's maritime rivals took quick notice of it; the tariff's preferential rate cut, a London newspaper observed, was even more formidable as a foreign trade mechanism than the Underwood Act's new apparatus of duties and schedules—through it America was "preparing to challenge the supremacy" that England had enjoyed so long as a carrier of world trade.[28]

But the tariff rider ran into problems that would presage in important ways those which would arise over the tolls rebate issue—it suggested an aggressiveness uncharacteristic of the direction Wilson's diplomacy was assuming at the time and promised to raise serious legal difficulties concerning America's treaty obligations. Both issues were outlined succinctly by editor and textile spokesman Daniel Augustus Tompkins, chairman of the National Association of Manufacturers' merchant marine committee. For thirty years, Tompkins had been the South's foremost proponent of an expanded merchant marine and was in close touch with most of that region's congressional foreign trade advocates. Notwithstanding the strong support southerners gave to the rider, Tompkins condemned the movement toward a differential tariff as simply an old remedy that had failed over and over again. Differential tariffs habitually bred preferential duties and then retaliatory duties, he argued. In the end confusion always reigned, followed by international conflict. Preferential duties, he pointed out, were also in violation of the many reciprocal treaties of commerce between America

27. House to Page, November 14, 1913, Edward M. House Papers; Peter Calvert, *The Mexican Revolution, 1910–1914*, p. 271; see also William S. Coker, "The Panama Canal Tolls Controversy"; Edward S. Kaplan, "William Jennings Bryan and the Panama Canal Tolls Controversy." Coker and Kaplan both emphasize that Anglo-American relations and the arbitration treaty were the most significant causes for Wilson's softening on the tolls issue.

28. London *Pall Mall Gazette*, quoted in *Outlook*, "What Foreigners Think of Our New Tariff."

and foreign nations. He concluded that in order to preserve an oceanic peace the best advice the Wilson administration could receive would be to drop the whole matter at once.[29] The Treasury Department did not respond to these fears of retaliation but agreed on the legal uncertainties. Foreseeing numerous and undesirable "international complications and diplomatic negotiations," McAdoo asked Bryan for an opinion. When the State Department replied that the governments having reciprocal treaties with the United States would not accept such discriminations with passivity, McAdoo backed off quickly. Consequently, when Congress passed the tariff act in early October 1913, McAdoo directed the United States collectors of customs to refuse to apply the 5 percent reduction.[30]

No sooner had the second of the great reform measures, the Federal Reserve Act, been passed in late December 1913, than Wilson, true to his promise, notified Ambassador Page that he was prepared to attack the tolls repeal issue. The president also sought to renew the Anglo-American arbitration treaty which the British had allowed to lapse the previous year as a protest both to the Panama Canal Act and to Taft's refusal to submit the argument to international mediation. In late January 1914, Wilson informed the Senate Foreign Relations Committee of his intentions, confirming these publicly shortly thereafter. It was a complicated issue that had importance beyond Mexico and the need for British cooperation. Japanese-American relations were at stake, and Pan-Americanism hung in the balance. The whole world, it appeared to Wilson, held America in blatant violation of the Hay–Pauncefote Treaty.[31] "It is not merely England that I am thinking of," he informed a friend. "The distrust runs all through Europe and all through Central and South America."[32] On these bases Wilson moved resolutely toward obtaining a congressional repeal.

At first he was not outwardly successful. So much political opposition developed that on March fifth Wilson felt compelled to take his argument

29. Tompkins editorials, March 27, May 20, 1913, Tompkins Papers, LC; Tompkins to Furnifold Simmons, October 6, 1913, ibid.

30. McAdoo to Bryan, May 26, 1913, McAdoo Papers; J. B. Moore to McAdoo, May 28, 1913, ibid.; U.S., Congress, Senate, *Papers Relating to Imports in Vessels with American Register*, 63rd Cong., 1st sess., S. Doc. 179.

31. Link, *The New Freedom*, p. 307.

32. Wilson to Albert Shaw, March 17, 1914, Woodrow Wilson Papers.

directly to Congress. This had a negative effect, however; it appeared for a short period that Wilson might actually lose control over crucial elements of his party. Underwood led the opposition. As he viewed it, the American merchant marine, "the key that unlocks the gate of commerce," had been sold down the river in an "un-American spirit of surrender."[33] In whole-hearted sympathy, coastwise maritime lobbies stormed Capitol Hill, and Bull Moose nativism in all its inbred Anglophobic forms came out of the woodwork. As one Progressive put it, Wilson's position meant that "the Stars and Stripes shall be pulled down from its place over the American canal at Panama, while in its place is hoisted a piece of muslin with the British Union Jack on one side and the white of nerveless neutrality on the other."[34]

Wilson met the challenge, as Arthur S. Link aptly described it, "with one of the most extraordinary displays of leadership of his entire career."[35] Employing all the political tools available, Wilson was able to fashion a favorable support for repeal. Late in the spring, a Senate majority comfortably sustained the president, and the repeal became effective on June eleventh. The free ships provision attached to the act also died. Not one application for registry of foreign built ships was filed, and as E. T. Chamberlain, commissioner of navigation, had predicted, "none were expected at the outset." Clearly, American registry could not override the prohibitively high costs entailed in American shipping.[36] Nevertheless, Redfield valued the effort and sought to add inducements to the provision by working for the removal of the five-year age limit stipulated by the canal provision.

Although in Wilson's initial year, three measures aimed at improving the nation's maritime position failed to achieve their designed purposes, it was clear that as an expression of public sentiment Congress was moving to take direct measures for the relief of the moribund overseas maritime system.

33. *Congressional Record,* 63rd Cong., 2d sess., March 27, 1914, pp. 5625–26.
34. Remarks of Melville C. Kelley (Pa.), *Congressional Record,* House, 63rd Cong., 2d sess., March 26, 1914, p. 5563.
35. Link, *The New Freedom,* p. 311. Link's discussion of the controversy is the best account. See pp. 304–14.
36. U.S., Department of Commerce, *Report of the Commissioner of Navigation, 1912,* p. 15.

This went so far as to lend support, in a so-called age of antitrustism, to the existence of combinations in the foreign and American shipping lines serving United States trade. In 1912, as a response to complaints that shipping combinations practiced discrimination, Congress called for an investigation by the House Committee on Merchant Marine and Fisheries. Chaired by Missouri representative Joshua W. Alexander, a longtime lobbyist for maritime growth, the committee unveiled the existence of seventy-six agreements, conferences, or understandings in American foreign and domestic shipping trade for the purpose of eliminating competition, pooling traffic, and fixing rates. But if unlookers expected the committee to conduct an attack on combinations, they received an abrupt surprise. After hearing testimony from shippers and steamship representatives for the better part of a year, Alexander's committee concluded in 1913 that while there were definite disadvantages and abuses built into the system, for the sake of American foreign and domestic trade the conference arrangement was highly desirable. Two alternatives had faced the committee: prohibiting conferences or recognizing them. The first course was rejected because it would have deprived American exporters and importers of important services conducted for the most part fairly and honestly: greater regularity and frequency of service, stability and uniformity in rates, the maintenance of parity in American and European rates to foreign markets, a better distribution of sailings, economical service, and equal treatment for shippers through the elimination of secret arrangements and underhanded methods of discrimination.

Consequently, the House committee recommended government recognition of the combinations, seeking at the same time to eliminate the system's worst abuses through federal regulation similar to that which the Interstate Commerce Commission exercised over the railroads. All agreed that the termination of existing agreements would guarantee cutthroat competition of the most vicious sort: "The entire history of steamship agreements shows that in ocean commerce there is no happy medium between war and peace when several lines engage in the same trade. [The consensus was] overwhelmingly in favor of some form of government regulation of steamship carriers engaged in this country's foreign trade." Although its recommendations would not be incorporated into legislative form for three years, the committee's hearings and reports demonstrated the degree to which government and business were steadily meshing for greater cooperation in the development of efficient foreign trade systems.[37]

That the Wilson administration was making long strides toward increasing America's access to the world marketplace was recognized openly by American business interests. Speaking in October 1913 before the American Manufacturers' Export Association (AMEA), James A. Farrell, president of United States Steel and the business sector's most respected spokesman for foreign trade, warmly praised Wilson for his "keen interest" in bringing about commercial expansion."[38] The main item on Farrell's and the AMEA's agenda, therefore, was how to fuse the many and diverse segments of business expression into a single association that could cooperate with the Wilson government in the development of a unified foreign trade program. Consequently, the AMEA determined to call a national convention of foreign trade interests for May 1914. To give that meeting an identity, business and government leaders created the National Foreign Trade Council (NFTC) out of a nucleus of three groups—the AMEA, the American Asiatic Association, and the Pan American Society. The new National Foreign Trade Council's expressed goal was "Greater Prosperity Through Foreign Trade."[39] When developing European political instability caused a genuine international depression during the winter and spring of 1913–1914, the new merger took on added importance to its creators.

Meeting in Washington, D.C., some 341 of the nation's most powerful financial and commercial leaders spoke glowingly of the administration's efforts to support overseas business interests. This was especially true for tariff and currency reform, "two things of which we might be proud," remarked a spokesman for Wall Street.[40] Wilson, Bryan, and Redfield, the last being the major administrative spark behind the new organization, ex-

37. U.S., Congress, House, *Report of the Committee on the Merchant Marine and Fisheries on Steamship Agreements and Affiliations in the American Foreign and Domestic Trade Under H. Res. 587*, 63rd Cong., 2d sess., H. Doc. 805, pp. 308, 415–17; Alexander to Redfield, June 14, 1913, Wilson Papers; Lawrence, *United States Merchant Shipping*, p. 37; Daniel Marx, Jr., *International Shipping Cartels*, pp. 49–67.

38. Farrell address, September 25, 1913, *Congressional Record*, 63rd Cong., 1st sess., Appendix, vol. 50, pt. 7.

39. Kaufman, *Efficiency and Expansion*, pp. 82–83.

40. Remarks of John E. Gardin, National Foreign Trade Council Convention, 1914, *Proceedings*, p. 249.

pressed their absolute delight in the NFTC's endorsement of their work by pledging continued government initiative in matters concerning foreign trade.[41] With "the relief of adverse domestic conditions by the opening of new markets abroad," its stated aim (in reference to the continuing depression), the convention agreed that tariff and currency reforms were but a part of the desirable foreign trade program. All concurred that the complete, or vertical, trade system depended also upon a number of other factors, foremost of which was oceanborne transportation service. On the basis of sheer volume of rhetoric, the major portion of the convention was devoted to maritime matters which received their clearest expression in the remarks of Edward Hurley. Hurley couched the problem in military terms. The foreign sales branches of American business were the infantry and bore "the brunt of the fighting." But these were likely to be disadvantaged "unless supported by banks, which may be likened to artillery, and steamship lines, resembling the supply trains of an army." Perhaps American traders accepted the nation's dependency on foreign shipping, but from a national standpoint it was commercially inefficient and "fundamentally wrong" to pay competitors to carry American freight.[42]

NFTC conventioneers endorsed these remarks with enthusiasm. "I believe I voice the sentiments of all our Associations and our National Foreign Trade Convention when I say—We want an American Merchant Marine," remarked C. E. Jennings, president of the AMEA. Farrell, the convention's presiding officer, concurred in Jenning's feelings. "There is no question whatever that he represents the views of every American citizen."[43] As the congressional struggle over the Panama Canal tolls issue was still in heated progress at this time, the convention was greatly relieved to hear from Clarence J. Owens, the managing director of the Southern Commercial Congress, that President Wilson had authorized him to say that he hoped to settle partisan issues in the current session of Congress "in order that the remaining years of his administration might be given in a broad statesman-like way to the question of the merchant marine."[44] P. H. W. Ross, pres-

41. Sklar, "Wilson and the Political Economy of Liberalism."
42. Edward Hurley, "The Panama Canal and Latin American Trade Possibilities," NFTC Convention, 1914, *Proceedings,* pp. 289–90.
43. NFTC Convention, 1914, *Proceedings,* pp. 144–45.
44. Ibid., p. 88.

ident of the National Marine League, expressed the optimism with which business viewed Wilson's intentions: After 130 years, providence had endowed the nation with a president who combined "the intellect of a Hamilton" with the "Jeffersonian power of capturing the emotions of the people to achieve the Maritime Independence of the United States."[45]

But circumstances permitting a carefully developed and reasoned settlement of the maritime issue remained illusive. On June 10, the day preceding the Senate's repeal of the canal tolls measure, Alexander R. Smith, a veteran shipping lobbyist, posed the problem concisely when he cautioned the president:

> The question naturally arises. . . . Are we in danger through too great dependence on foreign ships? Our exports consists largely of articles that compete 'in the world's markets' with those of the most powerful and commercially aggressive foreign nations. May we safely depend upon their merchant ships to reach, hold, and develop foreign markets for our rapidly growing competitive surplus products?[46]

Whether Smith was sensitive to world politics at this time is a moot question, for he had predicted the problem as it would squarely face the nation just eight weeks later with the outbreak of the European war.

45. Ross to Wilson, May 29, 1914, Wilson Papers.
46. Smith to Wilson, June 10, 1914, Wilson Papers.

Chapter III

Legislative Defeat:
The Ship Purchase Bill

"If a general European war comes," wrote Henry Lee Higginson to Wilson on July 30, 1914, "all ships of considerable nations except ours will be unsafe. We might not be able to send our food . . . to the markets in Europe." The Boston banker added that Wilson had probably thought of it, remarking that a bill enabling American registry for foreign vessels would do much good.[1] Had Higginson known about happenings on Capitol Hill he could have saved himself the trip to the mailbox, for his letter had scarcely reached the Boston post office when Wilson met with congressional leaders to discuss the shipping problem. "Our bountiful crops are ready to harvest," explained the president. "Unless they can be carried to the foreign markets, they will waste in the warehouses." The meeting had been convened to "provide ships [to] carry our commerce to all ports of the world."[2] The legislators responded eagerly. The deliberations carried on that day culminated in the genesis of a "free ships" bill, similar to the undesirable provision of the Panama Canal Act, but without any restrictions on the age of ships. With the weekend assistance of Joshua Alexander and E. T. Chamberlain, Senator Oscar Underwood prepared and submitted a draft bill to the president. Then on Monday, August 3, Underwood introduced the measure on the floor of the House.[3]

1. Henry Lee Higginson to Wilson, July 30, 1914, Wilson Papers.
2. From a memorandum of the meeting taken by Representative William C. Adamson of Georgia, quoted in Ray Stannard Baker, *Woodrow Wilson,* 5:109.
3. *Congressional Record,* 53rd Cong., 2d sess., August 3, 1914, p. 13183. This was Underwood's reply to a question regarding the origin of the bill. At the same time,

Though the need to confront the war issue had been obvious to these men, no one, not even Wilson, could have foreseen the severity of the economic crisis that developed in the next few days. Still suffering from the depression of 1913–1914, the American economy shuddered with each report of intensified European combat. Panic swept the money market, and a banking failure was averted only by the emergency release of United States currency. The New York Stock Exchange closed its doors tight, not to reopen until December, and the foreign exchange market fluctuated wildly in the storm on Wall Street.[4] The financial difficulties were augmented by the paralysis of trade, in particular the disruption of shipping service. Prior to August 1914, by far the largest oceanic carriers had been Germany and Great Britain. With the outbreak of war, Germany's vessels scurried off to home or neutral ports for fear of British surface raiders, and Great Britain diverted most of its huge tonnage to war-related activities in the European theatre. France and Russia followed England's suit.

These withdrawals revealed the total inability of the American merchant marine to meet the exigencies of foreign trade. Although the United States was ostensibly the third largest shipholding nation in tonnage, the great bulk of its ships were not engaged in oceanborne commerce. On the eve of the war, less than 10 percent of America's exports were being carried in American bottoms, and of all the vessels in the world ocean-carrying trade, only 2 percent were of American registry. To complicate matters, exorbitant freight rates were charged for what little shipping space remained, and insurance rates became virtually prohibitive.[5]

The shutoff coincided with the harvest and interior shipment of one of the biggest bumper crops in American history. A great flow of agricultural

---

Senator John M. Weeks of Massachusetts sponsored a bill in the Senate authorizing use of naval transports in foreign trade. It had considerable following but was ultimately pushed aside by the administration's ship purchase bill.

4. U.S., Treasury Department, *Annual Report on the Finances, Dec. 7, 1914*, pp. 2–3; William G. McAdoo, *Crowded Years*, pp. 290–92; Alexander D. Noyes, *War Period of American Finance, 1905–1975*, pp. 56, 71.

5. Edward N. Hurley, *The Bridge to France*, p. 20; David Houston, *Eight Years with Wilson's Cabinet, 1913–1920*, 1:121; John G. B. Hutchins, "The American Shipping Industry Since 1914"; Joan Bentinck-Smith, "The Forcing Period," pp. 36, 39, 59–60. For statistical data see U.S., Commerce Department, *Report of the Commissioner of Navigation, 1914*, p. 79; Saugstad, *Shipping and Shipbuilding Subsidies*, pp. 28, 179.

goods suddenly halted at the coast and piled up in depots all over the country. As surpluses built up, prices fell disastrously. The great staples were most seriously affected, especially cotton. A prewar slackness had already depreciated cotton, and the South, dependent on the proceeds of the 60 percent normally exported, faced the prospect of an unprecedented disaster. By the middle of August, cotton prices had fallen to half their 1913 levels, and it was estimated that as many as four million bales might not reach external markets. Grain exchanges also expressed alarm. The shipping tie-up and consequent depression in prices aroused widespread concern, not only among farmers but also on the part of all the commercial agencies involved with agriculture—the railroads, merchants, and bankers. In addition, at the outbreak of war the United States had a debit balance in Europe of close to $500 million. Only the creation of credits through the movement of export commodities could counterbalance that indebtedness. One Minnesota congressman spoke for everyone when he observed that unless cotton, flour, grain, and lumber reached their foreign destinations, "the whole business of this country [would] be demoralized."[6] James Farrell of United States Steel remarked shortly thereafter that one week's war experience had done more to convince Americans that foreign trade was necessary to the domestic economy than two years of theoretical debate.[7]

The crisis implied, on the other hand, great opportunities to capture new markets now necessarily abandoned by British and German interests. Commercial expansionists envisioned their greatest chance in Latin America, which had suffered most from the Anglo-German withdrawal. What Missouri Democrat William Stone, chairman of the Senate Committee on Foreign Relations, saw as a "most opportunistic time" for the enlargement of United States commercial intercourse with the republics of the south, his Republican colleague from Vermont, Jacob Gallinger, predicted as a period of unprecedented "boom" for Pan-American trade and shipping "which would astonish not only our own people but the world."[8] The press was even less constrained. A protracted European war would give America "control of the trade of the rest of the world and would put us beyond

6. *Congressional Record,* 63rd Cong., 2d sess., August 3, 1914, p. 13179. See also McAdoo, *Crowded Years,* pp. 194–302; Baker, *Woodrow Wilson,* 5:97.

7. *New York Times,* October 23, 1914.

8. *Congressional Record,* 63rd Cong., 2d sess., August 3, 1914, pp. 13136–37.

reach of competition in years to come," *The New York Commercial* editorialized, and another major daily summed up when it screamed:

> TWO THOUSAND MILLIONS in trade is the prize which world conditions have set before the American people. Europe's tragic extremity becomes . . . America's golden opportunity—the opportunity not of a lifetime, but of a century of national life.
>
> The whole rapidly developing trade of South America—to say nothing of other parts of the globe—heretofore almost solely in European and especially in German hands, is invitingly open to the United States through the annihilation of Europe's foreign trade![9]

The administration demonstrated considerable anxiety over these dual aspects—the emergencies and opportunities—and devoted itself zealously to their eradication and realization. Many in government spoke to these issues, but none articulated them with more intensity and fervid commitment than William Gibbs McAdoo, secretary of the treasury, around whose office and activities the maritime issue immediately swirled. From the onset of war, McAdoo worked without respite to stabilize and strengthen the economy by breaking down the export tie-up through increased shipping services. McAdoo's support for an American merchant marine proceeded logically from his intense concern to enrich American commerce. He probably would have involved himself in shipping matters earlier had he not, like Wilson, been engrossed in achieving currency reform and the Federal Reserve System and marshalling the resources of the treasury to facilitate the marketing of cotton during the depressed winter of 1913–1914. Though it was characteristic of Wilson's southern-dominated cabinet to exhibit a special penchant for moving agricultural products, particularly cotton, McAdoo went much further in this respect, literally dedicating his office to the efficient and profitable disposal of the great staples. After his winter campaign to assist cotton movements, he vowed that so long as he held office "the crops of this country will move without any of the apprehension which has heretofore characterized American business operations."[10] When the war prostrated Wall Street, McAdoo moved quickly to under-

---

9. *Literary Digest*, August 15, 1914, p. 256; *New York American*, August 8, 1914.
10. McAdoo, Address before the Atlanta Chamber of Commerce and Atlanta Clearing House Association, Atlanta, February 4, 1914, McAdoo Papers.

gird the economy by releasing treasury funds. In short, McAdoo was eternally prepared to make bold and enthusiastic commitments to use the government vigorously in the interests of the public welfare. Consequently, he placed his support squarely behind administrative efforts to insure continued and augmented business prosperity through movement of American exports to their overseas destinations. Out of this came three major accomplishments in the early weeks of American neutrality: a Bureau of War Risk Insurance, a liberalized "free ships" act, and the introduction of a bill to authorize government ownership and operation of a national merchant marine.[11] Although these issues would reflect on the nation's foreign policy, McAdoo and Wilson completely bypassed the State Department and its secretary, William Jennings Bryan, assuming full responsibility for every aspect of the shipping program.

As soon as war broke out, the nation's most powerful export associations, centered in New York City, requested government assistance in order to solve the transportation problem. On August 2, a special committee of the National Foreign Trade Council met to consider the shipping emergency brought about by the European conflict. Commending the Wilson administration for its initial response to the crisis, the committee called for "not only the necessity of providing an adequate American merchant marine, but also the importance of subordinating partisan and sectional differences as to practical methods of accomplishing it."[12] Responding to an appeal from Secretary McAdoo, J. P. Morgan, James J. Hill (the latter the president of the Great Northern Railroad and owner of the two largest freighters in the world), and other influential members of the New York Chamber of Commerce met in emergency session on August seventh. The chamber concluded that congressional action was imperative if the stoppage imposed by the war on the nation's foreign trade was to be eliminated. The group sent an

11. Broesamle traces McAdoo's shipping and foreign trade programs for the period of neutrality. See John J. Broesamle, *William Gibbs McAdoo,* Chapters 10–11.

12. Robert H. Patchin to Redfield, August 2, 1914, Record Group 41, Bureau of Marine Inspection and Navigation, General Correspondence Files of the Bureau of Navigation/78131-N, National Archives. Hereafter cited as RG 41 plus file number, NA. Appointed by Farrell, the committee included James J. Hill, president of the Great Northern Railroad; Edward Hurley; P. A. S. Franklin, president of the IMMC; Robert Dollar, president of the Robert Dollar Steamship Company; Alba Johnson, president of the Baldwin Locomotive Company; and Willard Straight, president of the American Asiatic Association.

urgent memorial to McAdoo, who was now developing, an eminent banker observed, "into the strong man of the administration."[13] Stressing the war's economic dislocations, and confessing that it was in a "blind alley," the group advised passage of the liberalized ship registry law then before Congress and called for a measure to provide war risk insurance on American vessels.[14] Three days later, James Farrell reassured McAdoo and Secretary of Commerce Redfield that the NFTC was pledged to work for "national unity of action," that it stood squarely behind the new navigation bill and war risk insurance, and that it was "anxious effectively to co-operate with the Government and with all commercial and industrial organizations not only for the restoration of safe and economic transportation but for the permanent extension of American foreign trade."[15] Similar statements and resolutions poured in from across the country.[16]

Bolstered by the steady receipt of favorable memorials, McAdoo announced a meeting for August fourteenth to consider ways of reconstituting and revitalizing the nation's foreign trade. The Conference on Foreign Exchange and Shipping, as it was entitled, attracted an impressive assemblage of business personnel. McAdoo always thought of it as "the first publicly conducted conference of businessmen that government had ever held in Washington," and another participant described it as "the most solemn meeting of hard-headed business men he had ever attended."[17] In addition to a large number of government officials and congressmen, sixty-two representatives of banking, shipping, foreign trade, and maritime insurance attended. Pledging their cooperation, business representatives

13. Frank A. Vanderlip to James Stillman, September 26, 1914, Frank A. Vanderlip Papers. One must not forget that the president's wife died on August sixth and that the funeral did not take place until the twelfth. It would be difficult to exaggerate the crushing impact of her death on Wilson in the early months of the war.

14. Special Committee of the New York Chamber of Commerce to McAdoo, August 7, 1914, McAdoo Papers. The committee included, among others, Morgan, Farrell, Franklin, Jacob H. Schiff of Kuhn, Loeb and Company, and Frank A. Vanderlip, president of the National City Bank of New York.

15. Farrell to Redfield, August 10, 1914, RG 41/74303-N, NA; Farrell to McAdoo, August 10, 1914, McAdoo Papers.

16. See, for example, the statements to Wilson of the Firestone Tire and Rubber Company, American Cotton Manufacturers Association, New Orleans Association of Commerce, and National Association of Retail Grocers, August 12–19, 1914, RG 41/75303-N, NA.

17. McAdoo, Crowded Years, p. 292; New York Times, August 15, 1914.

expressed high appreciation for the government's prompt solution of the currency problem and urged the administration to continue to adopt such measures and to provide whatever assistance was necessary to break the embargo on foreign trade. The conference emphasized the need for government aid in three areas: stabilization of the foreign exchange market, passage of the ships registry bill, and provision for war risk insurance on American vessels in the European trade. Of the three proposals, the last was considered the most important, for ships obtained under the pending registry bill would be immobile without insurance, and foreign exchange would "find its equilibrium" only when the United States got the ships and moved its agricultural surpluses.[18] Besides, the convention regarded government war risk insurance as a useful solution to one of the root problems of the American maritime industry—Lloyd's of London's monopoly in marine insurance and the discriminatory ratings it customarily assigned to non-British vessels.[19] In conclusion, the conference resolved to support any effort to place American shipping on "equal competitive terms with all other maritime nations."[20]

McAdoo moved eagerly to meet the need. One major step was taken almost at once when Congress passed the ship registry bill into law on August seventeenth. On the following day, McAdoo submitted a war risk insurance bill to Underwood with the admonition that the ship registry bill would be largely valueless without it.[21] The measure was rushed to both houses with every assurance of passage. This accomplished, McAdoo carried the process a giant step further—he introduced a bill to authorize government ownership of a merchant marine by granting it the power to purchase vessels.

It seems apparent that the full concept of a governmentally owned and

---

18. U.S., Treasury Department, *Annual Report on the Finances, Dec. 7, 1914*, pp. 5–6; *New York Times*, August 15, 1914.

19. William W. Bates, *American Navigation*, p. 304. For an explanation of why the United States did not have an adequate marine insurance program on the eve of the war, see Bentinck-Smith, "The Forcing Period," pp. 376–88.

20. U.S., Treasury Department, *Annual Report on the Finances, Dec. 7, 1914*, p. 6; *New York Times*, August 15, 1914; for McAdoo's remarks before the committee, February 17, 1916, see U.S., Congress, House, Committee on the Merchant Marine and Fisheries, *Creating a Shipping Board, Naval Auxiliary, and Merchant Marine*, 64th Cong., 1st sess., (Hearings on H.R. 10500), p. 263 (hereafter cited as *Shipping Board Hearings*).

21. McAdoo to Underwood, August 18, 1914, McAdoo Papers.

operated merchant marine matured in McAdoo's mind simultaneously with the Conference on Foreign Exchange and Shipping.[22] Several factors appear to account for this. McAdoo later recounted that the government's experience in running the Panama Steamship Line had been a factor and that the plan had been the logical "outgrowth" of the study that resulted from the August 14 meeting.[23] But more than a single day's conferring and the government's limited maritime experience shaped the decision. A major rationalization came from the government–business cooperation that had been achieved over the two preceding weeks. Judging Wall Street's behavior, McAdoo felt that since a segment of business had been willing to support, even initiate, government overseership and subsidization of a huge insurance program conceived ostensibly in the public welfare, it might be similarly disposed in the emergency to look with at least some grace on the larger venture of government as shipping operator. Even if that assumption proved false, there was every justification for forging ahead. For while McAdoo's relationships with big business at this time were good, he nevertheless harbored serious doubts whether private enterprise would act in the national interest when the opportunities and their profits were more thoroughly revealed.[24] With respect to the issues immediately on hand, McAdoo was concerned that American shipping and business interests would attend only to those trades earning substantial profits and not to the broadbased general welfare of all trades and their necessary development.

McAdoo had Pan-American trade foremost in mind. Looking back, he likened South Americans to "customers of a store that has burned down; they were looking for a place to spend their money."[25] And as if the timing had been preordained, the Panama Canal opened to commercial traffic in the very midst of the international crisis. Not only were South Americans receptive to trade, they had a spanking new oceanic highway to connect them with American interests. Much energy was spent in Congress in anticipation of the Isthmian opening. By August 15, when the first vessel went

22. See McAdoo, *Crowded Years*, p. 296; Link, *The Struggle for Neutrality*, p. 86.
23. McAdoo's remarks on February 17, 1916 in U.S., Congress, House, Committee on Merchant Marine and Fisheries, *Shipping Board Hearings*, 64th Cong., 1st sess., pp. 268–69.
24. McAdoo, *Crowded Years*, pp. 240–41.
25. Ibid., p. 351. Pan-American trade possibilities preoccupied almost the entire Wilson administration. See, for example, Burton I. Kaufman, "United States Trade and Latin America."

through, no fewer than a dozen bills had been introduced in the previous week to authorize government establishment of a steamship line for Pan-American trade.[26] None had gone beyond advising the use of existing facilities and frameworks, however, and McAdoo felt compelled to add his own plan, a far more comprehensive and progressive, even radical, step toward the creation of a national fleet. McAdoo's lack of assurance that the ship registry bill would satisfy the needs of American commerce added weight to his decision. It was difficult to forecast tonnage transferrals, and there had already been protests that the provisions in the bill requiring American line and watch officers would render it ineffectual.[27] Ever in the background was the disruption in foreign exchange, still in limbo and still of crisis proportions.

No doubt McAdoo had fastened longing eyes on the splendid vessels of the German Hamburg-American Line, fifteen of which had tied up in United States ports pending the outcome of the war. Not only were these ships among the finest in the world, they included the *Vaterland*, second largest vessel afloat. McAdoo later credited the idea of purchasing the German ships to private enterprise and to P. A. S. Franklin, vice president of J. P. Morgan's International Mercantile Marine Corporation (IMMC). At the August 14 meeting, Franklin approached the treasury chief with an offer to purchase the ships for the IMMC, but added that "it would be difficult, if not impossible, to secure private capital for that purpose." Consequently, Franklin hoped the Wilson administration would consider endorsing or guaranteeing the bonds of his company so that it could acquire the vessels. McAdoo demurred. Instead he adopted the purchase idea and moved accordingly in government, rather than private, channels.[28]

News of the purchase scheme soon reached the British Embassy. It was obvious, wrote a member of the legation, that the United States had determined to purchase the interned German ships and that any efforts by the British to hinder this undertaking would have the most serious repercussions in America.[29] Certainly the Hamburg-American Line anticipated

26. *New York Times*, August 15, 1914.

27. See, for example, E. L. Doheny, president of Petroleum Transport Co., to E. T. Chamberlain, August 14, 1914, RG 41/78131-N, NA.

28. McAdoo's remarks of February 17, 1916 in U.S., Congress, House, Committee on Merchant Marine and Fisheries, *Shipping Board Hearings*, 64th Cong., 1st sess.

29. Counselor Colville Barclay to Sir Edward Grey, August 19, 1914, cited in Ross

selling the vessels to the Wilson government. Julius P. Meyer, secretary of the line in America, attended McAdoo's conference on the fourteenth. While there, he attracted national attention by receiving power of attorney from Germany to put all fifteen ships on the market. Either to impress this upon McAdoo or at the secretary's request Meyer remained in Washington an additional day in order to confer at the Treasury Department about the possibility of selling the ships to American interests. There was speculation in shipping circles that whoever purchased the vessels would place them in the promising South American service, as only one American line (under British registry) operated from New York to Latin America.[30] Weighing all the possibilities, McAdoo saw the moment as propitious, a halcyon period after decades of turbulent obstruction to maritime reform and hence suitable for the creation of a more perfect national foreign trade system.

Confident of success, McAdoo prepared a skeleton draft for a government merchant marine bill and presented it to Wilson. It was an emphatic statement of the veteran financier's formula for wealth—in time of crisis, invest. "There is a big sentiment," McAdoo informed the president on August 16, "for the purchase, by the Government, of a large fleet of ships to supplement our transportation facilities to Europe, and to establish immediately lines to South America and Central America. We have an unusual opportunity for South American trade, but without ships we can do nothing. With them we can quickly establish business and political relations that will be of inestimable value to this country—perhaps for all time."[31]

McAdoo then outlined his plan. Government backing of such an undertaking would have major advantages. It would (1) exercise a regulatory function upon rates, management, policy, and the trade routes of the ships; (2) be profitable to government; (3) be predictably stable and assured of capital on all occasions; (4) guarantee American shipping a position from which to compete successfully with foreign operations; and (5) serve in war as a naval auxiliary and reserve. Such a venture would also get ships

Gregory, "A New Look at the Case of the Dacia." The British Admiralty did not agree with the Foreign Office. See Winston Churchill to Grey, August 19, 1914, cited in Ernest R. May, *The World War and American Isolation, 1914–1917*, p. 15.

30. *New York Times*, August 15, 16, 18, 1914.

31. McAdoo to Wilson, August 16, 1914, McAdoo Papers; Mary Synon, *McAdoo*, pp. 179–80.

immediately. The ship registry act and war risk insurance legislation could not produce vessels with sufficient alacrity, and private enterprise had been prostrated by the war.[32] Later McAdoo remarked that in principle he had always opposed government ownership except in "extraordinary circumstances where the intervention of the government [was] urgently demanded in the interest of the public welfare." The shipping dilemma "presented a perfect picture of such a case."[33] Wilson wholeheartedly endorsed McAdoo's proposal. It was in every respect the epitome of his own outlook. "We'll have to fight for it, won't we?," remarked the president. "We certainly shall," replied McAdoo. "Well, then, let's fight," Wilson concluded.[34]

Wilson and McAdoo were acknowledging that the proposed ship purchase bill would have rough sledding in Congress. For one thing, there had been ominous warnings from abroad that a transferral of German vessels would be considered inimicable to Allied interests. The French, for instance, had put the State Department on notice that they would not recognize a change of German registry under any circumstance.[35] And the announcement in the United States that the Hamburg-American Line intended to dispose of its vessels to Americans brought instant protests from overseas.[36] Second, there was strong opposition in the United States to government competition with private business; for many, the proposal for a state corporation of this magnitude raised the spectre of a nation edging menacingly away from free enterprise toward socialism. Wilson had acknowledged as much on his decision to go ahead. "Government ownership of merchant ships, no matter how desperate the need," he remarked, "would arouse the hostility of every reactionary in the United States."[37]

Nonetheless, Wilson and McAdoo were so caught up in the emergencies and opportunities that they determined to ignore the weather warnings. Forging ahead, they opened their campaign on August nineteenth by calling

---

32. Synon, *McAdoo*, pp. 179–80.
33. McAdoo, *Crowded Years*, p. 295.
34. Ibid., p. 296.
35. French chargé d'affaires to Bryan, August 4, 1914, U.S., Department of State, *FR, Supplement, 1914*, p. 485; Myron T. Herrick to Bryan, August 7, 1914, ibid.
36. *New York Times*, August 18, 1914.
37. McAdoo, *Crowded Years*, p. 296. A summary of the tremendous opposition marshalled against the bill is contained in Lawrence C. Allin, "Ill-Timed Initiative."

together congressional leaders disposed toward administrative solutions for expediting trade. McAdoo presented the situation: There was a paralysis in shipping, the result being complete inability to move the record bumper crop, either internally or externally. Much of the crop, especially cotton, was yet to be harvested. It was a "radical situation that required heroic treatment." Pressed by Wilson, the committee approved McAdoo's plan, whereupon the secretary submitted it the following day to the House and Senate commerce committees.[38] The plan authorized the establishment of a corporation run by a shipping board composed of the secretary of the treasury, the secretary of commerce, and the postmaster general which would purchase vessels and operate them in Latin American trade. The bill did not restrict the use of the government's vessels to that trade alone; McAdoo and Wilson did not intend to limit their range of commercial activity solely to the Western Hemisphere.[39]

As many expected, the presentation of the administration's shipping proposal to the appropriate congressional committees resulted in a furious outburst of opposition to the concept of government ownership and operation. Warnings from Europe intensified domestic concern. France restated its earlier position, noting that it would not even permit the use of German ships to repatriate the estimated 200,000 Americans stranded in Europe, no less allow the use of German ships for other purposes.[40] Although the British Foreign Office did not oppose the transfer on legal grounds—in fact much consideration had been given to purchasing the vessels for England— it was obvious that London would also object seriously if those vessels sailed to enemy ports or ports to which the Central Powers had access.[41]

But Wilson turned a deaf ear to all criticisms. When J. P. Morgan forwarded advice from his London firm on the British position, the president replied irritably that the British were "in danger of taking a very unjusti-

---

38. Link, *The Struggle for Neutrality*, p. 87; *New York Times*, August 20, 21, 25, 1914.
39. U.S., Congress, House, Committee on Merchant Marine and Fisheries, *Government Ownership and Operation of Merchant Vessels in the Foreign Trade of the United States*, 63rd Cong., 2d sess., pt. 1. See also *New York Times*, August 31, 1914; McAdoo to J. H. Lewis, September 14, 1914, McAdoo Papers.
40. Herrick to Bryan, August 20, 1914, U.S., Department of State, *FR, Supplement, 1914*, pp. 482–83.
41. Page to Bryan, August 18, 1914, U.S., Department of State, *FR, Supplement, 1914*, pp. 481–82.

fiable and high-handed action."[42] Taking their cue from the developing opposition, the congressional committees began entertaining second thoughts about reporting the bill. Wilson, however, notified the press that he would nevertheless continue to push for the legislation and expected it to be enacted within the next few weeks.[43] Wilson also disregarded protests that the ship purchase bill represented a radical departure from the staid traditions of laissez faire and downgraded suggestions that it would be better to ride out the crisis than submit to government control and restrictions on private profits and investments. When Oswald Garrison Villard wrote that the shipping proposal would "put a tremendous argument in the mouths of the Socialists," Wilson returned that his proposal did not represent a permanent undertaking. Government had taken the initiative, he pointed out, because private enterprise had neither the capital nor the inclination to put into affect a shipping system concerned with the nation's total welfare. Government intercession under these circumstances was the "immediate and necessary thing" to do.[44] McAdoo took the same position. Directly after Morgan had called on him to express Wall Street's antipathy, the secretary noted that he was convinced that big business did not represent the will of the people and that the shipping bill had been the "essential thing to do in the present emergency."[45]

Wilson and McAdoo were absolutely convinced that private enterprise did not have sufficient funding to underwrite a shipping service that would meet administration requirements. In confirmation of this, the very same commercial interests opposing the ship purchase bill began to press upon the administration the P. A. S. Franklin plan—private entry into the ship purchase business with government guaranteed corporate bonds.[46] This development led Wilson and McAdoo to intensify their adamant support of a government corporation. It was not a question of the government's

---

42. From the notes of the president's secretary, Joseph Tumulty, on the contents of the letter from Morgan to Bryan, August 21, 1914, Wilson Papers; Wilson to Robert Lansing, August 22, 1914, ibid.

43. *New York Times,* August 25, 1914.

44. Villard to Wilson, August 27, 1914, Wilson Papers; Wilson to Villard, September 4, 1914, ibid.

45. McAdoo to Redfield, August 22, 1914, McAdoo Papers.

46. See, for example, E. J. McCormack (of the Moore & McCormack Steamship Co.) to Alexander, August 21, 1914, RG 41/75303-N, NA.

willingness to assume major risks. That had been demonstrated. Rather, it was a question as to whether the taxpayers' money was going to be used to underwrite big business or the entire national economy and all of its beneficiaries. Wilson emphasized this on the twenty-fourth,[47] and later that week Alexander and McAdoo elaborated on the same point with depth and emotion during hearings conducted by Alexander's House Committee on Merchant Marine and Fisheries. McAdoo pointed out that, in calling for guarantees, private enterprise had demonstrated conclusively its financial inability to provide shipping services concerned with eliminating the crisis and capitalizing on the unparalleled opportunities in the name of national interest: "It seems to me that if this enterprise must depend upon the credit of the Government to succeed, or to raise the necessary means, the Government might as well do the thing directly."[48] Alexander agreed: If the government had to "pay the fiddler, [it wanted] the right to name the dancers."[49] The private sector had failed to meet the needs of American foreign trade. "How much longer must we wait?" demanded the majority report.[50]

The shipping enterprises had a ready answer. In their opinion, government could expect to wait indefinitely. They offered new developments and sent, as McAdoo subsequently came to describe them, "swarms of lobbyists" to Washington to prove their significance. While big business voiced the now normative arguments that government's shipping proposition violated laissez faire and invited international complications, its back had also stiffened as the result of a turn of events in the economic picture. Almost simultaneous with the submittal of the ship purchase bill, a break had appeared in the economic crisis. The haze covering domestic and international finance had begun to lift, and the military storm at sea had subsided as the result of British naval superiority. Combined with these developments, government assistance to private enterprise broke the impasse and unleashed a deluge of business optimism. Anticipating large profits, the

47. *New York Times,* August 25, 1914.
48. U.S., Congress, House, Committee on Merchant Marine and Fisheries, *Government Ownership and Operation of Merchant Vessels in the Foreign Trade of the United States,* 63rd Cong., 2d. sess., Hearings on H.R. 18518. See Alexander's comments on August 28, 1914; McAdoo's on September 1, 1914.
49. Ibid., p. 15.
50. U.S., Congress, House, *Government Ownership and Operation of Merchant Vessels in the Foreign Trade of the United States,* 63rd Cong., 2d. sess., H. Rept. 1149, pt. 2.

shipping industries turned on their benefactors of the previous weeks. The Department of Commerce abetted their cause. Unlike McAdoo and Wilson, William C. Redfield at this time disfavored government involvement in shipping, which he thought premature and unnecessary. Although he was no less concerned than they with the economic emergencies and opportunities and later changed his mind on the shipping bill, Redfield decried the cabinet's impetuosity, argued the need for patient and planned growth, and maintained that government's responsibility was to assist business, not take it over.[51] He had taken pains therefore to inform McAdoo on August twenty-fourth that wheat had begun to move and that the embargo was likely to pass within the week.[52] Redfield and his assistant secretary, Edwin F. Sweet, labored to publicize this development, for both also viewed government ownership and purchase as a violation of international neutrality.[53] Redfield also opposed war risk insurance as a policy born of panic and a break with all economic precedents, despite the public clamor for it.[54] McAdoo was disturbed with the commerce secretary. He responded by placing the war risk insurance program under his own jurisdiction, although he had intended originally to put Redfield, a former insurance executive, at the head of its managing board.[55] Nevertheless, Redfield and Sweet continued to emphasize the positive change in the economic scene. The opposition gained considerable strength from their views. The House minority report to Alexander's hearings, for example, scoffed at the administration's ship purchase plan and cited as its main evidence Sweet's testimony that the War Risk Insurance and Ship Registry acts would augment the American merchant marine by no fewer than 125 ships, or, as Sweet put it, a supply "ample to meet all the needs of the nation's agricultural exporters."[56] Shortly before, Franklin had stated Wall Street's position when he main-

51. Redfield to McAdoo, August 8, 1914, Josephus Daniels Papers.

52. Redfield to McAdoo, August 24, 1914, McAdoo Papers.

53. Sweet differed somewhat from Redfield in that, while he opposed the ship purchase bill, he did not disfavor a government ownership scheme. See Sweet to Wilson, September 4, 1914, Wilson Papers, in which he makes clear this variance of opinion.

54. Redfield to Wilson, August 12, 1914, McAdoo Papers. Redfield's posture remained fairly consistent throughout the war and served as an important, if ineffectual, counterargument to the feverish degree with which administration shipping proponents worked for commercial expansion. Redfield also pushed for cooperation with the Allies to a much greater extent than did the president and other members of the administration.

55. McAdoo to Redfield, August 17, 1914, McAdoo Papers.

56. See note 50.

tained that shipping shortages were virtually nonexistent, now that business confidence was returning. As Franklin saw it, the main problem lay in inadequate credits and in the selfish decision of the wheat industry to raise its prices. Staying calm was Franklin's remedy. The crisis would pass shortly, and private enterprise would be more than up to the task.[57] Villard cautioned Wilson along similar lines. Perhaps the president was moving "too hastily," Villard advised, for the problem could well change in a few weeks.[58] These men concluded that McAdoo and Wilson had acted so quickly that business had been deprived of the opportunity to respond to the crisis on its own initiative. Looking back, the National Foreign Trade Council argued that the government decision had caused considerable disarray in private circles and that it had seriously stalled the investment of private capital in American shipping during those crucial summer weeks. The administration's ownership plan, it concluded, had been "launched before commercial and financial enterprise had recovered from the initial shock of war and before plans for any large [private] shipping venture could have been inaugurated."[59]

The amelioration of the economic crisis upon which Wilson and McAdoo based their program and the vociferous development of an invigorated and hostile opposition from the private sector put a halt to congressional efforts to push the administration's shipping proposal. No amount of effort could prompt the House into further consideration of the ship purchase bill, and the Senate committee never even reported the measure. The bill was dead by early September, and Wilson admitted as much toward the end of the congressional session that same month.[60] But neither Wilson nor McAdoo was prepared to call it quits. Both had come out of the fracas politically bruised, and neither would be satisfied until he had gone at least another round. McAdoo was particularly upset, for he was convinced that the administration had been deceived.[61] The remarkable accomplishments of the first two weeks of August, imbued with unprecedented government involvement in the economy and unusual business–government understanding and

---

57. *New York Times*, August 29, 1914.

58. Villard to Wilson, August 27, 1914, Wilson Papers.

59. National Foreign Trade Council, Report of the Merchant Marine Committee, *Effect of the War Upon American Foreign Commerce*.

60. Link, *The Struggle for Neutrality*, p. 91.

61. McAdoo, *Crowded Years*, pp. 304–305.

cooperation, had led McAdoo and his chief to believe that they could negotiate a step further. But they had gone too far: At practically no expense,
big business had secured enormous government assistance in the Treasury
Department's revivification of the economy and its export trade. Private
enterprise was satisfied. Once righted and attended to by a kind corner, the
shipping industries wanted to fight their own fights and reap their own
rewards. The president of the National City Bank of New York, Frank A.
Vanderlip, expressed it thus: "If we can get the government here in a
frame of mind where the making of profits is not considered a crime, and
make some profits and put those profits back into productive work, rather
than spending them for useless luxuries, we will get on our feet sometime.
That is the salvation of the situation, it seems to me."[62]

McAdoo and Wilson, however, were not about to accept this as the final
judgment. Neither would be content until he could know that the American
shipping industry would never be knocked down again, that it would enter
the fight for the international marketplace on at least even (if not superior)
terms, and that its struggle would be conducted along lines concerned with
the efficient, scientific, and immediate utilization of the vast opportunities
made available by the war. From experience, they were convinced that only
government control and direction could achieve this. Correspondingly, while
they admitted defeat in September, they went on notice that the fight would
recommence at the earliest possible moment.[63]

———— · ◆ · ————

This resolve had not diminished in the slightest when Congress recon-
vened in early December 1914. In fact, it had intensified. For if shipping
interests considered their own requisites satisfied after receiving the government's financial "hypo" during the month of August, little had occurred in
the intervening period to solve the administration's concerns—even par-
tially. Despite the restoration of optimism in shipping circles, a scarcity of
vessels for foreign trade still existed, and surplus goods continued to pile
up at alarming rates, a combination that precipitated a frightening rise in

62. Vanderlip to Stillman, September 18, 1914, Vanderlip Papers.
63. Wilson to Frank E. Doremus, September 4, 1914, Wilson Papers. This was an
open letter to the National Democratic Congressional Committee.

freight rates. Moreover, in addition to costing exorbitantly more, what shipping was available too often ignored less profitable trade and trade routes for more selective trade offering rapid and lucrative returns.

Beyond this remained the administration's concern to perfect the foreign trade system, now practically complete, with tariff and banking reforms. McAdoo pounded home this principle incessantly. He expressed this conviction to Major Higginson in mid-December:

> With our new tariff laws, and our new banking laws, which, for the first time in many years, have given our merchants and manufacturers the opportunity of conquering foreign markets, and with the favorable situation created for this purpose by the European war, but one thing more is needed, and that is the establishment of reliable sea transportation lines equal in character to those of our competitors, and operated at reasonable rates for freight and passengers. The opportunity is here now, and must be seized quickly.[64]

Wilson was in full accord. "What interests us just now," he remarked before packed congressional galleries on the eighth of December, "is our duty and our opportunity. How are we to build up a great trade if we have not the certain and constant means of transportation upon which all profitable and usefull commerce depends?" The shipping bill, he continued, was badly needed and could not be wisely postponed, and only the government, could "open these gates of trade, and open them wide."[65]

The following day, the bill was reported out of the Senate Commerce Committee, where it had been stalled since September. Although William F. Stone of Missouri and Duncan U. Fletcher of Florida were designated the administration's senatorial floor leaders for the controversial measure, McAdoo once again planned the strategy. Two major problems had to be pushed to the front, he informed Fletcher: the usurious and discriminatory freight rates and the lack of sufficient American vessels to service overseas trade. Both were seriously detrimental to the nation's foreign trade, and both could be readily solved by government operation and control of its own merchant fleet.[66] When the Senate passed a resolution calling on

64. McAdoo to Henry Lee Higginson, December 14, 1914, McAdoo Papers.
65. Woodrow Wilson, *Public Papers*, 2:219–20.
66. McAdoo to Fletcher, December 14, 1914, McAdoo Papers.

McAdoo and Redfield for detailed information on ocean rate increases, McAdoo reinforced these views: The whole world desired American goods, and American producers were more than prepared to supply the demand, but the means of transportation were not sufficient. Nothing prevented the further growth of the increasingly favorable balance of trade than "the absence of ships and the presence of high rates."[67]

McAdoo carried these views into the public arena. In early January 1915, he visited the West Coast, ostensibly on nonmaritime treasury matters. But he managed to deliver addresses for the shipping bill in San Diego and San Francisco, making a strong pitch for the measure on nonpartisan grounds. After all, he pointed out, economic matters transcended political considerations, and the shipping question as a purely economic concern was one that went "absolutely to the root of our republican institutions and . . . the root of the prosperity and welfare of our people." What difference did it make what type of political interest proposed it, so long as it was essential to the economy of the country.[68]

In the meantime, Fletcher's Senate committee was putting the final touches on its own bill. Its primary objective, the committee majority contended, was to alter American dependency upon the merchant marines of foreign competitors. Not only was American commerce subject to foreign interests and foreign risks, but foreign control compromised America's ability to capitalize on the commercial opportunities produced by the war. "At a time . . . when the world . . . is calling as never before for the products of our mines and factories, we are all but helpless in the face of the largest opportunity we have ever known."[69] Senator Stone introduced the bill on January fourth.

Wilson had probably made a mistake in selecting the junior Senator from Missouri as a manager for the shipping bill. Unlike Fletcher, his sedate and always cordial colleague, Stone had a fiery and impetuous temper and a fierce hatred for the G.O.P. Upon his report of the measure he intimated that the Democrats would force the bill, boasting outright that "we have

67. "Preliminary Report on Ocean Freight Rates," December 26, 1914, McAdoo Papers.
68. McAdoo speech manuscript, January 4, 1915, McAdoo Papers.
69. "Promotion of Foreign Commerce of the United States by Providing Adequate Shipping Facilities," draft of a report by the Senate Committee on Commerce, December 28, 1914, Wilson Papers.

the votes to put it through," and then tactlessly accusing the Republicans before the fact of planning to defeat the bill with the use of "inexcusable and unpardonable obstruction."[70] This behavior only served to solidify Republican opposition, and enmeshed the issue in partisan conflict. The essence of the conservative position was made clear when Henry Cabot Lodge accepted the challenge by retorting: "If any attempt is made to cut off proper discussion of the bill, I for one shall be ready to . . . use every possible means of parliamentary obstruction," thereby confirming what the Democrats feared.[71]

Stone's insensitive commentary was no less tactless than the words Wilson publicly used to castigate Lodge's position. Speaking in Indianapolis on the occasion of the Jackson Day celebration, the president ran away with himself, overcome by the "psychology of the stump," he later admitted.[72] Wilson railed against his Republican opponents and disloyal Democrats, calling them "misguided, blind, [and] ignorant. Who commissioned them, a minority, a lessening minority?" he thundered, and promised that they would be soundly whipped in the next election. Central to the shipping question was the national economy. "These Gentlemen are now seeking to defy the Nation and prevent the release of American products to the suffering world which needs them more than it ever needed them before. This country is bursting its jacket, and they are seeing to it that the jacket is not only kept tight, but is riveted with steel."[73]

McAdoo summed up the administration's case for a shipping bill before the Commercial Club of Chicago on the ninth of January. The address stressed the importance of the shipping bill for American economic expansion.

Not only has the war emphasized the imperative necessity for the quick creation of an American merchant marine, but it has created an exceptional opportunity for the extension of our trade in the open markets of the world.

How can we expect our enterprising men to make large capital outlays to produce the particular goods required for the South American trade, or

70. *Congressional Record*, 63rd Cong., 3rd sess., January 4, 1915, p. 904.
71. Ibid., p. 906.
72. Wilson to Mrs. Crawford H. Toy, January 31, 1915, cited in Link, *The Struggle for Neutrality*, p. 146.
73. Wilson, *Public Papers*, 2:242.

any special trade, and to enter upon an active campaign to get their share of the business, unless they have the certainty of transportation, at reasonable rates, for a sufficient length of time to establish the trade upon a firm and profitable basis? We must stand back of them through governmental action if we want them to succeed. We must develop South American and other foreign trade relations through the fundamental of sufficient transportation of the right sort, just as we developed the great West in the sixties by building, with governmental aid, the transcontinental railways, thereby adding an empire of territory and wealth to our national resources. . . . American trade in foreign markets will follow transportation under the American flag and thrive as it never did before. The markets of the world are before us—the Orient, as well as South America. Enterprise and courage are needed to secure them.

The objection that "the Government must never go into private business," even though private capital refuses to engage in such business, when the interests of the people imperatively demand it, is always urged against any progressive step of this character. Are we to be bound by a mere dogma of this sort? Are we to be deterred from doing, through the agencies of Government, what is essential to the welfare of our people, when private capital can not be secured? . . . . I am not afraid of the Government going into business where private capital refuses, and where the business in which the Government is to engage is for the benefit of *all* the people of the country.[74]

Undaunted, the business opposition presented its case as clearly as McAdoo by arguing that times were good and hardly of the "emergency" nature described by the administration. In five short months, it pointed out, the United States had cleared its huge indebtedness to Europe—a sure sign of prosperity. The rewards of high rates, at the same time, were considered "just" after years of moderate and less gain. "We deny," petitioned the maritime committee of the Boston Chamber of Commerce, "that there is any such extreme emergency. Chartering is active; vessels long idle are being employed; freight rates have advanced."[75] Its counterpart in New York seconded this contention. Vessel shortages and high rates were a great boon to shipping, it declared, "making it possible for the first time in years for American vessels to profitably engage in foreign trade." That in itself,

74. U.S., Congress, Senate, *The Shipping Bill*, 63rd Cong., 3rd sess., S. Doc. 713.
75. *New York Journal of Commerce*, June 11, 1915.

commercial interests insisted, could serve as a mighty stimulus to increase private maritime investment.[76]

The frank admission by business that freight rates were high, albeit desirable, corroborated the contentions of the administration. Consequently, the shipping lobby did not bother to deny allegations along those lines but staked its campaign on the two primary issues left hanging in September: first, that the adoption of the shipping bill guaranteed serious international complication, if not involvement in war; and second, that government construction and ship purchasing were inimical to private business interests and laissez faire.

The first issue was concerned largely with the means by which the government would acquire vessels. The shipping lobby maintained that on two accounts the government would have extreme difficulty in constructing its own fleet: For one, the booming shipbuilding industry was completely engaged, every American shipping way was filled with domestic and foreign orders. Also, the normal period to complete a standard oceangoing steamship was two years, a prohibitive length of time. And since the Ship Registry Act had failed to remedy the shipping shortage sufficiently, the government's last recourse would have to involve the purchase of available vessels. With almost every nonbelligerent bottom engaged in the immensely lucrative transatlantic trade, the interned ships of the German and Austrian commercial fleets appeared as the only solution. But with France and England clear in their opposition to such transfers, the business community had no desire, as one eminent shipper argued, "to take hold of the hot end of a poker by buying international complications."[77]

Wilson's early support of the Declaration of London of 1909 and his continued adherence to some of its principles were central to the controversy. When war broke out, rather than base his position as a neutral on existing international law, Wilson determined to adopt codes spelled out in the London Declaration early in William Howard Taft's administration. It was to America's advantage to do this because the declaration not only avoided the ambiguities of existing law but also granted neutrals unprec-

---

76. Irving T. Bush to Joseph Tumulty, December 15, 1914, Wilson Papers.

77. Agnes C. Laut, "Will the Shipping Bill Help or Hurt our Commerce?" Quoted here is the same Irving T. Bush (see note 76), who owned a sizable amount of New York's waterfront terminal facilities.

edented rights during time of war. These rights included, among others, the authority to register or purchase belligerent vessels for neutral use. No nation had ratified the rules, but France and Germany had incorporated them into their prize codes. When England resolutely refused to adopt the regulations of the declaration without modification, on the grounds that the rights it granted to neutral trade would damage if not seriously impede the Allied war effort, Wilson backed off. He was prompted by the realization that English naval supremacy demanded it and by the unavoidable reality that the preponderance of American trade was with the Allied nations. Consequently, on October 21, Wilson and Lansing agreed to table the American position and accept existing international codes.[78]

Nevertheless, while Wilson's decision indicated, on face, American willingness to adhere to British definitions, in reality the president continued to champion neutral trade rights. If British policy as outlined by Sir Edward Grey was "to secure the maximum of blockade that could be enforced without a rupture with the United States,"[79] Wilson pursued a policy aimed at securing the maximum trade and maritime access to foreign markets short of provoking Great Britain into ruinous recriminations. Clearly, the president was willing to push this policy to great lengths. His involvement in the well-known case of the *Dacia*, an international *cause célèbre* which was played out from start to finish during the congressional second session debate over the administration's shipping bill, emphasized the point.

The *Dacia* was a German merchant vessel that avoided capture at the outbreak of war by taking refuge in Port Arthur, Texas. Subsequently, it was purchased by an American, Edward N. Breitung, who claimed he made the transaction for "purely business motives."[80] He then announced that he would outfit the ship for a commercial voyage to either Bremen or neutral Rotterdam with cotton for Germany. Breitung justified his purchase and destination on the opinion written by the solicitor to the State Department on the right to buy the ships of belligerents as authorized by the now, for all practical purposes, defunct Declaration of London. Wilson's unwillingness to circumscribe Breitung's activities can be interpreted as his determi-

---

78. Link, *The Struggle for Neutrality*, pp. 105–25.
79. Edward Grey (Viscount Grey of Fallodon), *Twenty-Five Years, 1892–1916*, 2:107.
80. "Affidavits of Officers of the Hamburg-American Line and Breitung & Co., Ltd.," March 22, 1915, Wilson Papers.

nation to champion his concept of neutral rights despite British and French restrictions.

It is significant that the *Dacia* case became prominent at precisely the moment of a marked deterioration in Anglo-American relations. The antagonism between London and Washington arose primarily from Wilson's loss of patience with British impositions on American trade and from British concerns over two developments. The British felt that the German-American lobby on Capitol Hill was gaining prominence and that the pending ship purchase bill would not only pay demoralizing dividends to the enemy if passed but also be used aggressively by Wilson to increase American neutral economic gains by redressing the imbalance between the British and American mercantile fleets.[81]

Wilson drove the opening wedge on December 26, 1914 with a scorching note asserting that British policy was bankrupting American business and, consequently, eroding Anglo-American friendship. The note had implications for the *Dacia* case, for Wilson also insisted upon the right of Americans to carry on commerce with neutral nations contiguous to the belligerents.[82] Breitung's tentative destination of Rotterdam would fit within this classification. Although Wilson was informed at once by both the Foreign Office and his own State Department of the certainties of Allied refusal to recognize the transfer, he obdurately refused to influence Breitung's preparations to sail.[83] A barrage of accusations from the British press that the United States had pushed its efforts to increase its neutral trade growth and prosperity to extremes had no apparent affect either.

Two things were at stake for Wilson: the theoretical rights of neutrals to engage in commerce during time of war and the practical need to augment American maritime services. The first involved Wilson's determination to push England to the limit on neutral shipping rights. It is evident that he had no intention of guaranteeing Breitung's efforts to reach German markets. What concerned the president was the need to champion the

---

81. For an assessment arguing that Anglo-American relations were improving, rather than deteriorating, see Gregory, "A New Look at the Case of the Dacia."

82. Bryan to Page, December 26, 1914, U.S., Department of State, *FR, Supplement, 1914,* pp. 372–75.

83. Spring Rice memorandum for Bryan, January 2, 1915, U.S., Department of State, *FR, Supplement, 1915,* p. 675; Lansing to Wilson, January 9, 1915, Wilson Papers; Bryan to Wilson, January 11, 1915, ibid.

international rights of neutrality, especially the right of neutrals to buy belligerent vessels and use them in neutral trade. Otherwise there would have been little purpose in supporting the ship purchase bill at all. Josephus Daniels, secretary of the navy, observed that Wilson had

> expressed faith that the ship bill would pass [and] combatted the suggestion that we might declare it was not the purpose to buy the German merchant ships interned, but that we should insist upon our right even though we should not exercise it.[84]

More to the point, it is doubtful whether Wilson ever seriously considered not exercising the right. In November 1914, Wilson and McAdoo corresponded actively on this subject. As the latter remarked, there was "no other way in which to get [ships] quickly."[85] Fletcher, Alexander, and Furnifold Simmons, chairman of the Senate Committee on Finance, were well aware of Wilson's line of thought. Although by January 1915 the president had resigned himself to the practical impossibility of using German ships for trade in the war zone, as late as February there was discussion in the White House about placing the belligerent vessels in coastwise trade. Such an action would release bonafide American ships for European commerce and make German bottoms available for Latin American trade.[86] As McAdoo saw it, America would "cease to be a nation" if it compromised its neutral rights to purchase belligerent vessels.[87]

Given these attitudes, Wilson ignored protestations from Bryan and Page that allowing the *Dacia* to proceed would seriously violate the spirit of neutrality. Spring Rice's uncompromising denunciation of the *Dacia* as an American test case impressed Bryan, and he informed Wilson that he and the counselor to the State Department, Robert Lansing, had concluded that it was incumbent upon the president to announce that the government

---

84. Daniels, *Cabinet Diaries,* January 26, 1915, p. 94.
85. McAdoo to Wilson, November 7, 1914, McAdoo Papers. See also Wilson to McAdoo, November 8, 1914, ibid.; McAdoo to Wilson, November 21, 1914, ibid.
86. Wilson to McAdoo, February 8, 1915, Wilson Papers; Wilson to Charles Eliot, February 18, 1915, quoted in Baker, *Woodrow Wilson,* 5:132, note. There was considerable talk about placing military vessels in the coastal trade, but this would have necessitated a revision of existing laws and would not have passed, given congressional feelings. See McAdoo to Wilson, February 9, 1915, Wilson Papers.
87. McAdoo to George W. Norris, February 24, 1915, McAdoo Papers.

would not employ the shipping bill to purchase German ships. Wilson rejected their position at once,[88] calling the embargo and any effort at seizure "arbitrary, unnecessary, and irresponsible" and instructing Page to notify the British that the belligerent ships would be used solely for the trade of the United States: The need for ships to permit the release of American goods was so acute that if they could not be purchased the government would build its own. It was Wilson's conviction that the British were naively acting as if they felt that the mere apprehension of the *Dacia* would end his efforts to establish government maritime service.[89]

All of this served to strengthen congressional opposition, which increased in formidability with each passing day. Lodge's contention that "there is all the difference in the world between the dangers to be apprehended from the privately-owned ship getting into trouble, which are insignificant dangers, and the international dangers arising from Government-owned ships," spelled out clearly the position of the lobby against the shipping bill.[90] Wilson's position on the *Dacia* played an important role in intensifying antagonism to the measure.

As Breitung's vessel prepared to slip her hausers in Galveston in late January, attention focused on the second essential concern of the opposition, the so-called "treacherous" entrance of government into the sanctuary of private enterprise. Former secretary of state Elihu Root denounced the measure as a "complete departure [and a] repudiation more signal than has ever yet been made of the principles of the great leader of the party which 'has the votes' to put this bill through."[91] The National Foreign Trade Council, meeting in St. Louis for its second annual convention, had serious reservations about the permanency of a government merchant marine, despite its support of McAdoo in the early stages of the war. Its president, James J. Hill, uttered the sentiments of most of its membership when he called the bill "an unwise and . . . disastrous experiment" and concluded that "private enterprise cannot possibly compete with a government which

88. Bryan to Wilson, January 22, 1915, Department of State, File No. 195.2/200a, National Archives. Hereafter cited as SD, plus file number, NA.

89. Wilson to Page, January 23, 1915, Wilson Papers.

90. Lodge to Higginson, February 5, 1915, cited in John A. Garraty, *Henry Cabot Lodge*, p. 310.

91. *Congressional Record*, 63rd Cong., 3rd sess., January 4, 1915, p. 909.

pays no interest on the cost of its ships, and throws aside considerations of profit and loss."[92]

Secretary of Commerce Redfield, a guest speaker at the NFTC convention, jumped up in heated and extemporaneous rebuttal. Now converted from his earlier opposition to the shipping bill, Redfield dismissed Hill's contentions as insubstantial: Private ownership was not concerned for the welfare of the nation but only for itself. He called business support of high rates "extortion," and a situation that "cries out to Heaven as a foul stench." American commerce had a right to move, Redfield argued. The administration had waited disappointedly for long months for private enterprise to solve the dilemma, but only government effort appeared capable of doing the job.[93] Redfield was talking facts on the basis of the final report he and McAdoo had prepared for Congress on the phenomenal rise of ocean freight rates. Supported by scores of letters, the report was an impressive corroboration of their reasoning that shipping greed was seriously checking American foreign commerce. First considerations, they contended, belonged not to a few usurious vessel owners, whose investment in foreign commerce was practically infinitesimal, but to "our farms, merchants, manufacturers and business men whose activities produce our great export trade."[94]

"I am not wedded to government ownership and operation of anything," McAdoo elaborated in debate before the United States Chamber of Commerce, "but I am opposed to the American Government sitting still in the face of an acute crisis when our vital interests are at stake." It was not a case of government going into business for the first time, he asserted. Private capital had failed to build the Panama Canal or the railroad that paralleled it. For eleven years, the government had operated the Panama Railroad Steamship Company with rates lowered since its inception by as much as 50 percent. A revenue cutter service had been maintained by the Treasury Department since 1790. The postmaster general's office had assumed parcel post responsibilities, previously in the hands of private enterprise, and the government's construction of an Alaskan railroad for the purpose of making available the mineral wealth of that territory for the

92. National Foreign Trade Council Convention, 1915, *Proceedings*, p. 191.

93. Ibid., pp. 194–95, 200–201.

94. U.S., Congress, Senate, *Increased Ocean Transportation Rates*, 63rd Cong., 3rd sess., S. Doc. 637, pt. 2.

benefit of all had met with national acclaim.[95] In short, to McAdoo the argument that the shipping bill represented a new departure was a subterfuge. It was all the more infuriating because of the necessity to take advantage of the wartime opportunities for enlargening foreign commerce. "This opportunity will not last—it must be grasped now," he counseled the secretary of the interior. To editor Albert Shaw he vented his spleen and declared: "I . . . condemn them for opposing a measure so imperatively demanded in the interest of our commerce and in the interest of the prosperity of the country."[96]

But McAdoo's resolve was not sufficient to bring about a change in the opposition. Nor was it capable of insuring solidarity in his own political camp. On February 1, seven Democratic senators bolted the party on its shipping position, censuring the measure as a monumental and dangerous step toward state control. The crux of the problem lay in Wilson's unwillingness to compromise and his failure to speak clearly as to whether the proposed government maritime fleet was to be temporary or permanent. On a number of earlier occasions, Wilson had spoken of the bill as a temporary expedient. In his December address to Congress he declared that "when the carriage has become sufficiently profitable to attract and engage private capital and engage it in abundance, the Government ought to withdraw."[97] But after another hint of the same kind in his Jackson Day peroration, the president had become conspicuously silent on the subject. The rhetoric of Wilson's congressional and administrative leaders complicated matters. Unlike the president, Alexander never equivocated as to the need for permanent state control. But Fletcher, after first taking an identical position, withered under Republican attacks in the Senate in early January and reversed himself. Ironically, McAdoo and Redfield attempted to steer clear of the issue. When forced to confront it, they suggested a willingness to compromise, but on account of their vociferous and aggressive support for the bill, they were construed by the opposition as supporters of a permanent merchant marine.

95. U.S., Congress, Senate, *The Opposition and the Shipping Bill,* 63rd Cong., 3rd sess., S. Doc. 949.

96. McAdoo to Franklin K. Lane, January 25, 1915, McAdoo Papers; McAdoo to Shaw, January 25, 1915, ibid.

97. Wilson, *Public Papers,* 2:220.

If the people at large were unclear as to Wilson's position, however, those moving in White House circles were not. They realized that despite the president's public statements one of the major impediments to the shipping bill was Wilson's staunch marriage to the concept of permanent state ownership. This has been made clearer by notes left by the House majority leader, Claude Kitchin.[98] Convinced that a program of permanent government control would destroy the prospect of the bill's success and, more important, the solidarity of the Democratic party, Kitchin, Simmons, Fletcher, Albert S. Burleson (the postmaster general), and McAdoo attempted on the eleventh and twelfth of January to change Wilson's mind. They asked the president to accept an arrangement wherein government control and operation would cease no later than two years after the end of war. Simmons, Fletcher, and Kitchin were unsuccessful at first, but Burleson and McAdoo tried again and felt that they had succeeded in gaining the objective. On the following morning, however, Wilson informed Burleson that he would not move from his former position. It is evident, therefore, that by mid-January Wilson's advisers and a number of Democratic congressmen were prepared to compromise in order to obtain the immediate legislative goal, while the president was not.

In late January, the president's political managers used strong-arm tactics to get the party in line. Nevertheless, although most would support the bill, only thirty-seven of fifty-three Democratic senators would pledge to bind themselves to the measure. Although compromise politics were absolutely the order of the day, Wilson's political obstinacy and his predilection for long-term commercial growth and preparedness ruled out a temporary merchant marine. Wilson's refusal to compromise was all the more important because, after the bolt on February first, six of the seven Democratic dissidents indicated a willingness to accept temporary government ownership. Still, with the passage of the bill frequently swinging upon the hinges of a single vote, Wilson would not yield. Prompted by one of the dissidents, a House committee modified the bill to strike out the permanent feature, but Alexander, the one close presidential supporter who had refused to compromise, amended it with a provision that would have transferred the

98. These abbreviated notes, scribbled on a copy of the Gore bill introduced on February 3, 1915 in the Senate, are located under that date in the Claude Kitchin Papers.

temporary government fleet to the navy two years after the cessation of hostilities. This rider hardly met the requirements of the seven outlaws, and it certainly did not satisfy the Republican filibusterers who determined, in the words of Senator Jacob Gallinger, to "beat the shipping bill if it takes all summer."[99]

On February 28, the announcement that the *Dacia* had been captured in the English Channel by a French cruiser slammed the lid on the administration's case. The dangers implicit in the dispatch of government vessels to the war zone, combined with successful Republican filibustering and the disunity of the Democrats, killed all hopes for passage of the shipping bill. Accordingly, the Democrats soon laid down their arguments, and the session ended on March fourth.[100] Four days later, McAdoo released a statement, authorized by and jointly drafted with the president: "The shipping bill never did have in view the purchase of the interned German ships, or any specific ships." The evidence suggested, however, that McAdoo was less than candid. A more plausible part of the statement was McAdoo's explanation for the president's refusal to surrender an essential neutral right: "To preserve this vital right did not mean that it must be asserted, but it did mean that this Government felt keenly its responsibility as the chief representative and trustee of neutral rights."[101]

Wilson's commitment to the overall expansion of American trade paralleled the moral and political considerations. A primary concern had been to meet national commercial emergencies and take advantage of the unmatched wartime opportunities. The opponents of the shipping bill, he concluded on March 3, had failed to take these needs into consideration: It was a time of extraordinary crisis and need, yet, the shortsighted forces of reaction had struck hard on behalf of privilege and self-interest at precisely a time "when all the rest of the world needed what America produces,

---

99. Gallinger to James O. Lyford, February 6, 1915, Jacob H. Gallinger Papers. This analysis differs from that of Arthur Link, who blaims the bolters for reneging when Wilson "was willing to concede most of their demands," including the question of permanent government ownership, on or about February 2, 1915. See *The Struggle for Neutrality*, p. 154. To this reader, however, the behavior of Wilson's floor managers, especially Alexander, suggests a policy to the contrary.

100. For an account of the political struggle for passage of the bill see Allin, "Ill-Timed Initiative."

101. Untitled paper, March 8, 1914, McAdoo Papers.

and America was ready to supply that need,—when the whole foreign trade of the country was threatened with a disastrous congestion and the fortunes and opportunities of thousands of her people put at jeopardy."[102] The president's remarks were an indication that the issue of shipping and the national interest was as vibrant as ever and that he had no intention whatever of putting it aside. An opportunity to reinitiate the battle took place several months later when the elongation and intensification of the European war created a rationalization for a national program of military and commercial preparedness.

102. From a statement that Wilson prepared but did not release, circa March 3, 1915, cited by Link, *The Struggle for Neutrality*, p. 159.

Chapter IV

Legislative Victory:
The Shipping Act of 1916

Although some mention of the need for a military preparedness program had been made in 1914, the crises created by the devastations of underseas warfare generated a genuine movement toward armament in the spring and summer of 1915. The sinking of the *Lusitania* on May seventh turned the tide in favor of such an effort. While the loss of the ship made clearer than ever how ill equipped the nation was to wage war, men with commercial vision feared also that it would seriously complicate an already faulty transportation system for the carriage of American goods. For if the Germans were able to construct submarines capable of commanding the seas, then serviced almost entirely by Allied and neutral ships, ocean trade to America would collapse. Under these circumstances, the need for an American merchant marine was even more imperative. Redfield noted as much in June when the president of the International Paper Company complained that he could not secure transportation for his wood products. The secretary bemoaned the lost opportunity, admitting the humiliation of being so dependent upon foreign ships. If Great Britain should fall victim to Germany, he noted ruefully, "the jaws of disaster would close upon our foreign trade like a trap. To be in a position of this kind is the serious thing, beside which other considerations are trifles."[1] Benjamin J. Rosenthal, a close supporter of McAdoo's maritime policy, agreed: It seemed incredible that the United States played with fate, trusting that England and France would

1. Redfield to Philip T. Dodge, June 5, 1915, McAdoo Papers.

continue to control the seas. America was sitting on a time bomb which at any moment was likely to explode and "smash its oversea commerce to smithereens."[2]

Because he was an official of the National Business League of America, Rosenthal backing a government merchant marine represented a striking exception to the rule, for the vast majority of the nation's commercial and financial moguls remained dead set against the administration's shipping position. As the result of the past year's struggles, McAdoo's pessimism about the willingness or ability of big business to alleviate the shipping shortage had increased markedly. "It is simply fatuous to hope that private capital will provide . . . ships," he complained on August 1, 1915 to the president of a southern chamber of commerce: "Our capitalists are not interested in the shipping business—not because they cannot make money in the shipping business, but because they can make more money in other directions. [Moreover] they are not familiar with shipping enterprises and will not engage in them in any large scale, no matter what inducements may be held out."[3] McAdoo had in mind two important examples illustrating the failure of private shipping interests to tend to the nation's important oriental trade. The first concerned the administration's efforts to assist American business in establishing a new transpacific steamship company.

In mid-December 1914, the American minister to China, Paul S. Reinsch, had informed the State Department that the Chinese government was desirous of establishing a Sino-American merchant marine company to operate between New York, Gulf ports, and China. It contemplated the creation of a small fleet of five to six 8,000 ton, twelve knot vessels. Two forms of organization were proposed by the Chinese minister of finance. The first would be capitalized entirely by the Chinese, but its operations would be run by an American general manager and American officers and engineers. The second would be a joint Sino-American venture with similar American operational staffs. For the first year, chartered ships would be used, but construction was also being considered.[4] In early January, responsibility for advertising the Chinese government's plan to American capital

2. Benjamin J. Rosenthal, *The Need of the Hour*, p. 54.

3. McAdoo to Charles W. Gold, August 1, 1915, McAdoo Papers.

4. Paul Reinsch to Bryan, December 16, 1914, SD 800.8890/81, NA; Reinsch to Bryan, December 21, 1914, SD 800/8890/89, NA.

was assigned to E. T. Chamberlain, commissioner of navigation in the Commerce Department. Chamberlain immediately contacted the nation's ten leading foreign trade and shipping interests. These were James Farrell of U.S. Steel, P. A. S. Franklin of the IMMC, R. P. Schwerin of the Pacific Mail Steamship Company, W. A. Burns of the American-Asiatic Steamship Company, James J. Hill of the Great Northern Railway, William H. Libby of Standard Oil, the National City Bank's Frank A. Vanderlip, J. Parker Kirlin of the Barber Line, and Robert Patchin and John Foord, secretaries respectively of the NFTC and the American Asiatic Association.[5]

Six of the ten responded to Chamberlain's overtures, none of them favorably. To the IMMC, for instance, the operation was unfeasible. The company had all of its tonnage tied up in other trades. Hill and Schwerin were frankly discordial. They seemed to resent the invitation, arguing that it was foolish to attempt such a venture as it was financially impossible on account of government marine laws for American registered vessels to operate in competition with ships of other nations using cheap Asiatic crews and covered by substantial government subsidies.[6] In summary, the best organized, financed, and largest American shipping interests were less than lukewarm, some even hostile, to the opportunity. Ultimately, the only taker was a firm in Cumberland, Maryland—F. Merten's Sons. Marginal at best, the Pacific & Eastern Steamship Company, as the firm named its line, ran into all sorts of organizational difficulties, not the least of which was its inability to charter ships. By midsummer 1915, the new line was still only a paper fleet.[7] Moreover, the whole enterprise frustrated and angered McAdoo. "It ought to make our great Government realize how impotently it is acting in a situation where it is depending upon weaker and less finan-

5. E. T. Chamberlain to James A. Farrell and others named in the text, January 11, 1915, SD 800.8890/84, NA.
6. Franklin to Chamberlain, January 13, 1915, RG 41/78131-N; Hill to Chamberlain, January 13, 1915, ibid.; Schwerin to Chamberlain, January 13, 1915, ibid.
7. The Pacific & Eastern Steamship Company (PESC) was organized finally in October 1915, but still could not purchase or charter ships, none being available. By March 1916, the firm had fallen out of favor with the State Department and especially with Reinsch, whose impatience to inaugurate the line was frayed beyond repair. See, for example, Reinsch to Lansing, March 13, 1916 SD 800.8890/143, NA. The history of the PESC and the negative impact it had on Sino-American relations is covered in Noel Pugach, "American Shipping Promoters and the Shipping Crisis of 1914–1916."

cially strong nations to back up and provide the facilities which we should be only too willing to provide ourselves," he pointed out to Redfield.[8]

To make matters worse, The Robert Dollar Line switched to Canadian registry and Schwerin's line, the Pacific Mail Steamship Company (PMSC), announced plans to sell out. These moves threatened to leave United States shipping service on the Pacific, minimal as it was, in even sorrier condition. Japanese interests were moving quickly to increase their control of trans-pacific shipping by making offers for PMSC vessels, much to McAdoo's indignation, and by adding new lines. Such was the situation when McAdoo complained in early August that private enterprise cared less for shipping as a national trade requirement than it did for making handsome profits on the Atlantic: "It was time for all American people to look this momentous shipping problem squarely in the face . . . . and we must resort to extraordinary measures, if necessary."[9]

War events added new dimensions to the scenario in late summer 1915. Much has been made of the successful efforts of McAdoo and Lansing to persuade Wilson to rescind the strict ban on loans to belligerents imposed by the president and the now departed Bryan the previous year. In short, McAdoo and Robert Lansing, secretary of state after Bryan's resignation following the *Lusitania* sinking, were so intensely concerned with the economic welfare of the United States that they were willing to compromise what Lansing termed "the true spirit of neutrality" in order to extend massive credit to the Allies, who were now running seriously short of cash reserves.[10] Ideally, the policy should be applied worldwide, McAdoo noted; America's resources had assumed such remarkable proportions in just one year that a global credits program would be the perfect way to add icing to the cake. On the very brink of unparalleled prosperity, the United States had only to enable its customers to buy. But the mere extension of credit would not be sufficient on its own: While the Allies had the resources to transport the goods secured on credit, other nations, particularly those of

---

8. McAdoo to Redfield, October 6, 1915, McAdoo Papers.

9. McAdoo to Gold, August 1, 1915, McAdoo Papers.

10. McAdoo to Wilson, August 21, 1915, Wilson Papers; Lansing to Wilson, September 6, 1915, quoted in Carlton Savage, ed., *Policy of the United States toward Maritime Commerce in War*, 2:378–81. See also Paul Birdsall, "Neutrality and Economic Pressures, 1914–1917."

Latin America, did not. In other words, McAdoo's concept of a functional credit arrangement required an integrated and efficient transportation system to move goods to interested consumers everywhere. "If we can only deal intelligently with the shipping situation," he informed North Carolina senator Claude Kitchin, "we can put our commerce upon a secure foundation from which it never can be shaken and from which our people will derive inestimable benefits."[11]

McAdoo conceived of the campaign for military preparedness as a solution to private capital's resistance to a government shipping program. After first promising to modify the shipping bill so as to satisfy even the most reluctant Democrats, the treasury head pieced together a propaganda platform from which he proposed to market the merchant fleet as an auxiliary force necessary to buttress the United States Navy. In essence, McAdoo determined to subordinate the commercial argument for shipping to the age-long rationalization of its requirement as a vehicle for military efficiency. It was the expedient thing to do, he later remarked, since experience had convinced him that, "people as a rule are far more interested in fighting, and in preparation for fighting, than they are in any constructive commercial or industrial effort."[12] On October 13, three weeks in advance of the administration's official delineation of its preparedness program, McAdoo undertook a long speaking tour to the Pacific Coast in support of his proposals.

The secretary's "first-nighter" before the chamber of commerce in Indianapolis keynoted the new emphasis: "A merchant marine is just as essential to the effectiveness of the Navy . . . as the guns upon the decks of our battleships!" The very essence of preparedness was for the navy to have auxiliaries where they could be quickly and easily secured. By building the necessary naval auxiliaries, moreover, the nation could develop a type that would provide a more efficient merchant marine than any other nation on earth. Besides their role as supplements to national defense, these ships would help to "enlarge our foreign trade and carry our influence, both financial and commercial, into the open markets of the world." The maintenance and extension of that foreign commerce was imperative to the

---

11. McAdoo to Kitchin, August 24, 1915, Kitchin Papers.
12. McAdoo, *Crowded Years*, pp. 311–12.

national economy. "We must have foreign markets to absorb our surplus products. Without them we shall have stagnation and depression and idleness and want." He then argued that Americans would have to "move swiftly" to take over the oriental and South American markets abandoned by the belligerents, for "if we do it now, we can establish ourselves so firmly that we can not be dislodged." Unparalleled prosperity was in the offing if only the United States would avail itself of the opportunities. But the timidity of private enterprise would not permit the ready realization of this promise. In sum, the United States was confronted by a situation demanding prompt and vigorous treatment by some agency strong enough, financially and otherwise, to be effective. There was no question in McAdoo's mind—the United States government was that agency.[13]

McAdoo used his western tour in an effort to cultivate agricultural support for a national merchant fleet. Speaking in Nebraska, North Dakota, and Montana, the secretary threatened that agrarians would slumber into ruin if they did not increase their efforts to solve the nation's oceanic transportation problems. Without foreign markets, he reminded an audience in wheat-wealthy Fargo, "the farmers of this country will suffer more than any other class of people." An American naval auxiliary would enable the producers to meet the wheat competition of the world by giving the farmer a "square deal and a fair chance." McAdoo did not lose the opportunity to harp on the old populist strains of antimonopolism. The shipping bill, he promised, would crush maritime monopolies and their extortionate rate systems through the creation of a shipping board. In the end, government control would serve the needs and prosperity of all the people and not just a privileged few.[14]

McAdoo's arrival in Seattle provided him with new targets in the infidelities of West Coast shipping. At the beginning of the war, America's only full-fledged overseas runs had been conducted on the Pacific. By 1915, however, every major West Coast shipping concern had either sold out to the foremost competitor, Japan, reregistered its vessels under foreign flag, transferred its fleet to the routes of the more profitable Atlantic trade, or

13. McAdoo address, "A Naval Auxiliary Merchant Marine," copy of in McAdoo to Wilson, October 9, 1915, Wilson Papers.
14. McAdoo addresses at Fargo, North Dakota, October 29, 1915, and Helena, Montana, October 28, 1915, McAdoo Papers; *Kansas City Times*, October 15, 1915.

prepared to do so. Ostensibly, the shipping companies claimed that the provisions of the LaFollette Seamen's Act signed by Wilson in March 1915 raised expenses prohibitively by forcing American shipowners to employ fewer foreigners and by upgrading wages and working conditions. The consequences, they argued, were making it impossible for American ships to compete with the less expensively operated Japanese merchant fleet.[15] But Redfield and McAdoo had essayed the problem thoroughly. Both were convinced that while the Seamen's Act had its shortcomings, it was being used mainly as an artifice to cloud the realities of fast-buck opportunism on the part of the shipowners.[16] The case of the Pacific Mail Steamship Company continued to occupy McAdoo's mind, especially now that he was face to face with its actual operation. He became so alarmed at the gap developing on the Pacific that he telegraphed the White House for authorization to use army and navy transports as replacements for the Pacific Mail's vessels. But this request was turned down by Daniels and secretary of war Lindley M. Garrison on the grounds that it would be legislatively unfeasible.[17]

Nevertheless, McAdoo felt the tour had done much to help the cause. "I had a great trip," he wrote Colonel House, "and found the interest in the Naval Auxiliary Merchant Marine question very great wherever I went."[18] While McAdoo continued to stress military preparedness, he was actually much more concerned with the nonmilitary nature of the shipping issue. On one of the last legs of his tour, in an interview conducted on the train between Minneapolis and St. Paul, he said: "The providing of suitable naval auxiliaries is not the only purpose of the administration in advocating

15. Emerson E. Parvin, secretary of the IMMC, gives the clearest defense of his company's position in "The Working of the Seamen's Act"; an impartial analysis is Earl A. Saliers, "Some Financial Aspects of the International Mercantile Marine Company"; for the reasoning of The Robert Dollar Steamship Company, see Dollar to Bernard N. Baker, October 26, 1915, McAdoo Papers; the background of the Seamen's Act is covered in Jerold S. Auerbach, "Progressives at Sea."

16. Redfield to McAdoo, July 8, 1915, Wilson Papers; McAdoo to Wilson, August 27, 1915, McAdoo Papers.

17. McAdoo to Wilson, October 26, 1915, Wilson Papers. On account of rising freight rates on the Pacific, the PMSC did not remove all of its vessels from oriental service; see Broesamle, *McAdoo*, p. 217.

18. McAdoo to House, November 4, 1915, McAdoo Papers. Robert Dollar listened to McAdoo on the West Coast and reported that he had changed his mind and would favor certain forms of government ownership; see Dollar to Bernard Baker, October 26, 1915, ibid.

a merchant marine, I may say that it is not even the principal purpose."
What concerned him was the phenomenal growth of America's commerce
and the paramount need for outlets, especially to Latin America. Without
American ships, both would be seriously impeded.[19]

From the war's commencement, the Wilson administration stressed the
need for increased Pan-American trade. Its effort to bring about maritime
reform in August 1914 was designed to help bring those aspirations into
actuality. Business recognized that. The ship purchase bill, an NFTC
spokesman noted, was "an emergency provision to pioneer business in certain undeveloped fields, to establish a merchant marine in South America,
to connect South American countries more closely with the United States
by fast steamship lines and good freight lines, at moderate prices."[20] The
effort to develop Pan-American commercial ties, however, went beyond the
fundamental desire to increase American foreign trade. Many officials were
able to rationalize such a policy on moral grounds as well. Wilson had long
argued that in contrast to that of other nations, American foreign trade
always had a liberalizing influence. To "supply and serve" the world was
an important thrust of the president's foreign policy. In his address at
Mobile, Alabama late in 1913, Wilson applied this notion specifically to
the Western Hemisphere. The American ambassador to England, Walter
Page, recalled that speech and hastened, once war began, to remind Wilson
and Colonel House of its importance: An English victory would result in
British omnipotence and probably leave the United States isolated in world
affairs. But a German victory would destroy America's hemispheric influence. The alternatives were twofold: First, the United States could
support Great Britain in order to gain a seat at the postwar peace conference.
Or it could organize European and South American neutrals into an independent pressure bloc. Page favored both, but while the first could wait
temporarily, the second could be best achieved by moving quickly while
the European powers were entangled in mortal combat.[21] House also considered the creation of a Pan-American system as a means of guaranteeing

19. *St. Paul Dispatch,* November 1, 1915.

20. W. L. Saunders to Redfield, December 17, 1914, Record Group 40, General Records
of the Department of Commerce, Office of the Secretary, General Correspondence/72155/18,
Part 1A, National Archives (hereafter cited as RG 40 plus file number, NA).

21. Bell, *Righteous Conquest,* pp. 94–95.

the United States an important role at the peace conference. He called for a union that would protect the Western Hemisphere from external aggression and provide the machinery to settle disputes on a worldwide basis. Employing these arguments as guidelines, Wilson and House drafted a Pan-American pact in mid-December 1914.[22]

At no time, however, did the administration believe it could achieve these ends without first creating the communication and transportation means. Not until shipping was established on a regular basis, this argument held, could the fruits of the union be fully realized. McAdoo's conviction that the shipping bill would pass in the winter of 1914–1915 led him to suggest to Wilson the next step in that sequence—convening a Pan-American conference to formulate the commercial ties sure to develop from the government's new shipping services.[23] That the bill failed to pass emphasized the significance of such a conference for the creation of important maritime publicity and support. The Pan-American Financial Conference of 1915 was held in Washington, D.C. on May 24–29.

The conference drew a distinguished assemblage of the Western Hemisphere's leading statesmen, financiers, and businessmen. Taking no chances, McAdoo dispatched emphatic briefs to key delegates explaining the deliberations and outlining the necessary conclusions that had to be reached.[24] His efforts were more than rewarded; after five days the conference decided unanimously in favor of the two requisites McAdoo had stressed in his instructions. First, ample financial credit had to be granted to Latin America along with the prompt provision of the necessary facilities and organizations enabling its use. Second, steamship service between the Americas was imperatively needed and had to be established at once.[25] As for the shipping requirement, Wilson said as much when he greeted the delegates on the White House lawn. "There is one thing that stands in our way," he remarked. A commercial union between North and South America was out

22. Ibid., p. 95.
23. McAdoo to Wilson, October 28, 1914, McAdoo Papers.
24. See, for example, McAdoo to Redfield, May 12, 1915, McAdoo Papers; McAdoo to A. H. Wiggin, May 11, 1915, ibid.; McAdoo memorandum for Eduardo Saurez Muvica, May 17, 1915, ibid.
25. "Letter to the President of the United States from the Secretary of the Treasury Transmitting the Proceedings of the Pan American Financial Conference," September 6, 1915, in U.S., Treasury Department, *Annual Report on the Finances, 1915*, p. 88.

of the question so long as there remained without correction "the physical lack of communication, the lack of vehicles—the lack of ships, the lack of established routes of trade."[26] As a concluding matter of business, the delegates resolved to call a follow-up conference of a new body, the International High Commission (IHC). To be composed of hemispheric commercial and political leaders, the High Commission would assemble in Buenos Aires in April 1916. When the conference adjourned, the delegates were taken on the customary tour of such industrial installations as the Baldwin Locomotive Works in Philadelphia and the General Electric plant in Schenectady. All told, McAdoo had shrewdly used the conference to give the administration's maritime program a tonic shot in the arm.

McAdoo then publicized the conference results in a broad extrapolation bearing major relationship to the Wilson–House–Page concerns to develop a neutral bloc for liberalizing purposes. McAdoo contended that the commercial advantages and mutual strengths that would inevitably redound from Pan-Americanism would do more than increase standards of living. In view of the European conflict, these could serve as a bludgeon with which to command the respect of European competition and as a mighty lever with which to tip the scales of the European conflict toward a peace desirable to the Western Hemisphere. Economic Pan-Americanism had the potential of becoming a "powerful agency for world peace," he pointed out. By the simple denial of its collected resources it could "exercise a persuasive power of irresistible force upon other nations of the world in the settling of international disputes." All of this depended upon a "wholesome materialism" concerning the basic essentials of trade and communication.[27] It was a compelling way to advertise for hemispheric commercial consolidation and an effective argument for augmented maritime services.

Wilson confirmed this tactical direction when he skillfully blended preparedness, Pan-Americanism, and the question of ships before the new Sixty-fourth Congress on December 7, 1915: What the United States wanted was a "community of interests" with Latin America. The unparalleled opportunity to link the two continents had to be affected in the name of national and hemispheric defense. Hence the prosecution of a program

26. Wilson, *Public Papers*, 2:334.
27. McAdoo, "The Pan American Financial Conference." See also McAdoo to Bryan, July 31, 1916, McAdoo Papers.

of preparedness to protect and facilitate the "unmolested development" of the economic and political interests of the Americas. It was a program that went beyond the conventional stockpiling of arms by broadening the parameters of national defense to include not only military matters but also domestic and foreign commerce and transportation, the conservation and mobilization of the nation's industrial and natural resources, and the cooperative defense of all Latin America. Above all, no such policy could hope to work without the development of commercial self-sufficiency and independence. Ships were absolutely essential, the "only shuttles that can weave the delicate fabric of sympathy, comprehension, confidence, and mutual dependence in which we wish to clothe our policy of America for Americans," and the sole way by which the hemisphere could hope to avoid the entanglements of European affairs. In sum, the military and commercial strengthening of the United States, including the crucial establishment of ocean shipping service, would fortify the resolution and the ability of the Americas to remain removed from the corrosive elements of European influence.[28]

Wilson elaborated a week later: America's ability to bring about an international peace would be predicated to a large degree upon the nation's success in securing and maintaining trade on a worldwide basis. In consequence, it was imperative "that no impediments should be put in the way of [America's] commerce with the rest of the world." Commercial interference from German submarines would not be tolerated, and neither would British efforts to prevent American merchants from gaining new footholds in markets formerly dominated by England.[29]

Wilson believed that a major impediment would be removed when the United States embarked upon a campaign for commercial efficiency. It would be a signal service to America, he pointed out early in 1916, if the country could be aroused to take quick advantage of the great opportunities available in wartime world trade. But in order to do this, "we must show an effectiveness in industrial practice which measures up to our best standards." A program was needed calling for industrial efficiency, education,

28. Wilson, *Public Papers*, 2:406–28.

29. Notter, *Foreign Policy of Wilson*, p. 463; Baker, *Woodrow Wilson*, 6:312; Kaufman, *Efficiency and Expansion*, pp. 170–75.

and scientific research.[30] In the same light, the president stumped hard for a government merchant marine, considered measures to prevent the belligerents from dumping surpluses in the American postwar marketplace, and ardently supported the creation of a scientific tariff commission "capable of looking at the whole economic situation of the country with a dispassionate and disinterested scrutiny." It was time for the United States to pay heed to the rapid changes taking place in the world's economy and take effective steps through industrial efficiency to insure the economic prosperity and development of the nation.[31]

The Wilson administration had sound grounds for believing in the inevitability of postwar economic conflict. Having usurped, as few denied, the legitimate prewar markets of the belligerents—the development of which had taken years, lives, and vast sums of money—Americans could not avoid acknowledging the probability of European efforts, even during the war, to hinder United States commercial growth and ultimately recover its own commercial forfeitures. Manifestations of this were already evident. In the year since the failure of the shipping bill and the attendant flare-up between Great Britain and Wilson over neutral trade privileges, the British, rather than lessening the severity of their restrictions governing American trade, had intensified them. In addition to unabated and particularly irritating British search and seizure policies, the contraband lists had grown, causing the inevitable delays and disruptions of schedules and trade that never failed to infuriate American exporters and shipping personnel. Where the British had maritime dominance, moreover, evidence of discrimination cropped up over and over—in the Pacific, for example, where the Anglo-Japanese alliance appeared to work particularly well against American shipping interests. The year 1915 also saw Great Britain and France restricting the sale or transfer of ships to foreigners and thereby cutting down considerably the opportunity of Americans to acquire needed cargo carriers and oil tankers.[32] Further, in December 1915, the entire British

30. Wilson to the Editor, February 11, 1915, *Scientific American*, 114(March 4, 1916):237.

31. Wilson to Kitchin, January 21, 26, 1916, Kitchin Papers.

32. Bentinck-Smith, "Forcing Period," pp. 66–67; for Redfield's testimony, February 10, 1916, see U.S., Congress, House, Committee on Merchant Marine and Fisheries, *Shipping Board Hearings*, 64th Cong., 1st sess., pp. 128–29; idem, Commerce Department, *Annual Report of the Commissioner of Navigation, 1916*, pp. 185–90.

commercial fleet was put under centralized control, a move that Redfield saw as "revolutionary," for it not only authorized the British government to requisition any vessel under British registration, which included hundreds of American-owned ships, but also subjected all vessels in the British foreign trade to government supervision.[33] Though it was unlikely to happen, such a measure could bring the whole mechanism of America's export trade to Europe to a numbing standstill. In addition, the British, depending upon the concentration of neutral shipping in the Atlantic trade, had purposefully fixed a highly profitable rate scale to hold it. This system worked contrary to Wilson's hope for Pan-American trade expansion—by the winter of 1915–1916 over 95 percent of the world's shipping had been attracted to the North Atlantic.[34]

Finally, it became painfully apparent that a great deal of economic collaboration was taking place in the belligerent camps. The Central Powers, for example, appeared to be well along in a plan for economic federation which included dumping cheap surplus goods on the postwar world so as to undersell Allied and neutral industry and recoup lost trade. Redfield was especially disturbed and even suggested punishing foreign dumpers with the antitrust laws.[35] The Allies, at the same time, were formulating plans to combine their economic efforts so as to create a more coordinated war effort. This combination, already exhibited in British and French coordination in the purchase and transportation of foodstuffs from Latin America and in efforts to establish colonial preference systems, was bad enough for America while the war lasted. It had vastly more ominous implications should it appear on the postwar trade scene.[36]

One of the government agencies Wilson relied upon heavily to cope with

33. Redfield address, "The American Merchant Marine," before the Civic Club of Brooklyn, New York, December 16, 1915, Wilson Papers; Saugstad, *Shipping and Shipbuilding Subsidies*, p. 208.

34. Agnes C. Laut, "The Tremendous Boom in American Shipping."

35. Kaufman, *Efficiency and Expansion*, p. 151.

36. See, for example, "Preliminary Report of the Special Committee on Trade during and after the War," London Chamber of Commerce, January 13, 1916, SD 641.001/6, NA. The United States Chamber of Commerce was considerably disturbed. See D. A. Skinner to Lansing, February 4, 1916, SD 641.001, NA; Skinner to Wilbur J. Carr, February 29, 1916, SD 641.001/2, NA. For a French explanation of what was taking place between the Allies see Étienne Clémentel, *La France et la politique économique interaliée*, pp. 59–63, 68.

these difficulties was the Federal Trade Commission. Wilson did not simply chance upon the FTC; its vice chairman, Edward N. Hurley, was prepared to assist the campaign for commercial preparedness to the utmost of his capabilities. Hurley had expressed concern for industrial preparedness and efficiency in an address to the Rubber Club of America in February 1916: The war, while it brought America "great opportunities," had also presented the nation with "equally great dangers." The thought that American businessmen had to keep eternally in mind was "after the war, what?" Was it sufficient for America simply to while away time and energy in anticipation of the return to normality and the reconstitution of competition with comparatively much better organized and efficiently managed European industries, or should the country use the opportunity to grow, expand, and solidify its position while the growing was good? Hurley quickly ruled out the first alternative: What was necessary was the immediate mobilization of American industry to a degree of prepeace strength "no foreign competition [could] dislodge. *Industrial preparedness must be our watchword*"; the European business conditions confronting American industry demanded it.[37] Under Hurley's direction, the FTC was making its own contribution by working on cost accounting systems, urging the legalization of export trade associations, and conducting investigations of business that would be used, among other things, to augment South American trade. In addition, the FTC was investigating the international tariff system, information from which would be employed by the government to adjust trade policies to meet anticipated European postwar competition. Two of Hurley's special agents were at that moment in South America gathering data for McAdoo's use at the forthcoming IHC meeting in Buenos Aires.

Hurley's estimation of the opportunities and dangers in the nation's neutral foreign trade position testified in important ways to the split character of America's commercial policy. For the industrial or commercial preparedness deemed necessary by the administration for national and hemispheric defense was nurtured on the dual roots of opportunism and apprehension. Opportunism displayed itself in the successful efforts of

37. Hurley address, "Industrial Preparedness," New York City, February 2, 1916, Wilson Papers.

American commercial interests to avail themselves of neutral markets abandoned by the belligerents and ready for the picking. Apprehension, on the other hand, was represented in the belief that the war would culminate before American commercial interests could entrench themselves. This was compounded by the conviction that the displaced interests would wage fierce economic warfare to regain lost ground and further complicated by the recognition that America's trade mechanisms were defective, or at best lacked essential components to give them sufficient competitive efficiency.

Hurley devoted considerable space to these issues in his book, *Awakening of Business*. The war, he maintained, had brought out once and for all the dangers of clinging to old industrial ideas and methods. "Industrial inefficiency, reckless individual competition, and the absence of cooperation" were no longer tolerable in a modern business world. In no part of the globe had this struck home with greater impact than in wartorn Europe. While Americans had become enormously prosperous as a result of the conflict, an attitude of self-complacency would be fatal, for Hurley believed that forces were gathering amongst the belligerents that would "lead to the fiercest kind of commercial rivalry after the war." Not only would European businessmen seek to retrieve commerce lost to the war (and to the neutrals), they could be counted upon to compete heatedly for America's markets as well. Unless the United States availed itself of the opportunity to reorganize "the whole fabric of our business system" along lines of efficiency, American commercial interests would suffer seriously at European hands after the war.[38] The business sector, of which Hurley was such an important part, strongly agreed. Charles Muchnic, vice president of the American Locomotive Sales Company, put it thus: "However gratifying this experience may be at the present time [American war-gained wealth], it carries with it elements of disaster unless we are far-sighted enough and prepare now for the inevitable reaction that is to follow the cessation of hostilities

38. Hurley, *Awakening of Business*, pp. xii–xiii, Chapters 9–12, Conclusion. See also U.S., Congress, Senate, *Cooperation and Efficiency in Developing our Foreign Trade*, 64th Cong., 1st sess., S. Doc. 459. This was an address delivered by Hurley before the American Iron and Steel Institute in New York, May 26, 1916. See also Hurley's address on industrial efficiency, "Trade Associations and Better Business Methods," before the Boston Commercial Club, March 28, 1916, Wilson Papers. Wilson's laudatory comments on this speech are the foreword to Hurley's *Awakening of Business*.

in Europe."[39] And the National Foreign Trade Council, for example, held its January 1916 convention under the very banner of "Commercial Preparedness" and devoted its entire program to discussion of what one of its members, Frank Vanderlip of the National City Bank of New York, had called the "war after the war," the commercial struggle guaranteed to take place immediately following the end of the European conflagration. While Wilson and McAdoo had been calling attention to this from the outset of hostilities, the winter of 1915–1916 was significant because it marked the first time they were joined in their views by men and organizations encompassing an effective working part of the American business community.

All of these developments intensified American resolve to retain the trade won and to perfect the means to service and expand it. While many preparedness issues were discussed at the NFTC's January convention, prominent attention was given to the question of a government merchant marine, a subject about which the NFTC had become strikingly solicitous after so many months of antagonism to the principle of public ownership. The conference program committee invited representatives from the Wilson administration to speak to the issue. Edwin Sweet, Redfield's assistant secretary of commerce, sympathized with the council's kindling apprehensions. "After the war is over," he warned the gathering, "we are going to have a fierce commercial competition—you might almost say antagonism." In these circumstances the capacity to deal with postwar competition depended upon the ability of the United States to entrench itself in such markets as Latin America and the assurance to the manufacturers and producers "that the means of delivery will be continuous." In a trade war, the United States could not count upon her competitors to supply the means of carriage; American ships backed by the government were central to the whole question of commercial preparedness.[40]

Sweet's counterpart in the Department of Agriculture seconded these

---

39. Charles Muchnic, "Relation of Investments to South American Trade." See also Wilson's address before the Railway Business Association, New York City, January 27, 1916, in U.S., Congress, House, *Addresses of President Wilson, January 27–February 3, 1916*, 64th Cong., 1st sess., H. Doc. 803.

40. National Foreign Trade Council Convention, *Proceedings, 1916*, pp. 209–10. Sweet's colleague, chief of the Bureau of Foreign and Domestic Commerce Edward Ewing Pratt, was vociferously outspoken in his support for commercial preparedness. See, for example, Pratt, "Commercial America and the War."

observations. Forecasting "an era of commercial and industrial warfare unparalleled in history," Carl Vrooman argued that the great maritime powers would unhesitatingly take advantage of nations like the United States, which were handicapped and commercially hamstrung for want of ships. In such an environment, the economic lot of the American producer would become "untenable and preposterous. The tribute levied by the robber barons of the Rhine was infinitesimal, as compared with the loot which, as long as our present condition of shipping dependence continues, will be exacted from us . . . by these gigantic transportation tyrants of the high seas."[41]

McAdoo emphasized similar concerns at hearings on the shipping bill held late that winter by Congressman Alexander's House Committee on Merchant Marine and Fisheries, one exchange of which was especially revealing. In what must have been one of the longest sentences to go on public record, Arkansas representative W. S. Goodwin initiated conversation with McAdoo by inquiring:

> Is not this primarily the thought back of this whole legislation, that inasmuch as the European Governments now at war have taken over practically all of the railway and steamship transportation lines, and the same being nationalized—usurping, so to speak, the functions and rights of private and corporate interests that formerly owned them—that when the war is over there will be the greatest commercial rivalry the world has ever seen, and the nations that have lost their trade will seek to regain it and to extend it, and every country will attempt to be in the vanguard of this commercial activity, and inasmuch as European countries have nationalized those activities, thus overcoming and outstripping private and even corporate interests, that therefore they are outstripping us in this commercial conquest as long as we permit our commerce to remain exclusively in the hands of private and corporate interests, and therefore we should ourselves nationalize in a measure, or seek to do so, so as to give an impetus to that increased activity which we ourselves expect to take part in?

To which McAdoo replied: "I think that is undoubtedly true and that it is essentially a part of preparedness. . . . to the extent the foreign governments have extended their powers over the shipping of their respective

41. U.S., Congress, Senate, *The Farmer and the Shipping Bill*, 64th Cong., 1st sess., March 30, 1916, S. Doc. 395.

countries, it is absolutely necessary that we organize and concentrate the powers of this Nation to enable us to protect our own commerce."[42]

The American delegation had these thoughts deeply in mind as it shipped out on March 4, 1916 for the meeting of the International High Commission in Buenos Aires. It also had the report of the Federal Trade Commission's mission which returned from South America only hours before the delegation's embarkation. The FTC report confirmed all of McAdoo's positions. It stressed the need for reciprocal trade agreements which in turn depended upon business and financial cooperation, foreign branch banks, and steamship lines controlled by Americans. These last were required because without the assurance of equitable freight rates and nondiscrimination American producers would find it impossible to compete with European firms.[43] Armed with these observations, the American representatives prepared their program as they steamed southward.

Upon arrival in Buenos Aires, the American delegation made it abundantly clear that the main object of Pan-Americanism was to develop South America's resources and to freeze out undesirable European competition. McAdoo advised his hosts in the Brazilian capital that the realization of mutual prosperity depended only upon reciprocal trade and the attendant release of South America's economic wealth. It was necessary to create a solid insurance against the recurrence of financial and economic disaster because of uncontrollable happenings across the seas. "We were determined that the cause of our economic dependence upon Europe should be definitely and permanently removed," McAdoo added in an aside.[44] At the same time, it was stressed that an additional aim was to secure profitable trade and financial investment for North American businessmen. Paul Warburg of the Federal Reserve Board spoke of the "gigantic efforts" Europe would exert to "regain her lost ground," and declared that the only guarantee against such an occurrence would be for Americans to "increase their efforts in gaining a strong foothold in Central and South American countries." That did not necessarily mean that the United States desired to "crowd out"

42. Remarks before Alexander's committee in U.S., Congress, House, Committee on Merchant Marine and Fisheries, *Shipping Board Hearings*, 64th Cong., 1st sess., p. 275.
43. U.S., Federal Trade Commission, *Report on Trade and Tariffs in Brazil, Uruguay, Argentine, Chile, Bolivia, and Peru*, pp. 20, 22.
44. U.S., Congress, Senate, *International High Commission*, 64th Cong., 1st sess., Doc. 436. McAdoo gave this address on April 4, 1916. For his aside, see undated manuscript, IHC papers, McAdoo Papers.

European nations that had previously serviced the commercial needs of Latin America but that because of America's new role as the world's banker, it was now inevitable as the result of "mathematical certainties."[45]

While Latin dignitaries associated with the IHC and most newspapers appeared uniformly receptive to such statements, several representatives of the South American press accepted them less graciously, in the process putting their editorial fingers on an issue that would cause considerable Anglo-American difficulty. To *La Prensa,* the Southern Hemisphere's most influential newspaper, Pan-Americanism was primarily an effort by the United States to "subordinate the destinies of all the countries of the New World to its own, to eliminate from them European commerce and to substitute for it American commerce in the guise of continental fraternity."[46] The Santiago *La Union* adopted a similar attitude: "Let us speak the truth. Both this Congress as well as others recently held seem to have been called together for the exclusive benefit of the United States." The end result would guarantee "mere satellite" roles for the Latin Republics.[47] Caught in an interview with another antagonistic Argentina daily, McAdoo admitted that America's eyes were indeed focused on Latin markets, but attempted to extricate himself by arguing that such a scheme could hardly materialize because no means had been devised to establish the principal and necessary part—the means of communication.[48] Despite these particular press criticisms, it was difficult to deny the validity of McAdoo's remark. The facts were clear: Latin America had enormous untapped economic resources, and the United States had unparalleled surpluses of industrial and agricultural goods. Given the European shipping tie-up and the lack of American maritime service, however, there would be little chance of constructing the "permanent moving bridge," as an American delegate described it, required to develop the reciprocal trade necessary to create mutual advantage during the war. The IHC's final report on maritime transportation stressed an identical viewpoint.[49]

45. Warburg address, Buenos Aires, April 4, 1916, McAdoo Papers.

46. *La Prensa,* Buenos Aires, March 6, 1916, McAdoo Papers.

47. *La Union,* Santiago, Chile, April 11, 1916, McAdoo Papers.

48. *El Diario,* Buenos Aires, telegram to the Santiago, Chile, *El Mercurio,* April 18, 1916, McAdoo Papers.

49. Senator Duncan U. Fletcher address, *Ties that Bind the Americas,* Buenos Aires, April 12, 1916, in U.S., Congress, Senate, 64th Cong., 1st sess., Doc. 479; "Report of the

Crossing the Andes into Chile, the American delegation concluded its tour in Santiago where McAdoo summarized the need for reciprocal trade and reemphasized his concept of economic Pan-Americanism as a potent weapon for international arbitration. By virtue of sheer market force, he declared, a united and economically powerful New World "could prevent any nation from going to war, and could make an end of the crime of killing human beings to settle needless controversies." To that he attached the habitual amendment—provided the means of communication were developed.[50] McAdoo knew, of course, that the Latin republics could not develop adequate maritime services on their own. That aspect of his remarks was largely good public relations. McAdoo was determined to use the publicity generated by the mission as a persuasive force in the campaign for a shipping bill at home. Consequently, he encouraged every statement endorsing transportation and reciprocal trade needs and sent the results posthaste with much fanfare to the news media in the United States. Congressional proponents of the bill were also on McAdoo's mailing list. William Stone, chairman of the Senate Committee on Foreign Relations, received a typical encouragement:

> The great cry throughout South America is for merchant ships to carry on trade between the United States and these countries. I wish every Republican and Democrat who opposed the ship bill in the last Congress could come here in person and know at first hand the way in which our trade and prestige is suffering and realize the wonderful opportunity we have, not only to stimulate trade between the United States and Central and South America, but also to strengthen our political ties and influence in a way that will be beneficial to the entire American Continent.[51]

The tour concluded in mid-April. His portfolio brimming with reports, recommendations, and resolutions, McAdoo sailed for home determined to carry on the congressional battle for a government merchant marine.

The bill had already been reintroduced in both houses in late January after McAdoo, Alexander, and Fletcher thrashed out an acceptable draft.[52]

Sub-Committee on Maritime Transportation," IHC, McAdoo Papers; McAdoo's official news release on the results of the IHC Conference, May 4, 1916, ibid.

50. U.S., Congress, Senate, *The Republic of Chile*, 64th Cong., 1st sess., Doc. 437. This was McAdoo's address given on April 18, 1916.

51. McAdoo to Stone, April 6, 1916, McAdoo Papers.

52. McAdoo to Wilson, January 10, 1916, McAdoo Papers.

With Fletcher and McAdoo in South America during March and April, Alexander, Stone, and Kitchin led the reinitiated fight for the bill's passage. Despite repetition of the customary invective, the new concern over commercial preparedness had such an effect that congressional opposition steadily eroded. Stone epitomized concern on Capitol Hill over the growing trade menace, especially that of Great Britain. The junior senator from Missouri envisioned descrimination in every switch of the Lion's tail. Forecasting the defeat of the Central Powers, he warned Wilson that England's maritime supremacy would present America with an "over-mastering rivalry" in the postwar commercial world. The one thing needed above all was direct action to provide facilities for the transportation of American exports.[53] Wilson pushed Kitchin to move quickly and inexorably for the early passage of the shipping bill and replied to Stone with an expression in wholehearted support of the obligation to meet the challenge of Allied postwar competition: "The present moral seems to be that we should push forward with the greatest zeal such action as is involved in the pending shipping bill."[54] Stone pressed the attack in the Senate: "I want to see the ship bill—the merchant marine measures—brought to the front and kept there until some great policy of commercial preparedness is definitely entered upon."[55] Emphasizing the need for a shipping board with broad regulatory and developmentary powers to serve as a preparedness counterpart to the British Board of Trade, Alexander's House Committee on Merchant Marine and Fisheries submitted a bill on May ninth.[56] Under Kitchin's whip it passed the lower house eleven days later.

Two additional events of importance at the time added weight to the urgency behind commercial preparedness and the passage of the shipping bill, which was now in the hands of the Senate. For over a year, Wilson had been trying to mediate the European war. His representative, Colonel Edward House, first visited the belligerent capitals in 1915, and in the

53. Stone to Wilson, March 25, 1916, Wilson Papers.

54. Wilson to Kitchin, March 27, 1916, Kitchin Papers; Wilson to Stone, March 28, 1916, Wilson Papers.

55. Stone address, "Three Kinds of Preparedness," given in the Senate, April 13, 1916, *Congressional Record*, 64th Cong., 1st sess., pp. 6025–26.

56. U.S., Congress, House, Committee on Merchant Marine and Fisheries, *Creating a Shipping Board, a Naval Auxiliary, A Merchant Marine, and Regulating Carriers by Water Engaged in the Foreign and Interstate Commerce of the United States*, 64th Cong., 1st sess., H. Rept. 659.

spring of 1916 he went to London in another effort to arbitrate. House's purpose was to persuade the British to call a peace conference. If Germany should refuse to agree to a cessation of hostilities, then the United States would in all probability enter the war in support of the Allies. But the British foreign secretary, Sir Edward Grey, pointed out in March that the complications and complexities of war policies among the Allies ruled out arbitration, adding that in any event war participation for the United States was the only alternative to being excluded from the peace negotiations. House responded by asserting that the United States would then force itself upon the deliberations by arming itself to the teeth. Grey agreed to resubmit House's arbitration proposals for Allied consideration but did not reveal the final negative outcome until late in May. Incensed at being put off so long, House concluded by mid-May that the Allies had no intention of seeking an armistice. In his opinion, they were determined to fight it out to the bitter end in anticipation of winning and reaping the rewards, a policy which would have ramifications beyond the redefinition of European affairs. "A situation may arise, if the Allies defeat Germany, where they may attempt to be dictatorial in Europe and elsewhere," he cautioned Wilson. An Allied victory, in other words, could mean considerable trouble for American interests.[57]

Wilson's demand for "freedom of the seas" as part of the arbitration package caused considerable irritation in Allied circles; the concept was introduced by House and greatly disturbed the British cabinet's war committee. When the final decision was made to turn down the American proposal, Arthur J. Balfour, first lord of the admiralty, made it understood that the "best" chance for House's plan would be American entry on the Allied war side in favor of Allied interests, whereas the "worst" chance would be represented by a status quo (or pro-German) peace "accomplished, perhaps even promoted, by diplomatic friction between the Allies and the United States over maritime affairs."[58] Such attitudes could only have strengthened the determination of House and Wilson to accept the alternative of military and commercial preparedness as a means to emphasize American views.

57. House to Wilson, May 14, 1916, Wilson Papers.
58. Arthur J. Balfour's draft reply to Colonel House, May 24, 1916, in John Milton Cooper, Jr., "The British Response to the House–Grey Memorandum."

On the heels of the arbitration failure came another disappointment. The Paris Economic Conference of June 14–17, 1916 certified American convictions that the Allies planned to subject the United States to postwar trade discrimination. The stipulations of the conference seemed to indicate to Americans that the Allies were intent upon establishing an exclusive economic union which, while ostensibly a declaration of economic war on the Central Powers and their own postwar *Mitteleuropa* plan, was also to be utilized for special trade privileges in the reconstruction period following the war. Descrimination was the key to the plan and apparently the neutrals were not to be exempted from liability to its application. Moreover, the provisions outlined at Paris openly declared the Allies' mutual interest in recapturing their former trade privileges and holdings.[59] Americans could easily interpret the remarks of the Australian prime minister, W. M. Hughes, as a confirmation of their fears. A delegate to the Paris conference, Hughes summed up his participation as a condemnation of the neutrals for growing "rich while we grow daily poorer [and making] great preparations to capture the world's markets and oust us from our position. We must face them and we must master them. [This accomplished] all the world would be suppliant at [our] feet."[60] The Paris resolves, as a member of the Federal Trade Commission later described them, were sheer "militarism translated into commercial warfare."[61]

Writing to Wilson, Lansing summarized the administration's concern a week after the conference. It appeared to him that the harsh postwar commercial strategy outlined at Paris would prolong rather than terminate the conflict. More important, the commercial combination provided in the agreements had onerous implications for neutral nations. It would be a strong combination of nations "which on account of their colonies and great merchant marine will be able, I fear, to carry through their preferential program. [The results would cause a] serious, if not critical, situation for the nations outside the union by creating unusual and artificial economic conditions." Added to already serious restraints imposed upon the neutrals by the Allies through blacklisting, nonexportation agreements,

59. Carl P. Parrini, *Heir to Empire*, Chapter 2.

60. *Times*, London, June 22, 1916.

61. William S. Culbertson, *Commercial Policy in War Times and After*, p. 348. Culbertson led the FTC's factfinding mission to South America early in 1916.

influence upon steamship companies, monopoly control over insurance rates and ratings, and the censorship of mail, the Paris Conference had created a situation requiring a strong antidote. Lansing's policy, could he apply one, would be to confront the giant with its own weapons—a combination of neutral powers.[62]

As if designed to add salt to the injury, on July 18 Great Britain added eighty-five more American firms to its blacklist. The news created "tremendous irritation" and an explosive atmosphere in the White House. Weighing House's failure and the Paris Economic Conference, Wilson called this action the "last straw" and considered asking Congress for authorization to embargo loans and exports to the Allies.[63] Congressional maritime supporters interpreted the latest discrimination as one more powerful incentive for the shipping bill. The situation revealed more than ever the need for an American merchant marine, argued Alexander in the House—the blacklist was simply the latest means by which Great Britain intended to use "her sea power to protect herself and to cripple her enemies." In the Senate, Fletcher remarked that it was obvious that England was determined to "re-entrench itself in maritime supremacy as soon as possible." The blacklist, used as a means to that end, furnished "the strongest kind of argument in favor of American ships."[64]

The reactions to British policy that surfaced in the Congress and the White House were not isolated. A large cross section of the economic sector had now become vitally concerned over the lack of adequate American shipping. In hearings before the Alexander committee, it was demonstrated that farm organizations endorsed the bill as an instrument for strengthening their economic position. The bill especially appealed to them as a means of restricting or even reducing exorbitant freight rates, and agriculture's traditional animosity toward monopoly was satisfied by the regulatory

62. Lansing to Wilson, June 23, 1916, U.S., State Department, FR: The Lansing Papers, 1914–1920, 1:312. McAdoo's concept of a suitable combination, like House's, was Pan-Americanism. See his interview with George Creel, undated, but under August 19, 1916, McAdoo Papers.

63. Frank L. Polk to House, July 22, 1916, in Edward House, The Intimate Papers of Colonel House, 1:312; Wilson to House, July 23, 1916, ibid., 1:313.

64. Congressional Record, Senate, 64th Cong., 1st sess., Appendix, p. 1209; ibid., Aug. 9, 1916, pp. 12357–58, 12365.

provisions of the proposed measure.[65] Simultaneously, business interests, which had previously opposed the shipping bill as socialistic, adopted a new stance in the face of increased Allied discrimination and the promise of rigorous postwar commercial competition. Once a bastion of opposition to any form of government control, the National Foreign Trade Council began to question the inflexibility of its position early in 1916. As a result of the Paris Economic Conference, it came full circle and advocated the prompt enactment of the shipping bill as a retaliatory measure.[66] In another major turnabout, John Fahey, former president of the Chamber of Commerce of the United States who had presided over the chamber's referendum against the shipping bill early in 1915, decided that the impact of Pan-Americanism was a justification for maritime preparedness. As a delegate to the International High Commission in March and April, Fahey returned a transformed man on shipping matters. He confessed to Alexander that

> I have never been enthusiastic over the question of Government ownership and operation if there was any other way out . . . but I want to say that as a result of what I saw and heard in South America I am convinced that it will be long years before private interests will ever undertake the establishment especially of the fast lines which are needed in South American countries. These lines are vital to us if we are to hold and develop our business, and we should have them at the earliest possible moment. I, therefore, hope that the bill is going to go through the Senate without delay.[67]

As the preparedness argument in support of the shipping bill reached a crescendo in July and August, inveterate opponents of government ownership admitted their inability to stem the tide. Jacob Gallinger, veteran senatorial campaigner against the bill in the previous session, prepared to inveigh against it once more but acknowledged in early August that this would be a futile and symbolic gesture.[68] Senator Wesley Jones of Wash-

---

65. U.S., Congress, House, Committee on Merchant Marine and Fisheries, *Shipping Board Hearings,* 64th Cong., 1st sess., pp. 672–98.

66. NFTC, *European Economic Alliances,* p. 10.

67. John H. Fahey to Alexander, June 2, 1916, *Congressional Record,* 64th Cong., 1st sess., Appendix, p. 1212. Robert H. Wiebe traces the business sector's turnaround in *Businessmen and Reform,* pp. 145–47.

68. Gallinger to Dana W. Baker, August 8, 1916, Gallinger Papers.

ington maintained that as he understood the politics of the matter, the principles of public ownership still remained an anathema to the great majority of his colleagues, including even proponents of the bill, but that to cover this the shipping lobby was maneuvering to "avoid the funda-mental principle" by urging the bill on extraordinary grounds as a "special emergency" for preparedness.[69] When Senator John H. Bankhead of Alabama announced that he and the six other Democratic dissidents would not oppose the measure, it was clear that after two years of hard fighting the administration had accumulated sufficient votes to put the bill through.[70] In fact, support was so strong that the "ill-omened coalition," as Wilson had branded the seven, could easily have stayed at home. In addition to a unified Democratic party, all of Theodore Roosevelt's progressives except the La Follette peace groups staunchly supported the shipping bill as part of their economic and naval preparedness platform.[71] Already approved by the House in May, the bill passed with amendments in the Senate on August eighteenth. In its revised form, it was endorsed by the lower chamber and signed by President Wilson on September 7, 1916.

While McAdoo would call the final product "tremendously emasculated," passage of the Shipping Act of 1916 was significantly more than a Pyrrhic victory.[72] It is true that the act compromised McAdoo's efforts to maximize government operation by stipulating that lines operated by the new United States Shipping Board would have to cease business five years after the end of the European war, by forbidding cabinet participation on the board, and by prohibiting the purchase of belligerent vessels; but its strengths were exceedingly important, especially in their contribution to the overall devel-opment of an efficient, scientifically managed foreign trade program. Fore-most, as McAdoo acknowledged, the measure represented the creation of the Shipping Board, an overseer along the lines of the Interstate Commerce Commission and Federal Trade Commission to regulate maritime transpor-tation. Concern for the larger needs of America's overseas commerce was explicit: The authority of the Shipping Board was limited to the main violators of the "public trust," the service lines, and specifically did not

69. *Congressional Record,* Senate, 64th Cong., 1st sess., August 11, 1916, pp. 12432–34.
70. Ibid., August 12, 1916, pp. 12528–29.
71. Seager, "The Progressives and American Foreign Policy," p. 338.
72. McAdoo to Wilson, September 4, 1916, Wilson Papers.

extend to the much needed tramp shipping so crucial to the maintenance of a flexible trade system. Discrimination by foreign shipping companies against American exporters was forbidden, and the board was given the power to "disapprove, cancel, or modify" any shipping agreements between service lines which could be construed as inimical to the commercial interests of the United States. Finally, the Shipping Act of 1916 authorized the creation of an Emergency Fleet Corporation for the purpose of purchasing, constructing, and operating government vessels in time of dire national need.[73] It was that particular function that served the nation so well within the course of a year.

73. McAdoo to Lawrence F. Abbott, June 10, 1916, McAdoo Papers; Arthur E. Cook, ed., *A History of the United States Shipping Board and Merchant Fleet Corporation,* pp. 9–10; Darrell Hevenor Smith and Paul V. Betters, *The United States Shipping Board,* pp. 6–8; Zeis, *American Shipping Policy,* pp. 92–94.

Chapter V

Assembling the Fleet for War

The Shipping Act of September 1916 was a peacetime measure and did not authorize a government shipping operation except under extraordinary circumstances. The provision prohibiting the newly created United States Shipping Board from operating any of the vessels it was enabled to construct or otherwise acquire, except during a "national emergency," was one of the conditions McAdoo had in mind when he complained that Congress had emasculated the bill. Consequently, little was done during the remainder of 1916 save to constitute, with some difficulty, board membership. This was accomplished finally in January 1917. It was McAdoo's slate from top to bottom. The first chairman was William Denman, a well known admiralty lawyer from San Francisco. A close friend of the treasury head, Denman had marshalled West Coast support for the Shipping Act and contributed helpful advice which was incorporated into the administration's draft. Another intimate associate of McAdoo, Baltimore shipping magnate Bernard N. Baker, was named vice chairman. The three remaining members were John A. Donald of New York, John B. White of Missouri, and Theodore Brent of Louisiana. Miffed at not being selected chairman, Baker resigned within a week. He was replaced in March by Raymond B. Stevens of New Hampshire. A special counsel for the Federal Trade Commission, Stevens had formerly been a congressman and member of the House Interstate and Foreign Commerce Committee.

Germany's fateful decision on January 31, 1917 to employ a policy of unrestricted submarine warfare encouraged the administration to take safety measures. As the German policy caused a precipitous exodus of American vessels for registry under less vulnerable flags, Wilson issued an executive order that prohibited such transfers after February fifth. Then on April 6, the congressional declaration of war enabled the Shipping Board to unleash the full scope of its emergency powers.

Two important undertakings highlighted the initial activities of the Shipping Board directly following the war declaration. These were the commandeering of German vessels and the formation of the Emergency Fleet Corporation. The first was a rudimentary task, although some German crews sabotaged their vessels and thus prevented the board from putting them into immediate service. Also, a number of the ninety-seven vessels seized were berthed in such faroff American possessions as Hawaii, Samoa, and the Philippines, which complicated the repair process. By midsummer, however, the board had overcome these obstacles, and most of the freighters and tankers were either in government service on runs to Italy, Russia, and France or chartered to private firms for use in important war trade. Commandeered German passenger liners, including the world's second largest ship, the *Leviathan* (formerly the *Vaterland*), were turned over to the navy for the transport of American military personnel to Europe. Altogether, 638,000 gross tons of ships were acquired in that manner.[1] During the course of the war, the amount of enemy tonnage obtained by the board was supplemented through the purchase or charter of German and Austrian vessels interned in nations still at peace. In this manner, two Austrian ships were chartered from China and two German ships from Siam. Brazil, Peru, and Uruguay also supplied enemy ships. The Shipping Board did not purchase German vessels outright from neutrals at any time, but it did acquire nine former Austrian ships totaling 58,000 deadweight tons which it put into the American war service.[2] Eventually, through agreements reached at the Paris Peace Conference in 1919, the German vessels seized in American ports were permanently added to the American merchant fleet.

The formation of the Emergency Fleet Corporation (EFC) resulted from

---

1. Hurley, *The Bridge to France*, pp. 39–41.
2. Ibid., p. 41. Deadweight tonnage is the actual weight of a ship at full draft load, including cargo, fuel, stores, water, crew, etc. This was the normal American method of rating the tonnage of a vessel and was generally about 50 percent greater than gross tonnage, the British rating system. A gross ton is expressed in terms of 100 cubic feet to the ton, or the entire internal cubic capacity of the ship, with the exception of certain exempted spaces.

the provisions of the Shipping Act enabling the Shipping Board to create a private stock corporation for the purpose of actually operating the ships accumulated under government control. Under the original act, the board was not sufficiently empowered to grant the EFC the necessary means to carry out the awesome task required to underwrite American wartime transportation needs. Consequently, through broad authority granted him by Congress, Wilson from time to time clothed the board and the EFC with powers the original legislation was incapable of providing. On July 11, Wilson delegated directly to the EFC responsibility to construct, requisition, and operate ships—a right conferred upon him by Congress in the Urgent Deficiencies Act of June 13 and the Emergency Shipping Act of June 15. Thereafter, delegation of presidential authority, rather than the original Shipping Act, defined most of the powers of the Shipping Board and the EFC. Hence the wartime shipping program was related directly to the White House, an autonomous operation responsible to Wilson alone. The importance of this unilateral presidential authority cannot be overemphasized—Congress retained only the purse strings.[3]

While the creation of the fleet corporation was intended to provide an immediately effective means of unleashing the federal shipping authority, it simultaneously created an administrative morass that seriously restricted the scope of its efficiency. These difficulties encompassed a series of fratricidal disputes over shipbuilding authority, the type and number of vessels to be constructed, the prices to be paid, and the effects of the program on Anglo-American relations.

The first general manager of the Emergency Fleet Corporation, Major General George Goethals, of Panama Canal fame, was given wide authority over the business affairs of the EFC, including full control and responsibility for the shipbuilding program. He was not legally accountable to the Shipping Board for most of his shipbuilding and operational activities. Goethals was not, however, given the authority to let contracts. That right was reserved by the Shipping Act to the president of the fleet corporation, who was also the chairman of the Shipping Board, William Denman. Inasmuch as the EFC shipbuilding program was but one of the many activities of the board, and an emergency program at that, the sponsors of the Shipping Act had logically vested the board itself with ultimate authority.

3. Ibid., pp. 23–26.

This division of authority might have functioned efficiently in normal circumstances, but in the war environment tremendous pressures were put on the board and the EFC to produce vessels at a rate unparalleled in shipbuilding history. To add to the confusion born of a task never before undertaken in the United States, the whole shipbuilding program threatened to go into slow motion when Goethals and Denman began to fight over policy.

When General Goethals accepted the position of EFC general manager in early April, the Shipping Board had already mapped out a plan for ship construction. While the primary goal was a huge steel shipbuilding program, it was to be augmented by the construction of up to one million tons of wooden ships of one to three thousand tons. A few months earlier, the board had not contemplated the need to build wooden vessels, but the damage wrought upon Allied shipping by German submarines after the turn of the year accentuated the need for ships that could be built quickly and inexpensively. In February, F. A. Eustis, a well-known yachtsman, persuaded Denman to undertake a large project of building wooden ships to supplement the steel ships. This program was not unique to the United States; Great Britain had insisted that Australian, Canadian, and British shipwrights construct wooden ships as well as steel. The USSB proposed to utilize the wooden vessels in coastwise trade as replacements for more oceanworthy steel ships.[4] After in-depth study, this plan was approved by the Council of National Defense which, prior to the creation of the War Industries Board, controlled the national wartime distribution and processing of natural resources. The plan then received the blessings of McAdoo and Wilson and was announced publicly on April ninth. Goethals was hired to carry it out.[5]

Goethals had been in office only weeks, however, when two things became painfully apparent. First, he was not relating well to Denman—a serious conflict had arisen over authority. Second, Goethals questioned the emphasis Denman placed on ancillary wooden ships; the general preferred

4. William Joe Webb, "The United States Wooden Steamship Program during World War I."

5. William Denman to Wilson, July 18, 1917, Wilson Papers; McAdoo to Wilson, April 4, 1917, McAdoo Papers. General outlines of the controversy can be found in Hurley, *The Bridge to France*, pp. 27–29; and Smith and Betters, *The United States Shipping Board*, pp. 18–21.

to reduce commitments to wood as much as possible. Goethals also expressed the belief that he, as a tested and celebrated engineer with international credentials, had a much better handle than Denman on matters relating to ship construction. In addition, Goethals had impressive business and political connections—over the years he had built up a powerful clique of financial, industrial, and political moguls. These included such illustrious figures as James Farrell of U.S. Steel, W. A. Harriman of the Harriman–Rockefeller group, and prominent members of the National Foreign Trade Council and the American International Corporation, the latter a construction and foreign trade branch of the National City Bank of New York. Among his political allies, Goethals counted Colonel Edward House. In contrast, Denman, as House observed, had practically no political or economic clout at all.[6]

The debate smoldered throughout April and most of May. Goethals received assurances from House that Wilson was not unsympathetic to the general's position.[7] Denman, in the meantime, was causing concern in the administration for taking a hard line with the British. As early as March 1917, members of the State Department were convinced that Denman was "anti-British [and that] great trouble [was] brewing" for the future success of Anglo-American shipping relations. Denman's hostility toward the British war mission in early May added to their fears.[8] McAdoo, who at this time was easing himself out of shipping issues, also began to entertain doubts about his friend's capacity for leadership.[9]

The so-called Denman–Goethals controversy broke out in full flame on May 26. Speaking publicly before the prestigious Iron and Steel Institute in New York, Goethals denounced the wooden ships project as "hopeless," asserting that the contracts for wooden ships had been let in all directions, that he had been unable to locate plans or specifications, and that there had been no adherence to any plan of uniformity. Moreover, no ship ought to

6. House to Wilson, July 18, 1917, Wilson Papers.

7. House to Goethals, May 8, 1917, General George Goethals Papers.

8. Diary of William C. Phillips, March 17, April 17, May 8, 1917, William C. Phillips Papers; P. C. Williams to E. E. Pratt, June 29, 1917, Raymond B. Stevens Papers, Records of Shipping Board Commissioners and Fleet Corporation Officers, United States Shipping Board, Record Group 32, National Archives. Hereafter cited as RG 32, plus file or file number, NA.

9. McAdoo to Wilson, May 12, 1917, McAdoo Papers.

be constructed without concern for its commercial use after the war. In his mind there was no comparison between the commercial potential of a steel ship and that of a wooden ship. Goethals preferred to emphasize the building of steel ships and would make plans accordingly with the steel community. The steel producers rejoiced openly at his announcement.[10]

Incensed at this public affront to his authority and articulating an inate antagonism for the steel barons, Denman replied to the press: "We believe that the committees of Congress, and not a public dinner with the head of the steel trust, are the places for the discussion of matters of policy with regard to shipbuilding."[11] Goethals responded by firing F. A. Eustis, assistant general manager, and his assistant, F. Huntington Clark, after the two charged that the general was deliberately and without authorization blocking the wooden ship program.[12] To Denman's added grief, Goethals' public statements brought about a serious slackening in the efforts of the wooden shipbuilding industry—some builders gave up entirely.

When Congress appropriated $500 million in mid-June for shipbuilding and authorized Wilson to exercise his authority for its dispersal through any agency of his choosing, Goethals felt he had a free hand and accordingly arranged for contracts with the steel trusts to purchase steel for $95 per ton. Denman refused to sign the contracts, charging the industry with extortion. Personally threatening James Farrell with a congressional investigation of the steel producers and their pricing systems, Denman got a tentative price of $56 per ton in a sliding agreement instead.[13]

Conflicts also arose over contracts British firms had arranged independently with American shipyards. Between February 10 and April 1, 1917, the British government, working through the Cunard Steamship Company, contracted with American yards for over one million tons of ships. In so doing, the British pre-empted practically all of the ways that might have been utilized by the EFC. Taken by surprise, Wilson and the Shipping Board belatedly established a moratorium on further foreign contracts in April. Denman was greatly distressed by the British actions; in

10. *Washington Post*, May 26, 1917. See W. L. Saunders to Goethals, May 29, 1917, Goethals Papers, for supportive sentiments claiming to represent important industrial interests. Saunders was a ranking member of the NFTC.

11. *Washington Post*, May 28, 1917.

12. Ibid., June 9, 1917.

13. Ibid., June 19, 22, 1917.

a fit of anger he actually threatened to jail Sir Richard Crawford, commercial adviser to the British Embassy. When the British War Mission (the Balfour mission) arrived in early May, Denman again belligerently raised the question of the British vessels being built in American yards. He made it clear that he considered it an unusual and unjustifiable situation when Americans would assist the British in materially increasing the size of their merchant marine at the expense and to the commercial disadvantage of the United States.[14] Rumors began to fly that the Shipping Board would commandeer the contracts and ships being built for the British. When Sir Arthur Balfour requested a confirmation of this, Denman did not reply directly but accused the British of continuing their efforts to arrange contracts even after Wilson's moratorium. Accusations of this sort prompted British concern about American motives and alarmed the State Department which was cultivating a policy of cooperation rather than competition.[15] In order to effect a compromise, but apparently without informing Goethals, Denman promised to continue building wooden ships, which both parties realized had little or no postwar commercial value, provided the British would submit peaceably to a commandeering order.[16]

In the meantime, there was a breach and then a showdown on the Shipping Board itself. From the moment of Goethals' appointment, vice chairman Raymond Stevens had sided with the general on the question of authority. In April, Stevens at times actually controlled the majority. In early July, over Denman's objections, Stevens brought the question to a head when he forced a vote on his resolution that Goethals be given absolute authority, including the authority to let contracts. Stevens' motion was defeated by three votes to two only when commissioner John White rushed back from his sickbed to cast the deciding vote with Denman and Theodore Brent.[17] Responding to an earlier request, Denman then sent the White House an outline of an executive order, which he hoped the president would

14. Phillips Diary, April 17, 1917, Phillips Papers; Arthur J. Balfour to Page, August 21, 1917, Edward N. Hurley Papers.
15. Balfour to Denman, May 23, 1917, Hurley Papers; Phillips Diary, May 25, 1917, Phillips Papers; J. Parker Kirlin to Raymond Stevens, September 12, 1917, RG 32/Stevens, NA; John E. Barber memorandum to Hurley, July 17, 1918, Hurley Papers.
16. Denman to Wilson, June 21, 1917, Wilson Papers.
17. Phillips Diary, April 17, 1917, Phillips Papers; Denman to Wilson, June 29, 1917, Wilson Papers.

sign, clarifying the ideas of the majority of the board concerning the distribution of powers covering ship construction and commandeering. A modified version of this order was signed by Wilson on July 11. In essence, the order told Goethals to build ships, Denman to operate them. Denman would retain his right to approve all contracts, but the Shipping Board was not to interfere with Goethals' actual building program.[18] Wilson hoped he could force Denman and Goethals to subordinate their quarrels to the larger calling.

The president's hopes were not realized. Goethals rejected the plan to commandeer the British vessels; he favored a policy allowing the British to complete their ships under American contracts, arguing that it would save the board much money. To overcome the problem of full yards, Goethals was arranging privately with the American International Corporation to construct a massive shipyard on Hog Island south of Philadelphia on the Delaware River. Additional plants were in the planning stage. Denman interpreted this as an act of insubordination. He insisted upon commandeering the British ships as a partial answer to American shipping needs. Goethals' announcement, Denman complained to Wilson, threatened to compromise his diplomatic arrangements with the British.[19] On his part, Denman continued to refuse to sign Goethals' contracts, claiming that the general manager failed to supply the board with adequate information. Denman indicated to Wilson that he had concluded that Goethals, willingly or unwillingly, had completely succumbed to the steel lobby. Goethals responded that he would not be "bossed" by the Shipping Board.[20]

Wilson then took a strong position with Goethals. He made it abundantly clear that the general manager of the Emergency Fleet Corporation was responsible to the directors of the corporation of the EFC, of which Denman was presiding officer. Not only would Goethals act accordingly, he would never again resort to the public press, directly or indirectly.[21] Goethals replied that he interpreted his job as embodying him with "absolute and complete authority" over construction and that the USSB was to

18. *Washington Post*, July 13, 1917.
19. Goethals to Denman, July 13, 1917, Goethals Papers; Denman to Wilson, July 13, 1917 (two letters), Wilson Papers.
20. *Washington Post*, July 17–19, 1917; Denman to Wilson, July 18, 1917, Wilson Papers.
21. Wilson to Goethals, July 19, 1917, Goethals Papers.

have acted on his suggestion and initiative. He had endeavored to establish harmonious relations with the Shipping Board but had not succeeded. Goethals confessed that it had become "impossible to secure the unison of purpose essential to the success of the work." He could not work under the conditions Wilson had set down. He believed that the interests of the nation would be served best by replacing him with "some one on whom full authority can be centered and whose personality will not be a stumbling block."[22] Five days later, on July 24, 1917, Wilson acted by putting Goethals' resignation before Denman. It was time to wipe the slate clean, the president declared: "No decision we can now arrive at could eliminate the elements of controversy that have crept into almost every question connected with the programme; and I am convinced that the only wise course is to begin afresh."[23] Denman complied immediately. Thus repudiated, commissioners White and Brent also resigned.

In reflecting upon the nature of the controversy, Denman testified after the war that there had not been any insoluble disagreements between him and Goethals. The real problem had been over the matter of authority, for neither he nor the general had ever placed much value on wooden ships.[24] Commissioner Brent suggested other causes. He told Wilson that Goethals' position held back the war shipping effort and came near to forcing Denman's group to capitulate to the steel forces which proposed to "wreak vast profit for a war emergency, and then dissipate the concrete product—ships."[25] Still others felt that Denman's relationship to the West Coast lumber industry, and Goethals' to the eastern steel market, were predominant factors.

Goethals thought highly of his decision to resign—he considered his action "subject to congratulations." Wilson, he confided to a fellow officer, had insisted upon a divided authority which had made him more or less an employee of the Shipping Board. This had been enough of a handicap, but once Denman compounded difficulties by utilizing the occasion for an attack on the steel industry, Goethals' hope for a successful construction program

22. Goethals to Wilson, July 20, 1917, Goethals Papers.
23. Wilson to Denman, July 24, 1917, Goethals Papers.
24. U.S., Congress, House, Select Committee, *United States Shipping Board Operations*, 66th Cong., 2d and 3rd sess., pp. 3188–89.
25. Brent to Wilson, July 24, 1917, Wilson Papers.

had been stymied. Goethals admitted that he was relieved to be no longer associated with the fleet corporation: "I feel I am well out of a mess."[26] The State Department sympathized: It received the news of the resignations with a great sense of relief and as a welcome remedy to the difficulties the controversy had caused for Anglo-American relations. As the assistant secretary of state observed, "all hands agree that it is a fortunate solution, but should have been done sooner."[27]

———— • ◆ • ————

The new men appointed by Wilson to replace Denman and Goethals were Edward N. Hurley and Rear Admiral Washington Lee Capps. The two vacant spots on the commission were filled by Bainbridge Colby of New York and Charles R. Page of California. Hurley was by far the most important of these. His career is touched upon in earlier chapters, but his subsequent activities were so vitally important in the development of American shipping and the expression of Wilsonian foreign policy that a recapitulation and embellishment of his background and beliefs is appropriate.

Described by many as cast from the Horatio Alger mold, Hurley was a self-educated, self-made millionaire from Illinois. Born in Galesburg in 1864 of Irish immigrants, Hurley left school at the age of sixteen and worked at various railroading jobs, rising steadily until three years later he became the youngest passenger locomotive engineer for the Chicago, Burlington & Quincy Railroad. In 1896, he incorporated his own firm and pioneered in the invention and development of machine and pneumatic tools, including the ship's riveter. By 1902, at the age of thirty-eight, he had accumulated sufficient wealth and satisfaction to sell his tool business and go into early retirement. But he was back in business within six years, manufacturing labor-saving home electrical appliances. Hurley became involved in politics as well and is reputed to have played an important role in the Democratic Party's decision to run Wilson for the New Jersey governorship in 1910.

Hurley's basic orientation toward business efficiency had always been

26. Goethals to General H. F. Hodges, July 26, 1917, Goethals Papers.
27. Phillips Diary, July 24, 1917, Phillips Papers. See also Frank Polk to Lansing, July 28, 1917, Frank L. Polk Papers.

coupled with a staunch advocacy for the extension of American foreign trade. In 1912, he conducted a business tour of the Caribbean for members of the Illinois Manufacturers' Association, of which he was vice president. Recognizing his talents and interests, Redfield persuaded him to tour South America for similar purposes early in 1913. Subsequently, Hurley helped found the National Foreign Trade Council, and late in 1914 he joined the administration as vice chairman and later chairman of the Federal Trade Commission. Despite Wilson's disappointment, Hurley left government service in January 1917, but upon the declaration of war he joined the Red Cross. He then reentered the administration by accepting the vice chairmanship of the Exports Administration Council. By this time, he had achieved national recognition as a leader in the business efficiency and trade organization movements, in his outspoken belief in the necessity for government aid and direction to business and the expansion of its foreign trade, and in his marked competence at administering and facilitating the functions of government agencies. Consequently, Wilson overrode his initial protestations that he did not know shipping and appointed him chairman of the Shipping Board and president of the Emergency Fleet Corporation on July 27, 1917.[28]

Although Hurley replaced Denman, most of the applause for his appointment came from the forces that had rallied behind Goethals. They saw in him a man long influenced by the same industrial and administrative proclivities. W. L. Saunders, a colleague of Hurley on the NFTC, reflected opinion in the industrial sector when he remarked that Hurley's appointment should be interpreted as a "triumph [for the general] professionally and personally." In Saunders' mind, Hurley and Admiral Capps, the new general manager of the EFC and former chief of construction for the Navy Department, were both Goethals men. Hurley, he assured the departing Goethals, had been behind the steel ships program from the very start of the dispute. Most important, Hurley represented that "some one" Goethals had called for, on whom full authority could be centered and whose personality would not present a stumbling block.[29]

28. *Dictionary of American Biography*, supp. 1, s.v. "Hurley, Edward Nash"; Hurley, *The Bridge to France*, pp. 16–18; Kaufman, *Efficiency and Expansion*, pp. 120–21.

29. Saunders to Goethals, July 25, 1917, Goethals Papers. Clarification of authority did not actually take place, however, until the Shipping Board revised the EFC bylaws in November.

The demands on the new chairman were clear cut. Ships, thousands of them, were drastically needed to meet the requirements of war and service essential commercial needs. Four options were available. Ships could be requisitioned, purchased, chartered, or constructed. While the last would ultimately provide the largest source of ships, it promised to be of the least immediate benefit. Consequently, Hurley acquired his initial additions to the national fleet by requisitioning, purchasing, and chartering vessels.

Numerous considerations dictated a policy of haste, foremost of which was continued German submarine warfare. From February through June 1917, the British lost almost two million gross tons of ships, three times greater than output, and by July 31 had a net deficit of nearly three million tons after allowing for additions since the commencement of hostilities. In addition, the frightful carnage caused by the German undersea marauders had driven good numbers of neutral ships away from the war zone. The necessity of employing defensive navigational maneuvering caused additional delays. At the same time, the actual demands of the Allies for supplies increased many fold.[30] Moreover, the Denman–Goethals controversy had consumed four vital months and placed the ship construction and commandeering efforts behind the proverbial eight ball. A further complication came in the nature of American shipbuilding itself. When Hurley took office, every shipway in the United States, of which there were 234, was occupied in construction. Of these, 70 percent were in use for United States naval construction, and of the 431 contracts let for commercial vessels in excess of 2,500 tons, either under actual construction or still on paper, 57 percent were foreign, mostly British, Norwegian, and French. The work in hand, just over three million tons, was greater than the full capacity of all American yards for an entire year. To make matters worse, most contracts were for ocean liners, not cargo-carrying vessels.[31]

Hurley was in office only one week when he applied the authority Wilson granted to the board that Denman had desired to exercise. On August third, Hurley issued an order "to prevent American shipyards from working for any country but our own." As Hurley put it, his action was as if "431

30. C. Ernest Fayle, *The War and the Shipping Industry*, pp. 196, 245, 278–79; Maurice Hankey, *The Supreme Command, 1914–1918*, 2:639–40.
31. Hurley, *The New Merchant Marine*, p. 38; Saugstad, *Shipping and Shipbuilding Subsidies*, pp. 45–46.

bombshells, the number of ships involved, had exploded."[32] American shipyard and shipowner protest was vigorous and tied up the board for valuable days and weeks. But these demonstrations could be answered on patriotic grounds. Less easily dealt with were protests from abroad, from foreign shipowners from whom the majority (246 of 431) of the contracts were taken over and from the representatives of their governments who presented their grievances. As a result, while the board issued its confiscation order on August 3, Hurley held back from declaring whether the edict would encompass all foreign vessels without exception and whether the act of confiscation would be permanent—that is, would allow the board to retain the vessels after the war. Great Britain, with 163 of the 246 foreign contracts, a total of 1,200,000 tons, pressured the board to rescind its order, and when that failed attempted to induce Hurley to agree to return the vessels to England following the cessation of hostilities. As they had with Denman, the British continued to assume that the confiscation order was implimented without sufficient consideration of British war and post-war shipping needs. British ambassador Cecil Spring Rice and shipping delegate Thomas Royden reiterated British apprehensions after Hurley's takeover. They went to great lengths to point out that British war losses were catastrophic, to emphasize American maritime growth and growth potential, and to insist that the ships would be used by the British solely for war and not for commercial purposes. While Balfour and Royden did not favor pushing the issue into the realm of the unreasonable, other members of the British mission disagreed with a policy of acquiescence.[33]

Hurley was well aware of the British position and responded indirectly. "It has not been with any view to national advantage, but with the single-minded purpose of waging the war successfully," that his considerations were governed, he informed Lansing. America's ability to provide troops for the war in France, he added, would depend upon shipping, the uncertainty of which required drastic requisitioning measures. "Your position is impregnable," commented McAdoo when he saw the note.[34] Ultimately, the

32. Hurley, *The Bridge to France*, p. 32.
33. Cecil Spring Rice to Polk, July 24, 1917, Hurley Papers; Thomas Royden to Hurley, August 17, 1917, *FR, Supplement, 1917*, 1:616–17; Lord Northcliffe to William Wiseman. August 21, 1917, William Wiseman Papers.
34. Hurley to Lansing, August 29, 1917, Hurley Papers; McAdoo notation on Hurley to McAdoo, August 31, 1917, ibid.

entire issue was resolved by Hurley and the board on September 14 when they decided to take control of all ships built, being built, or about to be built by American labor in American yards, as well as the yards themselves. Four foreign vessels virtually completed on August 3 were excepted. All the rest were to be returned to their owners not later than six months after the war concluded, provided the costs of construction were borne by those accounts.[35]

Having commandeered shipyards and the vessels they were constructing, Hurley then took over American vessels already afloat. His order was given on October 12, 1917 and involved the requisitioning of all steel oceangoing cargo and passenger vessels of American registry in excess of 2,500 tons (657 ships). While private interests actually retained possession of their ships, both owners and vessels were put into the service and pay of the Emergency Fleet Corporation. By October, then, virtually every vessel under American flag or building in American yards and capable of oceanic voyage had been pressed into the war service, and Hurley was able to record with relief that "the controversy . . . is closed as far as the Shipping Board is concerned."[36]

———————•◆•———————

The Shipping Board's initial war-related requirements included the acquisition not only of a fleet but of an ample number of experienced sea-farers to man them. In early May 1917, Denman assigned to vice chairman Raymond Stevens the task of calling together representatives of the nation's shipowning and seamen's organizations to work out a policy that would increase the voluntary supply of American seamen for war trade. Conscription would be considered only as a last resort. Although the history of labor–management relations in the maritime industry was traditionally one of intense conflict and hostility, both sides agreed (with some exceptions) that patriotic considerations required cooperation. Consequently, they laid aside their differences for the most part and concurred on several measures.[37]

35. Hurley to Lansing, September 14, 1917, Wilson Papers.

36. Hurley Diary, October 12, 1917, Hurley Papers.

37. The war maritime labor story does not fall within the scope of this study. In short, the Shipping Board was put between the proverbial "rock and a hard place." Labor sought to use the war to strengthen its fledgling position; the shipowners sought to main-

First, wartime wages and bonuses were determined. Both the USSB and substantially all the ocean steamship lines agreed to pay a uniform and attractive monthly salary. In addition, overtime rates were fixed, as were war zone bonuses of 50 percent of wages, and compensations for loss of effects caused by war. Wages and bonuses were fixed at a high rate deemed sufficient to lure men back to the sea, and uniformity in wages would discourage job jumping and create greater efficiency in performance.

Even men without sea legs were in demand, and the agreements of May eighth obliged the shipowners to take on a certain number of boys and ordinary seamen for training purposes above their ships' regular compliments of able-bodied men. The unions pledged to cooperate with the ships' officers in teaching seamanship to the new recruits. In return, the owners would allow union representatives access to company docks and vessels for the purpose of enforcing labor's commitment. Finally, bonuses and other compensations arising from the war would terminate with the end of hostilities, but the wage levels would be retained for the duration of that year's agreement in order to maintain some stability and continue the inducement for men on shore to return to the sea.[38]

These agreements were ratified and confirmed at a second conference held on August eighth. Urgency was added to these proceedings when news reports indicated that the Scandinavian countries might be drawn into the European conflict and would recall their seamen from foreign employment. Danish, Norwegian, Swedish, and Finnish nationals, it was noted with some alarm, composed more than 50 percent of the crews on American merchant vessels. Under these circumstances, American mariners were all the more desirable.[39] Subsequently, the voluntary decisions reached at these two conferences in May and August of 1917 became known as the "Atlantic

---

tain as much as possible of the prewar advantage they had enjoyed; and the Shipping Board, in an often exceedingly frustrating and hostile environment, sought to please both sides in order to obtain cooperative and coordinated results for the war effort. Despite these difficulties, the board was remarkably successful in obtaining its objectives. However, whatever wartime working relationships with labor the board did acquire were lost in the depression of 1920–1921. See Joseph P. Goldberg, *The Maritime Story*, Chapter 4; Hyman Weintraub, *Andrew Furuseth*, pp. 143–49.

38. Report on conference of May 8, 1917, RG 32/General Files 1089, NA.

39. "Conference on Increase of Shipping Facilities," August 1–2, 1917, Record Group 280, Federal Mediation and Conciliation Service, File 20-16, NA. Hereafter cited as RG 280, plus file, NA.

Agreement." The essential thrust of the Shipping Board was to get American boys onto American ships, not only for the war effort but also for the postwar and long-run needs of the nation's maritime services.

Eight months later, in late April 1918, the Shipping Board called still another conference of seamen's and shipowners' organizations. The board did not desire to set aside the Atlantic Agreement, but concluded that developments brought about since the previous summer warranted changing some of the agreement's conditions. These new conditions included the increased cost of living caused by wartime inflation; the need to equalize wages with the Pacific theatre where shipowners had already made independent upward adjustments; a need to counteract the attraction of high shore wages, particularly in the shipyards; the necessity of bringing wages on the East and Gulf coasts up to levels recently fixed by a limited but significant number of Atlantic companies; and the continued desirability of offering inducements to men to come to the sea as apprentices, in addition to providing incentives for staying in the maritime services. Conference testimony justified these concerns, and on May 18, 1918, the Shipping Board adjusted its own wage scales upward and made the new rate of pay retroactive to May fourth, the last date of the meetings.[40]

The agreement to fix an attractive wage scale was only one of the methods the Shipping Board employed to lure men to the sea. Under the direction of Henry Howard, director of recruiting and training, the board instituted a vigorous recruiting program in every American community with a population over one thousand. Recruitment centers were located in almost seven thousand Rexall drug stores, so chosen because they were considered centers of social activity in those days and because they were open every day and evening. By the spring of 1918, training schools had been established on every coast and were working toward a goal of two hundred thousand seamen. Howard's training program covered the task enthusiastically; the new swabs were even required to train in the old art of chantey singing. The training of officers also fell under Howard's jurisdiction, with a goal of twenty thousand. In conjunction with the Commerce Department's Steamboat Inspection Service, Howard's department encouraged the

40. R. B. Gregg to Charles R. Page, May 20, 1918, RG 32/Marine Conference, Tray 31, Seamen's Correspondence, NA; Report by Page, May 18, 1918, RG 32/General File 1089, NA.

return of over six thousand former ships' officers, half of whom reacquired their licenses through USSB schools. Engineers got their own six-week Shipping Board training program, studying at eleven technical institutions including MIT, Johns Hopkins, and Case Tech. In addition, more than forty navigational schools were established. To cover the possibility of continued shortages in the interim, Howard also cooperated with the Officers' Association of England to bring retired British officers back to sea, paying their fares as they were needed and giving them board on USSB training ships until they could be employed. Howard also helped nongovernment steamship companies obtain officers.[41]

In addition to these responsibilities, Howard embarked on an effort to improve labor conditions aboard merchant vessels, attacking especially the universally wretched conditions in the forecastle sections, the notorious "glory holes" where seamen were berthed. Combining decent wages with improved working conditions, the board argued, would serve as an additional incentive for the recruitment of American personnel and measurably increase work contentment and efficiency. The Howard training, recruiting, and inspection systems were awarded high marks by both labor and management.[42]

The government's maritime labor policies also affected Anglo-American relations. At issue was the La Follette Seamen's Act of 1915 which the British asserted was damaging their effort to maintain a stable wartime maritime work force. Prior to 1915, desertion from the American merchant marine and from the merchant marines of most other countries had been dealt with in exceedingly harsh ways, sometimes by cruel punishment, often by imprisonment. This was enforced reciprocally—most nations were obligated to each other by treaty to arrest and return foreign deserters to their vessels of origin. The Seamen's Act forever freed American seamen from such punitive measures. The act also provided for the abrogation of all treaties which called for arrest and return agreements. In addition, section 4 of the act guaranteed American seamen the right to demand one-half of their earned and unpaid wages in any port. Combined, these two

41. Proceedings of May 1, 1918, RG 32/Marine Conference, 3:652–53, NA; USSB release, "Making an All-American Mercantile Navy," July 7, 1918, RG 32/Colby, NA; Daniels Cabinet Diaries, July 16, 1918, p. 321.

42. Proceedings of May 1, 1918, RG 32/Marine Conference, 3:652–53, NA.

provisions gave American seamen unprecedented mobility: They could now leave their vessels in any port, without fear of incarceration and with money in their pockets. In seafaring circles, the La Follette Seamen's Act was rightly called the American seamen's Emancipation Proclamation.

This situation did not prevail in British mercantile circles, and within days of Wilson's war proclamation, the British ambassador, Cecil Spring Rice, complained to the State Department that inasmuch as the Seamen's Act was applicable to all seafarers—American and foreign—who touched at American ports, it was encouraging British mariners to carouse and desert on American shores. British shipowners, Spring Rice maintained, were bearing increased financial burdens and the sailings of their vessels were delayed by the difficulty of getting disorderly men back on board and procuring replacements for deserters. Spring Rice argued that the results were causing severe damage to the war effort. To his mind, only a suspension of the onerous sections would remedy the problem.[43]

Lansing referred this protest to the Commerce Department, but Redfield advised him that the Department of Labor was a more appropriate place to obtain a decision. It was a natural place to go, for its head, William B. Wilson, had been a major factor in the passage of the Seamen's Act. A Pennsylvanian, Wilson had been secretary-treasurer of the United Mine Workers of America before gaining a House seat in 1910. Two years later, Wilson sponsored a seamen's bill for Andrew Furuseth, president of the International Seamen's Union and patron saint of the maritime labor movement. William Wilson's rationale in supporting the measure through to its final form in 1915 was consistent with Furuseth's in all major respects, including ethnocentrism, safety at sea, industrial efficiency, humanitarian concern, and support for the merchant marine.[44] Of these, Wilson emphasized most the relationships that he believed existed between upgraded seafaring standards and America's role in world commerce. Low pay and poor work standards, he and Furuseth avidly pointed out to a sympathetic President Wilson, had resulted in the progressive elimination of Anglo-Saxons from seamanship. Consequently, shipowners were obliged to seek out crews of Orientals or Hispano-Americans who were not adverse to

43. Spring Rice to Lansing, May 3, 1917, SD 196/115, NA.
44. For Furuseth's position see Jerold S. Auerbach, "Progressives at Sea."

serving under squalid conditions. It followed, they argued, that crews that would accept lower standards were inevitably composed of men of lower intelligence and, hence, incapable of performing at high levels of efficiency. Moreover, when such men deserted, the United States had been obliged to arrest and return them to American ships. In short, the United States was both interfering with efficiency and safety at sea and providing its competitors with an unfortunate commercial edge. Wilson and Furuseth pointed out that the passage of their bill would upgrade standards, level costs, and assure the nation a fair field in the world's marketplace.[45]

Secretary Wilson's reply to Lansing on June 21, 1917 emphasized this position: One of the purposes sought by the Seamen's Act was to force an equalization of the operating expenses of American and foreign vessels trading in American ports. Because seamen could now desert in American ports without fear of arrest, the natural operation of the law forced foreign shipowners to match American wage levels and adopt American standards in order to retain their men. Equalization of wages and standards would create fairer competition for American shippers. The remedy would be either lower rates for American seamen or higher rates for British seamen. Obviously, the British would either have to pay the higher rate or loose their seamen. As was typical of the Wilson administration, his secretary of labor was blending moral arguments with commercial tactics; and he had his chief's backing all the way.[46]

The State Department, however, did not agree with the president and Secretary Wilson. It considered the labor head's well-known prejudices as "unguarded," and as unwisely concerned with "theoretical" commercial justifications when the British complaint emanated from "practical" wartime considerations.[47] Undersecretary Frank Polk determined to withhold Wilson's note from the British Embassy. Following two more protests from Spring Rice, Polk finally responded obliquely: The United States had the question under advisement. In the meantime, Polk asked McAdoo to investigate Great Britain's grievances through the customs service. But

45. See, for example, W. B. Wilson to Woodrow Wilson, April 19, 1914, RG 280/20-16, NA; Andrew Furuseth to Woodrow Wilson, February 12, 1914, Wilson Papers.
46. W. B. Wilson to Lansing, June 21, 1918, Wilson Papers; Woodrow Wilson to W. B. Wilson, June 25, 1917, ibid.
47. Alvey A. Adee to Polk, July 14, 1917, SD 196/116, NA; W. B. Phillips to Polk, July 18, 1917, ibid.

McAdoo passed the buck back by arguing that Redfield had a better handle on such matters. That left Polk exactly where he had started. Subsequently, the State Department did nothing.[48]

Frustrated in his inability to raise a concrete response, that fall Spring Rice intensified his criticism of the Seamen's Act. Desertion rates were causing the British serious concern and threatened to disrupt the carriage of supplies to the war zone. The sections covering payment of wages in port were contributing factors, he admitted, but the real difficulties were an excessive demand for seamen, an insufficient supply, the natural desire of seamen to sign on for the higher wages paid on American vessels, and the preference of British seamen for work in American coastal trade rather than in British war trade. Spring Rice hoped that the United States would influence American shipmasters to deny employment to British deserters. As the result of these protests, in late November Redfield called for a formal meeting to decide on the matter.[49]

Events began to move swiftly at this point, and before the meeting could be convened representatives from the Commerce and State departments and the Shipping Board agreed that an effort was in order to assist the British materially by suspending the features of the Seamen's Act that encouraged desertion. This decision was spurred by news that naval intelligence services in New Orleans were prepared to take such action independently. Lansing and E. T. Chamberlain, commissioner of navigation in the Commerce Department, adopted a harder line. But Redfield did not agree with their arguments for a full suspension of the law, as he desired to retain the act's humanitarian features. He was prepared, however, to suspend those sections encouraging desertion. With attitudes such as these prevailing, representatives of the Labor, Commerce, and State departments and of the Shipping Board met in conference on the third day of the new year, 1918.[50]

Predictably, a large majority concurred that England's needs had to be met. The arguments of Lansing and Chamberlain for full suspension did not

48. Polk to Spring Rice, July 24, 1917, SD 196/119, NA; Polk to McAdoo, July 24, 1917, ibid.; E. L. Rowe to Lansing, August 16, 1917, SD 196/120, NA.
49. Spring Rice to Polk, October 25, 1917, SD 196/121, NA; Spring Rice to Polk, November 7, 1917, SD 196/128, NA; Redfield to Lansing, November 19, 1917, RG 41/94316, NA.
50. Chamberlain to Redfield, December 1, 1917, RG 41/94316, NA; Redfield to Lansing, December 8, 1917, ibid.

carry, but an agreement was reached calling for a legislative enactment authorizing American officers to seize and return to their ships immediately all seamen of foreign vessels deserting in United States ports. This provision also covered those mariners who demanded one-half of their wages and then refused to complete their contracts. There was one hitch: W. B. Wilson had not attended the meeting, and his representative from the Labor Department would not vouch for his approval. The meeting adjourned with the understanding that no suspensions would take place until Secretary Wilson's support was secured.[51]

Wilson kept his colleagues on edge for two weeks and then replied in a manner some had feared—he rejected the British Embassy's argument. The problem, Wilson maintained, was not in the unwillingness of British seamen to work in the war zones; in contrast, American seamen were not deserting in foreign ports. Hence some other factor had to explain the jumping of ship by British seamen in American ports. In Wilson's judgement, that factor was the wage differential. If British shipowners would but pay their seamen rates comparable to those paid by American operators, desertions would be almost entirely eliminated. As the remedy was in the hands of the foreign employers themselves, there appeared no reason to justify the use of American police power to compel alien seamen to fulfill contracts in American waters. Wilson pledged his department's constant assistance in all matters concerning the war labor situation, but he would not endorse a plan that promised to strengthen an already "decided economic advantage [for] the foreign shipowner." Lansing concluded that under these circumstances the British could not expect the Seamen's Act to be suspended. President Wilson endorsed this position.[52] And there the matter rested until later that year when Anglo-American postwar economic relations took on different and crucial dimensions in the environment surrounding the armistice.

51. A. L. Thurman memorandum of meeting, January 3, 1918, RG 41/94316, NA; Thurman to Lansing, October 18, 1918, ibid.

52. Louis F. Post to Lansing, January 19, 1918, SD 196/138, NA; Lansing to Wilson, February 6, 1918, ibid. President Wilson penciled his approval on this same note.

Chapter VI

Ships through Embargoes

When William Denman relinquished office on July 24, 1917, one of his last acts was to describe to Hurley what he considered were the major concerns of the board's majority. These covered commandeering, steel construction costs, lowering ocean freight rates, and the need to develop an embargo policy that would give the United States control of the neutral tonnage of the world.[1] It might have appeared ironic, perhaps hypocritical, that the Wilson war administration could contemplate putting pressure on the remaining neutral nations. Considering that the United States had objected vigorously for three hard years to British embargoes, one might have expected Americans to exercise a degree of compassionate restraint in their own wartime policies toward the neutral world. Instead, following some understandable deliberations and delays, in certain respects the Wilson government actually intensified the procedures employed by Great Britain. America's position on embargoing was predicated upon certain fundamentals. The administration brought pressure to bear upon countries directly or indirectly aiding the Central Powers and, where and when possible, forced neutrals to supply the Allied and American cause with needed materials. A number of programs were devised, and one of the most active entailed acquiring neutral tonnage for Allied and American war shipping service.

Utilizing America's resources as a means of putting pressure on the remaining neutrals was a natural result of Wilson's call to war. Hundreds of thousands of tons of neutral ships, aside from those of Germany and

1. Denman to Hurley, July 24, 1917, Wilson Papers.

Austria, were tied up in neutral ports or were being used in ways inimical to Allied interests. Many Americans argued that exports, especially the great amounts of food the neutrals required from the United States, ought to be parceled out upon the condition that neutral tonnage be deployed in the service of the Associated Powers.[2] Such attitudes were applauded by the British who wasted little time impressing on American statesmen how effective the blockade of Germany could become with American aid. The Balfour mission gave considerable emphasis to this, as did the British Embassy in Washington. Of greatest concern to the British was the question of cooperation. A basis upon which it might be achieved was outlined for the State Department on May 11 by Richard Crawford, commercial adviser of the British Embassy. Crawford pointed out the British experience with respect to neutrals prior to American entry into the war. The neutrals tended to retain their shipping in safe trade, sometimes utilized them in the commercial service of the Central Powers, often denied their use to the Allies, and on occasion even refused to allow them out of port at all. American cooperation would bring an end to most of these practices, largely because the Associated Powers would collectively control the major coal resources of the world, the primary source of maritime fuel. Given that fact, "any conditions, short of compelling the neutral shipowner to run his ships at a loss, [could] be imposed as a *quid pro quo* for the supply of coal." To secure laid-up shipping, which bunkerage control would not effect, the British Embassy suggested a food embargo. But the first requirement would be a policy of Anglo-American cooperation. Otherwise the neutrals might, as Spain had so far done with distracting effectiveness, play the Allies and America against each other.[3] Three days later, American and British officials concurred on a report stating the Allied conviction that American control of vital commodities would force neutrals to commit their maritime fleets to the Allied war effort.[4]

Intending to maintain its freedom in policy, the State Department made clear that it would not be bound to employ British embargo techniques; it

2. See, for example, the statements of Herbert Hoover, April 12, 1917, *New York Times.*
3. "Memorandum 'A': Control of Neutral Tonnage," in Crawford to Polk, May 11, 1917, U.S., State Department, *FR, Supplement 2, 1917,* 2:838–41.
4. "Report of the Joint Subcommittee on Export Licenses," May 14, 1917, U.S., State Department, *FR, Supplement 2, 1917,* 2:848–65.

would, however, pledge its cooperation in obtaining information about neutral shipping whether it agreed with the British in principle or not. This return expressed Wilson's determination to maintain a free hand in the administration of the American war effort. It also reflected his government's sensitivity to British violations of neutral rights in the previous three years. The British appreciated these difficulties and couched the embargo proposals in the manner of suggestions, trusting that the United States would recognize their importance in due time.

In the meantime, Congress considered how to empower Wilson legally with embargo controls as a means of protecting foreign trade and conserving important materials for the American war effort. After encountering some difficulty with southern senators, who feared the effects of the embargo on cotton exports, and with Progressives, who flailed at it as a sellout of neutral principles, both houses finally adopted an embargo as part of the so-called Espionage Act which Wilson signed into law on June 15, 1917. The purpose of the act was "to punish acts of interference with the foreign relations, the neutrality, and the foreign commerce of the United States."[5] One week later, by executive order, Wilson created two agencies to implement the new provisions, to one of which, the Exports Administration Board (EAB), he appointed Edward Hurley.

Still, Washington appeared less than hasty in its desire to enforce measures so thoroughly detested but a few months earlier. In late June, the British became impatient. Certain members of the Balfour mission had remained behind to work out a policy with the State Department. On the twenty-seventh, Lord Eustace Percy complained to the EAB and to Herbert Hoover, head of the United States Food Administration, that Britain's ability to deal effectively with the neutrals was suffering from the failure of the Wilson administration to promulgate leverage strategies.[6] British ambassador Cecil Spring Rice also emphasized the need for haste; he couldn't stress sufficiently the importance of forcing Dutch and Spanish shipping into the Belgian relief program and preventing those countries, along with Norway and Sweden, from trading with the enemy. To Spring Rice the whole question of "whether the war shall be shortened by a drastic restric-

5. Ibid., pp. 883–84.
6. Thomas A. Bailey, *The Policy of the United States towards the Neutrals, 1917–1918,* pp. 79–80.

tion of German supplies, or whether it is to be seriously prolonged by the absence of such restrictions" would be resolved by the United States, and the United States alone.[7]

In that light, Wilson's proclamation of July 9 declaring an embargo on a list of commodities was interpreted by the Allies as only half a loaf. Vitally important goods, including rubber, vegetables, chemicals, ores, and alloys, were not included on the list. The British Ministry of Blockade pointed out that while it was delighted with the proclamation, so long as some commodities were unrestricted, the neutrals would continue to supply the Central Powers with their products. The British were adamant in their assertion that "only a complete prohibition of all exports" to the neutrals would "cover the situation."[8]

Still, weeks went by without a decision from Washington. Certainly, the Denman–Goethals controversy, Hurley's abrupt ascendancy to office, and the tremendous amount of time and energy consumed in expediting the Shipping Board's requisition of shipyards and contracts were factors of importance in delaying a determination to fully employ the embargo. While Wilson expected Hurley to assume an important role in formulating an embargo policy, the new Shipping Board chairman spent late July and August disposing of shipping and shipbuilding problems.

Not until August 21, when Wilson reorganized the parent Exports Council and its working board, the EAB, was serious consideration given to implementing an embargo policy. Significantly, the Shipping Board was included for the first time as a member of both. Six days later, Wilson enlarged the list of exports under control. His second embargo proclamation clarified certain distinctions between European neutrals and the Central Powers on the one hand, and the Allies and all remaining neutrals on the other. To the former, exports of any kind were prohibited; to the latter, the list of July 9 applied, with a few additions. Although the State Department, Shipping Board, and Exports Administration Board combined their resources to control neutral shipping through export licenses, the EAB was handed the largest portion of the task. In essence an embargo department,

7. Spring Rice to Lansing, June 27, 1917, U.S., State Department, FR, Supplement 2, 1917, 2:886–88.
    8. The American Commercial Attaché in London to the EAB, July 12, 1917, U.S., State Department, FR, Supplement 2, 1917, 2:905–906.

as was the name of its counterpart in the British war administration, the EAB was headed by Vance McCormick, Democratic National Committee chairman. In a major turnabout, McCormick pursued a policy so blatantly antagonistic to the neutrals as to provide everything the British had called for and more. McCormick's first move was to isolate the northern neutrals. The board detained all vessels bound for those countries carrying or intending to carry goods on the embargo list, and then intensified the policy by withholding fuel bunkers from cargo ships bound for northern neutral ports without EAB approval.[9] In general, the EAB tightened screws to such a degree following the August 27 proclamation as to surprise the British. On October 7, William Wiseman, a British intelligence officer, noted his conviction that McCormick intended to go beyond putting pressure on the neutrals by actually forcing them into war with Germany. Only weeks earlier, the British had been concerned, as Lord Northcliffe, chairman of the British war mission, noted, that the United States would be too easy on the neutrals. Now the situation was such that the Foreign Office was "trying to restrain Washington from treating the neutrals too harshly in the matter of the blockade."[10]

On October 12, the same day that Hurley noted the termination of the requisitioning ordeal, Wilson revamped the two export control organizations for a third and last time by creating a more efficient single agency, the War Trade Board (WTB). Chaired by McCormick, the War Trade Board was composed of representatives from the State, Treasury, Commerce, and Agriculture departments and the Food Administration and Shipping Board. While it was primarily a policy-executing organization, it dispatched representatives to a great number of foreign countries who entered into detailed negotiations with their foreign counterparts. As the matters involved concerned foreign policy, the State Department had an overseeing responsibility which included handling the WTB's overseas communications. On several occasions, though, the War Trade Board worked quite independently and (once policies had been clarified) quite autonomously. McCormick later explained that as a short-term operation the WTB did not have to concern itself with setting precedents or de-

9. Bailey, *Policy towards the Neutrals,* pp. 88–90.
10. Wiseman to Secret Service Department, October 7, 1917, cited in Wilton B. Fowler, *British-American Relations, 1917–1918,* p. 87, note.

veloping lasting and troublesome enmities. Because it would exist only for the duration of the war, it operated as it saw fit and without concern for its future.[11]

Discussion revolving around a second British mission to the United States in late September and early October added emphasis to the need for adequate shipping. By that time, there was no question that oceanic transportation had become the crux of the war effort. "More and more the problem of the war revolves around the shipping," noted assistant secretary of state William Phillips, with which Royden, Northcliffe, and Lloyd George, the British prime minister, readily concurred.[12] To the Allies, the only chance to stem the expected German spring offensive and launch their own counteroffensive lay upon the degree to which shipping could be gathered to carry American food and supplies to France. Italy's huge war needs and the continuous demands of the Belgian relief program increased the need for shipping. Americans had their own demands for ships—there were numerous import and export trades absolutely essential to the war effort which stretched to all corners of the globe. Hurley outlined the shortages to the War Department and concluded on October 17 that in its present stage of development the Shipping Board could supply only slightly more than half the vessels needed to meet minimal requirements.[13]

Combined, those concerns heightened the American resolve to fill the gap with neutral tonnage and explained the strict policy of the War Trade Board. The basic method employed by the WTB—much as the British had been suggesting—involved bargaining with the countries involved: food and raw materials in exchange for vessels on charter. As Lansing explained, the United States adhered "to the policy of including in all our negotiations for rationing of the . . . neutral countries their chartering to the United States a part of their total shipping tonnage."[14] Other methods were also used: In October, the Shipping and War Trade boards

11. Bailey, *Policy towards the Neutrals*, pp. 91–93.

12. Phillips Diary, October 1, 1917, Phillips Papers; Lloyd George to Wiseman in Sir Eric Drummond to Wiseman, October 11, 1917, cited in Fowler, *British-American Relations*, p. 88; Northcliffe to Winston Churchill, October 14, 1917, Sir William Wiseman Papers.

13. Hurley to Baker, October 17, 1917, Newton D. Baker Papers.

14. Lansing to Joseph E. Willard, February 2, 1918, Polk Papers. See also Frank C. Munson to Hurley, February 14, 1918, RG 32/618-16, NA.

refused to allow neutral vessels, whether in American trade or not, to leave American ports unless their owners guaranteed to return. So successful was the American embargo over exports that by the end of 1917 the WTB estimated that it had cut off 65 to 85 percent of the northern neutrals' export trade with the Central Powers.[15]

While the war administration had come to the conclusion that a complete embargo was the sole way to deal with the neutrals, a number of factors forced it to moderate its policy in late winter 1918. For one, the British were less than convinced of the effectiveness of an absolute embargo. By Christmas 1917, disappointingly little progress had been made in levering neutral shipping into Allied and American war service. In a significant change of policy, London contended that a lessening of commodities under embargo would generate a willingness on behalf of the neutrals to negotiate. The British Foreign Office was also concerned that Germany was taking advantage of the strict embargo to entrench itself in Baltic export trade formerly held by England. Washington's reaction was to argue for the continued maintenance of a complete embargo and to discount Germany's increased export to Scandinavia as minimal in comparative importance. Late in January, the WTB softened somewhat by stating a disposition to defer to the opinion of its London representative who tended toward the British view.[16]

Factors beyond the administration's control also played a major role in bringing about a revision in the WTB's firm position. The winter of 1917–1918 was one of the most severe in American history. A monumental railroad freeze-up put tremendous demands on coastwise shipping and seriously hampered efforts by the Emergency Fleet Corporation, already beset by paralyzing labor unrest, to put into operation its new ship construction plants. Crisis calls from the British for increased food supplies added to the WTB's burdens, as did an emergency demand for shipping to supply anti-Bolshevik forces in Siberia. Finally, a congressional investigation of alleged shipbuilding extravagances subjected the Shipping Board to great pressures.

As the result of those difficulties and the satisfactory development in

15. "Report of the War Trade Board for the Period Ended December 31, 1917," U.S., State Department, *FR, Supplement 2, 1917,* 2:1011.
16. U.S., State Department, *FR, Supplement 1, 1917,* 2:950.

negotiations for shipping with Sweden and Holland, nonessential commodities were stricken from the WTB's embargo list for those countries on February 18, 1918. On account of the sensitive state of shipping talks with Denmark and Norway, however, the WTB did not accord them similar privileges. Those were not granted until April 16 when negotiations with Norway appeared settled and Denmark had been written off as a lost cause.[17] In the meantime, the Shipping Board had taken a stranglehold over all neutral ships using American ports. On April 1, the USSB restrained neutral vessels from leaving the United States until their owners agreed to American charters. At once every neutral vessel entering American ports was subject to a form of requisition, and it became literally impossible for neutrals to get anything out of the United States without coming to terms with the war administration.[18]

Given the application of these embargo and leverage tactics, by the end of the war the Scandinavian countries (including Denmark) had relinquished 1,254,000 deadweight tons in steamers and sailing vessels which the Shipping Board took under ninety-day charters.[19] In consideration of the vital economic needs of the neutrals, some tonnage was left in their control, generally 30 to 40 percent, but the volume forced into charter not only effectively reduced Scandinavian ability to aid the Central Powers but also diminished their capabilities of building and maintaining trade that could be directed to the commercial disadvantage of America and the Allies while the war lasted. That, of course, was true for the commerce of all countries unfortunate enough to be touched by American and Allied leverage policies.

The War Trade and Shipping boards attempted to negotiate with the Netherlands in an identical manner, but the Dutch were severely handicapped by their geographic proximity to Germany. Any acquiescence to the demands of the Associated Powers seemed certain to tempt the Kaiser to consider harsh or even warlike attitudes. It was a case, as the leader of the Dutch mission to the United States in the summer of 1917 put it, of being "between the devil and the deep sea."[20] Nevertheless, the American embargo of sixty grain- and feed-laden Dutch vessels in American

17. Ibid., p. 980.
18. Hurley, *The Bridge to France*, p. 110.
19. Ibid., pp. 110–11.
20. Cited in Bailey, *Policy towards the Neutrals*, p. 201.

ports on July 9, 1917 and their detention there for over half a year was largely responsible for the Dutch accession to charters for more than half a million tons of Dutch shipping cautiously laid up in American ports early in the war. However, when about 300,000 tons deadweight had been turned over, Germany exerted so much pressure on its neighbor that the Dutch were forced to renege. Consequently, Hurley appealed to the president who authorized their confiscation under the international right of angary, America's privilege as a belligerent to requisition for military purposes foreign vessels in American waters. When finally accumulated in ports throughout America and America's possessions, eighty-seven Dutch vessels of 533,746 deadweight tons were added to the American fleet and assigned to South American war trade or to Belgian relief.[21]

Spain proved much harder to deal with. The Iberian kingdom had early been a thorn in the Allied side, and the Balfour mission spared little time in introducing the problem. A suspected accomplice to various German military activities, providing supplies and information to submarines, Spain manipulated its control of valuable resources required by the Allies, in particular iron ore, copper, and lead. Britain could not retaliate with force because its imports from Spain considerably exceeded its exports. When the Germans instituted unrestricted submarine warfare, Spain refused to use its vessels in Anglo-Spanish trade, forcing the British to divert important tonnage to Spanish ports. In addition, the trade relationship between Spain and the Allies was so unbalanced in favor of Spain that the Allies experienced great difficulty in securing financing. The Allies needed a credit system with Spain like the one arranged with the United States in 1915, but Madrid would have nothing to do with it. The British saw American entry into the war as a means to redress the balance, for the United States supplied Spain with numerous commodities, especially coal which Madrid was securing from America in order to avoid being dependent upon Great Britain. That the United States Treasury Department did not favor advancing funds to cover Allied commercial obligations to Spain emphasized the desirability of using American embargoes to force Spain to establish a credit system for the Allies.[22]

21. Hurley, *The Bridge to France*, pp. 115–16.
22. Pierce C. Williams to Burwell S. Cutler, October 9, 1917, General Records of the Treasury Department, Office of the Secretary, General Correspondence, 1917–1932, Record Group 56, File Number 129, National Archives. Hereafter cited as RG 56 plus

While the Spanish squeeze on Allied finances and shipping was sufficient to warrant American sanctions, other factors added concern. In the first place, heightened Spanish commercial activity in the Caribbean following the American declaration of war was viewed with jaundiced eyes in Washington.[23] Spain also possessed twenty-one interned Austrian ships that could serve for the Allied war effort. By the fall of 1917, the War Trade and Shipping boards, encouraged by the British, had adopted a tough embargo policy, shutting down Spanish access to American coal for maritime fuel and withholding export licenses to Spain in virtually all important commodities. The WTB "intended to exert extreme pressure upon Spain" in order that the United States could secure shipping and certain other articles from Spain necessary to the war effort. That pressure could be secured most easily "where industries can be disorganized by the cutting off of supplies of raw materials or by the doing away temporarily with the market where supplies may be disposed of."[24]

By February 1918, the United States position had hardened to the point of demanding almost two-thirds of Spain's overall tonnage for the Allied war effort, excluding the Austrian shipping. It was that or nothing, Lansing informed the American Ambassador to Spain, Joseph E. Willard. If necessary, the United States was prepared to continue to apply the embargo until Spain more definitely felt the need to reach an accord with the United States.[25] In the meantime, War Trade Board negotiators first attempted to persuade Austrian interests to transfer their vessels to the United States and then tried to find a way the Swiss government could obtain them on the notion that this would relieve the USSB of the responsibility of furnishing Switzerland with ships. But Spain could not be cowed. Despite varied efforts, Spain sidetracked the bunkers discrimination by stoking her engines with Mexican coal (considered too inferior by the Wilson administration),

file number, NA. See also Oscar Crosby to Wilson, October 17, 1917, ibid.; Pierce Williams to Hurley, October 19, 1917, Frank C. Munson Papers, Records of Executive Office, General Correspondence of Members of the War Trade Board, 1918–1919, Record Group 182, National Archives. Hereafter cited as RG 182 plus file number, NA.

23. See, for example, Hoover to the War Trade Board, November 10, 1917, RG 182/Munson, NA.

24. Beaver White to Lord Eustace Percy, December 1, 1917, RG 182/Munson, NA.; Beaver White memorandum, January 29, 1918, ibid.

25. Lansing to Willard, February 2, 1918, Polk Papers.

ignoring other impediments, and temporarily making do without American commodities. In August, the American negotiations fell through completely. Madrid then closed a sudden and exclusive deal with the British for charters of Spanish bottoms for the metals trade to England, much to the chagrin of the War Trade Board which felt that it should have received a 50 percent share, as had been agreed upon for the disposition of all neutral shipping acquired through embargoes. "The British did what they could to put any negotiations of ours on the bum," complained a WTB operative from Spain.[26]

Despite the loss of Spanish vessels to the British, in all the United States secured close to two million deadweight tons of neutral ships. The administration assigned these vessels to various parts of the war trade touching at virtually every corner of the globe and operated them in American service throughout 1918 and into 1919.

While American use of embargo power to secure European neutral shipping for the war effort has received proper historical attention, scant consideration has been given to the application of the embargo in a seemingly unlikely and far removed area from the war zone—the Pacific—and to its most formidable occupant, Japan. While the United States obtained Japanese merchant vessels on the same basis as it obtained them from the European neutrals, the application of economic leverage in the Pacific had a significance beyond the basic effort to muster maritime force against Germany. Japan was a ranking military and commercial power and possessed the inside track to the legendary China market at a time when each of its foremost competitors was handcuffed by the great European war.

From the American standpoint, there was ample reason to be concerned with Japanese commercialism. From the very outset of war, Japanese exploitation of the ensuing shipping shortage on the Pacific was viewed in the United States as an ominous threat to American economic interests and ambitions in that area. The immediate withdrawal of German shipping

26. W. A. Chadbourne to T. L. Chadbourne, September 4, 1918, RG 182/Munson, NA. See also Thomas Fisher to Beaver White, June 19, 1918, ibid.; Munson to Fisher, August 17, 1918, ibid.

from the Pacific at the outbreak of war and the gradual reassignment of British and Canadian bottoms to war duties left the field open for Japanese and American investment. But American participation was short lived. Because of the greater trading profits on the Atlantic run, principal American lines were transferred there, and Japan gained control of more than 55 percent of the carrying trade in the Pacific. In comparison, American participation fell to 2 percent. In addition, Japanese lines penetrated to every corner of the Pacific, including Latin America, which the United States considered its special preserve. To consolidate this expansion, the Japanese government established a system of strict control and subsidization of its maritime and related industries. The Japanese also used their competitive advantage to raise freight rates and initiate a damaging program of freight-space discrimination. Summing up early in 1916, the Commerce Department concluded that the combination of Japanese shipping discrimination and the absence of American ships on the Pacific was "the main retarding influence" on United States trade expansion in that part of the world.[27]

Despite these disadvantages, it was again the British who initially broached the possibility of countering the Japanese by denying them essential materials, particularly those which could be used in maritime construction. Great Britain had its own scores to settle with Japan, and British interest in containing the advances of the Japanese economic empire was as long lived as that of the United States. Stanley Hornbeck, an American Far Eastern expert, noted: "The value to her of the open door in China is greater in its immediate aspect than it is to us."[28] But the British attempt to limit Japan's military participation in the Pacific failed, and Tokyo soon controlled all of the Asian territories previously held by Germany. In addition, Tokyo made every use of the Anglo-Japanese alliance to secure steel from England in exchange for policing the Pacific. Japan

27. E. E. Pratt to Redfield, February 7, 1916, RG 40/72155/18, Part 7, NA. See also Abraham Berglund, "The War and Trans-Pacific Shipping"; J. Russell Smith, *Influence of the Great War on Shipping,* pp. 90–91; Saugstad, *Shipping and Shipbuilding Subsidies,* pp. 325–27. The State Department, USSB, and WTB files contain many official reports of discrimination.
28. Stanley K. Hornbeck, "Trade, Concessions, Investments, Conflict and Policy in the Far East."

also managed to keep its vessels out of the Allied war shipping pool and use them instead for trade aggrandizement at English expense.[29]

British frustrations were openly expressed with the arrival of the Balfour commission in April 1917. In a meeting with Denman and the Shipping Board, Balfour requested that inasmuch as the English steel supply was seriously limited the United States should assume the Japanese need for steel, plates, forgings, and the like for shipbuilding, "conditional on the proper employment in the interest of the Allies of Japanese shipping."[30]

Nothing suggested that Wilson and the Congress had Japan in mind when the president's executive order of July 9 listing embargoed commodities was announced. Nevertheless, placing an embargo on steel and iron as war essentials played havoc with the Japanese economy. The Japanese minister for foreign affairs quickly protested that all industrial enterprises and particularly the current construction of ships would be "enormously" affected. He added that if Japan "should be shut off from the markets of this country [the United States] . . . her foundries and factories would have to shut down and great loss would ensue."[31] An American official in Tokyo reported that "the greatest apprehension is now felt by shipbuilding and dockyard companies" and observed accurately that the move was interpreted as a "weapon to force Japan to send ships into the Atlantic."[32] The Japanese news media corroborated his analysis. "The embargo problem . . . is a life and death problem to the Japanese," declared the *Osaka Asahi* on August 16. "It is like giving a cold bath to the prosperity-intoxicated people of Japan." The following day the *Asahi* added: "Japan seriously feels the lack of ships. Delayed goods are piled at every pier. . . . The decreased number of ships would mean increased

29. Charles Nelson Spinks, "Japan's Entrance into the World War"; Grey, *Twenty-Five Years*, 2:104–105; Smith, *Influence of the Great War on Shipping*, p. 90; Fayle, *The War and the Shipping Industry*, p. 246; Don Dignan, "New Perspectives on British Far Eastern Policy, 1913–1919."

30. Arthur J. Balfour memorandum for Lansing, May 15, 1917, U.S., State Department, FR, *Supplement 1, 1917,* 1:596–97.

31. Viscount Motono to State Department, July 12, 1917, SD 694.119, NA. See also Breckinridge Long memorandum to Frank Polk, July 30, 1917, Polk Papers. For an overview of the effects of the embargo see Kakujiro Yamasaki and Gotaro Ogawa, *The Effect of the World War upon the Commerce and Industry of Japan,* pp. 25, 248–51.

32. Post Wheeler to Lansing, August 12, 1917, SD 694.119/2, NA.

prices of commodities. The rise of the cost of living would likely bring about a great social disaster."[33]

The embargo intensified a situation that Japan considered both good and bad for its interests on the Asian mainland. American war involvement in Europe would allow Japan greater freedom in the Far East; but conversely, an armed America posed a serious challenge if it maintained its concern with the Open Door policy. American efforts to induce Chinese entry into the war had been viewed with alarm, and the Japanese determined to take preventive action. Under the guise of arranging suitable military and economic cooperation, Japan announced the forming of the Ishii mission in June 1917.

The seriousness of the Japanese reaction led the State Department to realize how formidable the embargo could be as a diplomatic weapon. Within several weeks, various members of the State Department were not only alloting considerable time to discussion of the embargo but also considering it as the primary means by which to counter Japanese strength in the Orient. E. T. Williams, head of the division of Far Eastern affairs, warned that the Japanese had taken advantage of the situation to "promote their own commerce at the expense of Europe and America." Williams argued forcefully that the embargo had to be maintained until a sufficient proportion of the Japanese merchant fleet was diverted to the Atlantic war effort.[34] Breckinridge Long, third assistant secretary of state, concurred. Informing Lansing that Japan's lack of steel gave the United States a formidable advantage, he advocated "aggressive use" of the embargo as a means of obtaining satisfactory settlement at the coming discussions.[35] A similar analysis came from M. A. Oudin, one of Hurley's associates as a founder of the NFTC and the manager of General Electric's vast foreign enterprises. Oudin had just returned from Tokyo where he had close contact with members of the imperial administration. He wrote to the assistant secretary of state, William Phillips, that the withholding of steel and iron had completely disarranged the program of the Ishii mission and placed Japan in the "disadvantageous position of having to obtain concessions from the United States of an entirely different character from those orig-

33. *Osaka Asahi*, August 16–17, 1917.
34. Report of E. T. Williams, August 4, 1917, Breckinridge Long Papers.
35. Long to Lansing, August 4, 1917, Long Papers.

inally in mind." Oudin advised immediate use of economic leverage: "In the present embargo, the United States has the most powerful weapon that it has ever possessed with which to deal with Far Eastern questions."[36] And Long, who had gone to San Francisco to welcome the mission, cabled the department that the steel issue was paramount in the minds of the delegates.[37]

The British kept up their own pressure on Washington, maintaining that the Japanese were falsifying their need for vessels in essential trade and were "employing their tonnage purely in their own interest and with a view to commercial expansion." They further suggested that the State Department consider the embargo as a valuable postwar economic weapon.[38] Moreover, London declared it would strengthen the American hand in the negotiations by abandoning its own efforts to acquire Japanese tonnage.[39] Following the British lead, France and Italy also entered into the agreement to give the United States the fullest degree of leverage.

By September first, a number of reasons seemed to suggest a powerful use of the embargo as a lever in the Lansing–Ishii negotiations. On the eve of the discussions, Oudin, fresh from a trip to the State Department, wrote an associate in Shanghai that the embargo was presently "just as important and certainly more pressing than the question of recognition of Japan's superior position in China. It is believed that our State Department will not make any concessions."[40]

Oudin, however, apparently had spoken to everyone at the State department except Lansing, for the secretary, while supporting the use of leverage on the European neutrals, opposed its application in the Pacific. After a cursory discussion of his hope to arrange for Japanese maritime support of

36. M. A. Oudin to Phillips, August 28, 1917, SD 694.119/18, NA.

37. Long to Lansing, August 19, 1917, SD 694.119/5, NA. See also Phillips Diary, August 22, 1917, Phillips Papers.

38. Memorandum to the State Department from Sir Richard Crawford, August 24, 1917, SD 694.119/7, NA.; Phillips Diary, August 23, 1917, Phillips Papers.

39. Memorandum, "Japanese Tonnage and Shipbuilding Material for Japan," British Foreign Office, August 31, 1917, RG 182/Munson, NA. The British Foreign Office went so far as to suggest the terms of barter. See the undated "Memorandum of Japanese Steamship Construction," given to the State Department by Crawford and presented by Gordon Auchincloss to Vance McCormick on September 11, 1917, ibid. See also Sir Thomas Royden's suggestions to McCormick, August 17, 1917, Executive Country Files, Japan, 1917–1919, RG 182/11, NA.

40. Oudin to Thomas F. Millard, September 1, 1917, Paul Reinsch Papers.

the war, the secretary abruptly dropped the subject and worked to invoke a spirit of cooperation.[41] Lansing, perhaps the only ranking American official realistic enough to appraise correctly the weakness of the American position in China and its contiguous areas, molded what was in effect a delicate compromise. Recognition of Japanese "special interests" was granted in return for a pledge to prohibit discriminatory acts against foreign commerce in areas under Japanese control. Oudin maintained that American commercial activities in China had been dealt a "demoralizing blow" and that American business interests in Asia had been "seriously and permanently injured" as a result of Lansing's unwillingness to get tough.[42] But Lansing replied indirectly that "the circumstances in which the world now finds itself are such that it is not desirable for us to compete with Japan."[43] Lansing's remarks set the stage for his subsequent efforts to contain Japan within a cooperative framework. His later support of the four-power consortium and joint Siberian occupation exemplified this.

While the Lansing–Ishii agreements were a genuine effort on behalf of the secretary to create an advantageous position for the United States, the Japanese claimed the agreements granted them permission to exploit their rights of territorial propinquity. The furor that arose from those who condemned the agreement as a sellout of American commerce, however, substantially clouded an important fact. Lansing's decision not to employ the embargo as leverage in the talks did not mean that other American officials would not favor an embargo. This became evident in the behavior of the Shipping and War Trade boards, whose chief policymakers vigorously disagreed with the secretary and considered containment through cooperation an impossible goal.

Lansing and Ishii had no sooner ceased discussing the transportation problem than the Exports Administration Board moved to use the embargo. Both the EAB and the Shipping Board were primarily concerned with the prompt and effective containment of Japanese maritime expansion and

41. "Memorandum by the Secretary of State of a Conference with the Japanese Ambassador on Special Mission (Ishii), September 6, 1917," U.S., State Department, FR: The Lansing Papers, 1914–1920, 2:432–33. See also Lansing, War Memoirs of Robert Lansing, p. 290.

42. Oudin to Polk, November 9, 1917, Polk Papers.

43. Lansing to Redfield, January 22, 1918, Long Papers. This was in response to a protest Oudin made to Redfield.

cared only secondarily whether Japanese ships were secured for the Atlantic war effort. Vance McCormick articulated this approach when he advised the Ishii mission that the United States fully intended to secure shipping from the Japanese and that if necessary economic force would be used. American steel, he remarked, would be released only in exchange for immediate delivery of ships, or, as the Japanese readily perceived, a payoff in vessels taken from active use in Japan's thriving commercial trade. When a member of the mission complained that the United States was "taking advantage of the situation," McCormick deceptively retorted that it was not a commercial issue but a war matter and suggested that the discussion be terminated and reopened at some later date.[44]

The Shipping Board strongly endorsed McCormick's approach. After Japanese Ambassador Aimaro Sato had called on Hurley several times to discuss the matter, the chairman recorded confidentially:

> I have impressed upon him the fact that we are obliged to consider this matter from a diplomatic standpoint, but in reality it is nothing but a business question. If Japan was an old customer of many years standing who had purchased their plates here, we would, in a measure, be duty bound to be very considerate of their requirements. While we have no feeling about Japan buying steel from England, as we had sufficient foreign markets to take care of our surplus, we do feel that we are not obliged to exert ourselves in taking care of new customers who only came to us when they could not purchase elsewhere.

> I further stated that he must take into consideration the fact that they cannot get steel from England or any other country for the next ten years, our market being the only one open to them. Any treaties they may desire to make with us which are not made on a fair and equitable basis will seriously hamper their future activities in the ship building industry.[45]

These remarks revealed several important things about America's position. First, like McCormick, Hurley was not overly concerned with the immediate necessity of obtaining Japanese vessels for the war effort. Second, the United States, believing that it held a stacked deck, had no intention of

44. Record of a conversation between Vance McCormick and Viscount Ishii, September 12, 1917, RG 182/Munson, NA.; Minutes of Meetings of the Exports Administration Board, September 13, 1917, RG 182/2, NA.
45. Hurley Diary, October 21, 1917, Hurley Papers.

being outfinessed in the intrigues of business. This attitude was representative of the old storekeeper's ethic that pervaded the entire period of bargaining. The favorable consummation of an arrangement for ships at Japanese expense was considered to be the acid test of American business acumen. Third, Hurley's revelation that the Shipping Board enjoyed a steel surplus belied the American argument that its actions were based largely on the existence of an acute shortage.[46] Fourth, Hurley was prepared to employ exactly what Lansing had spurned—the use of a monopoly on raw materials to exact favorable diplomatic and commercial concessions. The embargo would be used at the expense of the shipping industry vital to Japan, and no consideration would be given as to time of peace or war.

The War Trade Board translated such thinking into bitter economic warfare. Created out of the EAB on October 12, 1917, it assumed the major role in the embargo through its authority to issue export licenses, without which nothing could leave the country. Representing the Shipping Board on the WTB was Hurley's personal choice, shipping magnate Frank C. Munson. Munson was vested with full authority over the negotiations for Japanese vessels. One of America's largest charterers, Munson's own shipping line had developed a thriving Caribbean and South American trade during the years of neutrality. As a result, he had come to appreciate the extent of Japanese commercial extension into those areas. Accordingly, he strongly opposed the program of removing for Atlantic military uses what little American tonnage was left in the oriental trade, and developed a near frenzy over alleged Japanese discrimination against American trade. Thoroughly upset with what he termed profiteering on the part of Tokyo, Munson informed Hurley that every effort had to be made "to influence the policy that Japan is pursuing on the Pacific."[47] Given Munson's attitude, negotiations over steel came to a complete standstill. In late November, a

46. Six months later, on April 5, 1918, Hurley argued before the Senate Committee on Commerce that there had as of that date still been no shortage. He quoted Elbert Gary and James Farrell as saying: "There is plenty of steel." See U.S., Congress, Senate, Committee on Commerce, *United States Shipping Board Emergency Fleet Corporation,* 65th Cong., 2d sess., Hearings, 2:2446. See also RG 32/Verbatim Minutes, February 28, 1918, NA.

47. Munson to Hurley, October 17, 1917, RG 182/Munson, NA. See also Munson to Raymond B. Stevens, October 17, 1917, RG 32/Stevens, NA; Munson to J. R. Morse, October 18, 24, 1917, RG 182/Munson, NA; Minutes of Meetings of the WTB, Stenographic copies, October 18, 1917, RG 182/6, NA.

Tokyo daily reviewed the deadlock and predicted its continuation. "America naturally does not like to see Japan build many vessels which will be employed in obtaining the mastery of the Pacific," noted the *Mainichi Shimbun.* "If the intention of the United States is really such as we suspect, the removal of the steel embargo will be next to impossible."[48]

Consequently, Japan reconsidered its lack of resources and began developing its own supplies of iron and steel. As early as September, Tokyo sent a scientific mission into the interior of China to search for a supply of iron ore that could free Japan from dependence on the United States or Great Britain. Shortly thereafter, the Japanese government announced plans to increase the capacity of its own iron mines and to open new ones, both at home and in Shantung. In Peking, Paul Reinsch, the American minister, witnessed these and other moves on behalf of Tokyo to increase its share of Chinese steel production. When he asked Chinese officials for an explanation, they simply repeated what the Japanese minister told them: "Inasmuch as the United States refused to sell steel to Japan . . . the time has come for Japan to control China's ore deposits."[49] And from Tokyo, Reinsch's counterpart, Roland S. Morris, notified Lansing that the stalemate in negotiations was causing such "growing unrest and irritation" as to make imperative Japanese efforts to cease all dependency on American markets.[50]

At this point, a group of American and Japanese businessmen in Japan, convinced that diplomacy could reach no satisfactory solution, sought to open direct negotiations with the WTB. But the board stood firm, insisting on new tonnage in exchange for steel and refusing to pay prices for ships at anything near the market quotation. Moreover, the War Trade Board offered only silver bullion, not gold, as a medium of exchange. By early 1918, the negotiations had bogged down once again. The tactics of attrition seemed to be working. On January 12, Munson was able to report to Hurley that "one or two" of the large private shipbuilding concerns in Japan had run out of steel and were ready to do business on American terms: "This is a very important opportunity to take advantage of the embargo . . . and secure important additions to our American fleet."[51]

48. *Tokyo Mainichi Shimbun,* November 25, 1917.
49. Reinsch to Lansing, October 26, 1917, Reinsch Papers.
50. Morris to Lansing, December 3, 1917, SD 694.119/51, NA.
51. Munson to Hurley, January 12, 1918, Hurley Papers.

But other factors compromised aspirations of the War Trade Board for a Carthaginian deal. As is described previously, the shipping situation in midwinter 1917–1918 cornered the Shipping Board in a bad way. Inclement weather and serious transportation problems, coupled with shipping demands of unforeseeable proportions and a congressional investigation, plunged the operations division into a state of despair. Responding to its director's admonition that his department was in a "hopeless position, [and] up against the proverbial stone wall,"[52] Hurley revised his position on the values of stalling and determined that the time had come to place the needs of war before the satisfactions of business success. He informed McCormick that the stalemate of the WTB was making all departments "liable to the charge of woeful negligence. Each time we pause on the edge of making a decision, we unquestionably cause further distrust in Japan."[53] At the same time, Hurley suggested that the State Department, which was now concerned, circumvent the War Trade Board in the hope of obtaining a breakthrough.[54]

The strategy paid off. In March, Ambassador Morris negotiated an agreement to charter 150,000 tons of Japanese shipping for a six-month period. Fearing the United States might possibly assign these ships to competitive Pacific runs, the Japanese insisted that the vessels be used solely in the Atlantic war trade.[55] Munson was hardly pleased. He protested against this action, claiming it represented "intervention" in the affairs of his office and glossed over and ignored the serious realities of Japanese economic expansion.[56] Munson's resolve to prolong the purchasing negotiations was hardly diminished: "The embargo must be maintained to the limit. In every case an effort will be made to make some deal by which the United States will gain in ship tonnage."[57] But by that time, Hurley had interjected himself personally into the management of the negotiations from the United States. On March 18, he successfully pressured McCormick into concluding

52. Edward F. Carry to Hurley, December 30, 1917, Daniels Papers.
53. Hurley to McCormick, February 13, 1918, Hurley Papers.
54. Hurley to Lansing, February 12, 1918, Hurley Papers.
55. Although the Shipping and War Trade boards gave such assurances, they nevertheless employed the *Persia Maru* in the Manila trade (sending her via Japanese and Chinese ports!) and utilized Japanese bottoms on the West Coast in the South American nitrate trade. The *Persia Maru* case caused considerable ire in Japan. See, for example, Morris to Lansing, July 12, 1918, Food Administration Papers.
56. Munson to Gordon Auchincloss, March 4, 1918, RG 182/Munson, NA.
57. Munson memorandum, March 11, 1918, RG 182/Munson, NA.

contractual arrangements for the purchase of forty-five steel cargo carriers. The first vessels were to be received in June in exchange for 250,000 tons of American steel. Export licenses for the steel were to be granted by the WTB. The steel to be furnished had been ordered by Japanese shipbuilders before the enactment of the embargo and stored on the Pacific Coast for more than nine months in anticipation of a settlement.[58]

Overnight, optimism permeated Japanese business circles, and new plans for ambitious and expansive trade enterprises were announced. But the new vitality alarmed Ambassador Morris, especially in view of increased Japanese interests in Siberia. He hastily advised Lansing that export licenses should be screened carefully for fear that subsequent ship production would be used "not in the Allied cause but largely for Japanese trade purposes."[59] Subsequently, Morris urged the adoption of a "trickle-down" policy for steel exports and requested that he be consulted before any materials helpful to Japanese shipping were released.[60] When Japanese business interests endeavored to open an abandoned iron furnace in Talladega, Alabama, Morris advised against the concession. Though approval was given because the State Department deemed it an unprofitable enterprise, Morris was made personally responsible for allocation of the mine's iron ore in Japan.[61] In urging these considerations upon Vance McCormick, Morris noted that it would have the added effect of generating a feeling of respect on behalf of the Japanese for the favors granted them.[62] The WTB proved adept at following such advice. An intentional lethargy reigned. By early July, close to three months after contractual agreements had been signed, licenses for shipping steel had still not been issued by Munson's office. In consequence, the Japanese refused to deliver any ships until the steel was released.[63]

Procrastination served to achieve more than one end, for the Allies had

58. Hurley memorandum, March 18, 1918, Hurley Papers; United States Shipping Board, *Second Annual Report, December 1, 1918*, p. 53.

59. Morris to Lansing, April 30, 1918, SD 894.85/79, NA.

60. Morris to Lansing, May 13, 1918, SD 894.85/58, NA.

61. War Trade Board to Morris, May 18, 1918, RG 32/618-15, NA; Morris to WTB, May 27, 1918, ibid.; Munson to Fred L. Blackman, August 19, 1918, RG 182/Munson, NA. With minor exceptions, American steel was allocated for use only in Japanese maritime construction.

62. Morris to McCormick, June 14, 1918, RG 32/618-15, NA.

63. Minutes of Meetings of the War Industries Board, May 17, 1918, Bernard M. Baruch Papers; Munson to J. D. Duncan, May 29, 1918, RG 182/Munson, NA; Hurley to J. L. Ackerson, July 2, 1918, RG 32/618-15, NA.

pledged the previous summer to withdraw from the Japanese ship market in support of the embargo. Great Britain and France often exerted pressure on the WTB thereafter to lift this binder, but the clamps were kept on. And while the WTB did finally arrange in July to release the steel, the Allies were kept off balance by intimations that negotiations still had not been terminated. Fed up, an angry British Ministry of Shipping notified Hurley on August 13 that it was sick of McCormick's and the WTB's machinations. Arguing that the embargo was doing little to halt Japan's commercial expansion in the Pacific, that the embargo was "detrimental" to British commercial interests in the Orient, and that its success in procuring Japanese vessels for the general Allied war service was largely unsatisfactory, the ministry threatened to abandon its pledge of abstention by opening direct chartering negotiations with Japan.[64]

The final release of the steel and the growing disagreement among the Allies in their policy of twisting Tokyo's arm diminished the effectiveness of the War Trade Board's use of steel as an economic lever. Moreover, by late summer 1918 Japan was supplying itself with ship plates through its own manufacturing processes and through the furnaces and mines of its mainland possessions. American recognition that steel had substantially lost its force as a lever in Pacific diplomacy was succinctly documented by John Foster Dulles of the WTB. With the termination of hostilities, Japan would have little difficulty in securing iron and steel in the open market, Dulles informed Ambassador Morris in November, and the time had come to terminate the embargo on steel: "We believe that if it becomes necessary for us to exert pressure, . . . it can be done more effectively with other commodities." Dulles then informed Morris that the War Trade Board had decided not to issue export licenses for cotton or import licenses for silk.[65]

It is questionable whether the embargo did much more than temporarily

64. Thomas Fisher to Hurley, August 13, 1918, RG 32/618-15, NA.
65. War Trade Board to Morris, November 18, 1918, RG 182/11, NA. Four days later, the WTB rescinded the export embargo on cotton "on account of domestic considerations" and noted that "import restrictions will suffice for our purpose." See War Trade Board to Morris, November 22, 1918, ibid. By this time Washington was more concerned with Japan's exclusion of the Stevens Railway Commission from operation in Manchuria, for which purposes the silk and cotton embargoes were imposed. See the memorandum by Lieutenant A. A. Berle, Jr., December 10, 1918, "American Economic Intervention in Russia," U.S., State Department, FR, The Paris Peace Conference, 2:475.

delay the phenomenal increase of Japanese maritime strength. Despite its inability to obtain American steel, Japan still managed to double tonnage production in 1918. In fact, Japan reached the zenith of its ship construction that year, and related industries were stimulated to a growth and output never before conceived.[66] Of a certainty, the embargo demonstrated to the imperial government its vulnerability to the denial of raw materials in time of war. This factor and the additional prospect of an embargo in peacetime was sufficient to strengthen Japanese determination never to be deprived of its mainland interests. Accordingly, by the fall of 1918, Tokyo had taken major steps in that direction. At the State Department, the division of Far Eastern affairs acknowledged in late October that "the war, with its various embargoes and . . . the importance of owning a large merchant marine, has set the Japanese to work with feverish energy to develop what metals they have in their own islands, and in their colonies and protectorates, and acquiring special concessions and privileges in the mining areas of China."[67] It was an admission that the steel embargo, originally directed by elements of the Wilson war administration to restrict Japanese imperial growth and support Chinese integrity, had backfired. The American embassy in Tokyo agreed. Japan, convinced that it could not become a ranking industrial and military power until it could secure unimpeded access to iron and steel, had been furnished with a prime "motive for territorial expansion."[68]

In other analyses of American Far Eastern policy, much has been made of the various means by which Washington sought to limit the Pacific aspirations of the Japanese Empire during the war years, 1917–1918. Research has focused on the Lansing–Ishii agreements, on Woodrow Wilson's support of the four-power consortium, and on his decision to intervene in Siberia. The first was an effort to bind Japan morally to the Open Door; the second a restraining device whereby Japanese capital investment in China would be limited by the consortium's cooperative ordinances; the

66. "The Japanese Merchant Marine: A Confidential Report," September 16, 1918, RG 32/Operations, NA; Yamasaki and Ogawa, *Effect of the World War upon Japan*, pp. 235–46, 248–49.

67. "Iron and Steel Industry of Japan," confidential report of E. T. Williams, October 30, 1918, Roland S. Morris Papers.

68. American Embassy report, "On the Preponderance of Imperialistic Forces in Japan," undated but written between October 20 and November 7, 1918, Morris Papers.

third an endeavor to check Japan by working militarily to curtail its advances on the Manchurian and Siberian mainlands.[69]

Clearly, a fourth must be considered; the embargo on steel for Japan's shipbuilding industry, while less than effective and perhaps even counterproductive, should not be ignored in explaining how the United States attempted to maintain a modicum of control in Asia while handcuffed by a European war.

69. One of the first to articulate clearly the containment concept for Asia was A. Whitney Griswold, *The Far Eastern Policy of the United States*. By far the most able of the Lansing–Ishii studies is Burton F. Beers, *Vain Endeavor*. Analyses of the consortium tactic have received less play. The reports of actual participants still provide the best source of information. See, for instance, Paul S. Reinsch, *An American Diplomat in China;* and Thomas W. Lamont, *Across World Frontiers*. The motives for intervention have been "warmly debated," as aptly put by Daniel M. Smith in *The Great Departure*. At stake here is whether Wilson's despatch of American troops was to contain Japan or Bolshevik Russia. For the best treatment of the former argument, see Betty Miller Unterberger, *America's Siberian Expedition, 1918–1920;* William Appleman Williams presents a convincing case for the latter viewpoint in *American–Russian Relations, 1781–1947*. Smith's conclusion that intervention represented an effort to deal with both Japan and Russia seems the most acceptable.

Chapter VII
Anglo - American Wartime Shipping Rivalries

While the rapid growth of the American fleet was significant as a war expedient, Wilsonians also considered it a means by which to bring about an American solution in the peace that would follow. To the Wilson administration, the development of an international position advantageous to America in the postwar period and the economic and liberal rationalization and enrichment of the world depended to a good degree upon the extent to which the national fleet could be put to use. Wilson's world view, however, was not accepted with equanimity by the major powers. That was particularly so of Great Britain. Challenging the premises and logic of the argument that the moral and economic expansion of the United States would bring progress to all it approached, Great Britain judged American exceptionalism as an arrogant and deceitfully disguised attempt to dethrone England from its dominant position in world commerce. As a nation utterly dependent upon oceanic transportation, England immensely resented United States maritime growth. On the other hand, Americans were deeply antagonized by such attitudes. To them, such growth was justified on military and humanitarian grounds alone. Although the Anglo-American war alliance tended to mute these differences on the surface, American wartime shipping policy in fact evolved in an atmosphere intense with dark suspicions of Allied intensions to thwart American postwar commercial aspirations and significantly shaped the course Wilson adopted for the Paris peace negotiations following the cessation of hostilities.

No one supported the liberal, capitalistic mission and its relationship to ships more than the chairman of the Shipping Board, Edward N. Hurley. To Hurley, foreign trade expansion was axiomatic if the nation hoped to dispose of its huge surpluses and avoid economic and social stagnation: "Unless we continue to develop our foreign trade, after the war we can have no enduring prosperity."[1] To fulfill his commitment to trade expansion, Hurley put his authority over shipping to immediate use. "No nation can be great commercially unless it has its own manufacturing and its own shipping," Hurley informed the National Marine League. The war experience would supply both the means and the rationale. The goal of prosperity would be "passed in peace if we can reach it in war." There was no need to be clandestine about it, for the growth of American shipping represented the "central beam" in the Allied war effort: "If that fails, all else fails."[2]

At the same time, Hurley maintained that America could not expect to expand commercially during the war without accepting vital moral obligations: At stake was the liberal mission, selling America to the rest of the world—selling her ideals and her hopes as well as her goods.[3] Wilson had written into the record the lofty principle of "national unselfishness," to which ships were a vital adjunct. Built originally by the United States as instruments of war, they were "designed to serve equally well as the instruments of an enduring peace."[4] "We are building ships not alone for the war, but for the future of world trade," Hurley held.[5] Just as the railroad remade America in the late nineteenth century, United States maritime development would highlight an oceanic transportational "touchstone for a new world"

1. "The War and Foreign Trade," Hurley address, New York City, April 24, 1918, Hurley Papers.
2. Hurley address before the National Marine League of the U.S.A., March 26, 1918, McAdoo Papers.
3. "Shall Successful Business Be Penalized By Government?" Hurley address before the New York Chamber of Commerce, undated, circa April–May 1918, Hurley Papers.
4. Hurley address before Latin American diplomats at the Hog Island Shipyard, Philadelphia, June 26, 1918, Hurley Papers; "American Ships—Built by Manufacturers for Manufacturers," Hurley address before the Illinois Manufacturers' Association, June 28, 1918, ibid.
5. "The War and Foreign Trade," Hurley address, Hurley Papers; "The War as a Supreme Test of the Efficiency of Business Management and Labor," Hurley address before the National Coal Association, May 28, 1918, ibid.

in the early twentieth.[6] America's pride in the undertaking would be measured by the degree to which its ships brought prosperity to its neighbor's as well as to itself. In sum, American ships would not only ensure the defeat of the Central Powers and guarantee national economic growth and stability but also "open up international territory, carry new ideas along with new goods, furnish other countries new outlets for their products, increase their prosperity, and stimulate them to still greater production."[7] In all these matters, Hurley never ceased to emphasize his indebtedness to Wilsonian thought. As he put it shortly after Wilson's announcement of the Fourteen Points:

> One of the statements which you have made has had a large influence on my mental slant. I have frequently recalled that you pointed out that America no longer can be provincial; that she no longer can live within herself; that she has burst the jacket of a protective tariff. The great commerce of the United States in the future will be carried in the vast merchant fleet under construction. Our opportunities for service, as well as for trade, will be found in the markets of the world.[8]

Hurley, as one historian has described Wilson, not only "did not miss or fail to act on the economic implications of the frontier thesis, . . . he was the very model of Turner's crusading democrat."[9]

On the surface, Hurley never ceased to argue that the game was not going to be one of "blind competition for an inelastic volume of trade, but a game of international teamwork to expand trade and production."[10] In the private administration of his office, however, he worked under the assumption that few nations, if any, would conduct themselves in the American spirit. Arguing that in his opinion the European conflict represented to the warring powers primarily an interlude in a Darwinian struggle for commercial supremacy, Hurley worked to counter German and British preparations for the so-called commercial "war after the war."

Responding late in the winter of 1917–1918 to the Brest–Litovsk peace

6. Hurley, "American Ships on the Pacific."
7. Hurley, "Business on The Seven Seas"; See also idem, "What America's New Merchant Marine Means to the World."
8. Hurley to Wilson, March 2, 1918, Hurley Papers.
9. Williams, "Frontier Thesis and American Foreign Policy."
10. Hurley, "American Ships on the Pacific."

negotiations and apprehensive that Germany was about to force Russia into signing submissive political and commercial agreements, Hurley called for an economic, as well as military, war on the German regime. In his view, German behavior in Russia was simply a manifestation of a larger desire for world commercial conquest. Inspired by Wilson's appeal over the heads of the German government concerning the Fourteen Points, Hurley reasoned that a commercial war on Germany would move the people of that nation to put unrelieved pressure on Berlin. To affect his program, Hurley recommended sending commercial teams into Central and South America, China, Japan, and the Scandinavian nations to combat German commercial influence and propaganda directly. To his mind, there was but a single way to awaken the military, business, and financial war leadership of Germany to the fact that by continuing the war it was writing its own ticket to doom. "America [must] show that she is not merely willing to shed her life's blood for the cause of humanity, but is already moving to replace Germany in the markets of the world," he advised the president. In short, Hurley advocated a policy of commercial war that would make "Germany realize that her commercial demoralization is likely to prove permanent if her militaristic party continues in power."[11]

When Wilson expressed doubt about American ability to support such commercial missions at the peak of the war, Hurley acquiesced, but reiterated the importance of utilizing "the weapon which the German government cravenly fears the most—our commercial power." If properly advertised, the newly passed Webb–Pomerene Act by itself (a law legalizing business combinations in foreign trade) would "arouse more resentment against the German government, by the influential interests of Germany, than an appeal to reason." If the big commercial interests who ran the country could be impressed that prolonging the war would mean diminished opportunities for Germany to recover its lost trade, a wedge could be driven between them and the military leadership.[12]

Perhaps no statement better expressed the exceptionalist character of Hurley's *Weltanschauung* than the note he sent in late May 1918 to Bernard Baruch, chairman of the War Industries Board.

11. Hurley to Wilson, March 2, 1918, Hurley Papers.
12. Hurley to Wilson, April 20, 1918, Hurley Papers.

The more we study world conditions, with respect to commerce, the more convinced I am becoming that world peace in the future, as well as moral leadership, will swing upon the pivot of raw materials.

The President discussed this question with us at a recent meeting, and I am taking this opportunity to present the problem to you, as I view it from the shipping standpoint. I think we are all agreed that commercial conquest was the foremost thought in Germany's mind when she started this war. Diplomatic intrigue and secret diplomacy were born out of a desire for a stronger commercial position. Not only did the diplomats loose confidence in each other, but the commercial interests of some nations lost confidence in the commercial methods of other nations.

Many nations were suspicious of Germany's grasping trade practices and there was a similar suspicion with respect to England's commercial growth, backed as it has always been with supremacy on the seas. The altruistic methods of America towards China, Cuba, Porto Rico [sic] and the Philippines were in sharp contrast with the methods of other powers. Germany, by the use of kartels [sic] and trusts, forced every nation in the world to pay excessive prices for everything over which she possessed a monopoly, particularly on raw materials, such as potash, and on dyestuffs. Where she had to sell at a loss to enter a market, Germany did so unhesitatingly, the government making up the difference by paying a subsidy to the selling corporations.

The Webb law removes a handicap from American exporters, but all the European powers are engaged even now in preparing for the struggle for trade after the war. England is encouraging combinations of capital. Even the great combinations of Germany, which before the war divided a whole industry into three or four concerns, are now being consolidated so that where there were three or four doing business, after the war there will be but one.

The thing that Germany's business men are worrying about now is where they will get their raw materials after the war. Some of the German financiers and business men have been very frank about it recently. I have seen quotations from them, wherein they were reported as saying that unless Germany could obtain the raw materials she needed she would never recover from the war. If the world kept raw materials from her, they argued, her commerce would die from inanition.

While the bloodiest war in history is progressing, every nation is preparing not merely to get its share of foreign trade, but is trying to find out how much it can take away from other nations. The question as to what nation will control the raw materials of the world is uppermost in Europe. Whatever nation does control them (unless it be America) will make other nations pay a heavy toll. Great power may be used either for good or for evil. If possessed by the United States we may be sure it will be used for good. The nation, under President Wilson, has given ample proof of this in the present war.

We are spending billions to win a military victory; we can certainly afford to set aside one billion to prevent a recurrence of the present world-disaster. I doubt whether any other nation is in a position to put the same moral force behind trade-leadership.

If America would invest substantially in the essential raw materials of all foreign countries, such as the iron mines in Brazil, the manganese ore of Brazil, the nitrates of Chile, the tin of Bolivia, or perhaps also of the Straits Settlement, the chrome of New Caledonia, the tungsten and vanadium of South America, and in other raw materials of foreign countries, we would soon be in control of 60% of the cotton of the world, 73% of the copper, and, together with Mexico, 75% of the oil of the world. America would then be in a position to say to the rest of the world that these commodities would be sold at a fair price, plus ocean freight rates—the same price that producers in our own country would pay—and each nation would receive its share. If it were desirable to have an international syndicate for the distribution of raw materials, the United States, with even partial control established, could prevent any agreement that would be unfair, either to this country or any other country. A plan of this kind would be helpful in eliminating the rivalry that now exists to control the raw materials of the world.

To my mind, we are the only nation that has taken a completely unselfish position in the war. All belligerents were figuring very frankly on a division of the spoils until President Wilson raised the standard of America's moral leadership. He has convinced the world of American sincerety. This nation's whole thought has been to be helpful and serviceable to the rest of the world. In what better way could we be of real service than by the use of our financial strength to control the raw materials for the benefit of humanity, raising a protecting arm against the commercial blows that surely will be aimed at the smaller and weaker nations. If the Sherman law had been in force internationally, and governments had not been struggling for commercial conquest, there would have been no war.

It may be an ambitious program that I have in mind, but these are the days when great achievements are possible. We no longer think in provincial terms. These questions surely will arise at the peace conference, whether that conference is delayed for one or five years.[13]

Secretary of Commerce Redfield took exception to Hurley's benevolent monopolism. Although he too shared a concern for postwar trade, Redfield deprecated the statist implications of Hurley's argument. In his opinion, Hurley was also guilty of having cultivated an "atmosphere of suspicion and fear which seems to surround much of our commercial thought," and which assumed that the interests of the United States and Great Britain were "essentially hostile." Hurley responded that while he had once believed that there should be no planning for postwar conditions until the conflict was over, he had become reluctantly convinced as the result of every interview with the Allies that their foremost thought was not on a democratic peace but on postwar economic conditions and how the raw materials were going to be controlled. Baruch threw in his support: "As you say, when the war comes to an end there is going to be a terrific scramble for raw materials, and the men with the longest vision are going to be the more successful."[14] While nothing along these lines was instituted at this time, Hurley had revealed the extent to which the Wilsonian world view had come to dominate him.

Concern with Great Britain's wartime commercial program occupied a large portion of Hurley's time. In fact, until it became obvious in the early fall of 1918 that the German war effort and economic viability were exhausted, Hurley tended to perceive the two belligerents equally in terms of world commerce and American efforts to break into its mainstream. Redfield portrayed Hurley's position accurately when he accused the shipping chairman of treating England as "our ally in war, but our antagonist in peace."[15] As early as the British shipping mission of September–October 1917, Hurley became convinced that the "dominant" characteristic of the English, "even in a crisis of this kind, [was] to obtain trade." As the result of that mission, Hurley concluded that the British were not dealing openly and fairly with America in commercial matters. Unless they cooperated willingly concerning wartime trade and shipping, he confided to his diary,

13. Hurley to Baruch, May 21, 1918, Wilson Papers.
14. Redfield to Hurley, May 28, 1918, RG 40/77270, NA; Hurley to Redfield, June 4, 1918, ibid.; Baruch to Hurley, July 16, 1918, ibid.
15. Redfield to Hurley, May 28, 1918, RG 40/77276, NA.

"instead of being *associated with England* in the fight against Germany, [he would] watch England to prevent her from gaining some commercial advantage at the present time, and particularly after the war."[16]

Conflicts with the British throughout the winter of 1917–1918 over the disposition of neutral vessels acquired through embargo leverage and confiscation did little to assuage Hurley's fears. The British had agreed in November 1917 to an equal division of all neutral ships, however acquired. Under this agreement, the United States turned 50,000 tons of Norwegian ships over to Great Britain. But Washington quickly discovered that holding England to its end of the bargain was no easy task. When additional Norwegian tonnage became available, British shipping authorities did not divide it but retained it in European waters. Hurley and Munson were convinced that this action illustrated British reluctance to allow America shipping growth of any sort. In what seemed clearly an act of retaliation, Munson held up an equal distribution of Dutch vessels in March 1918.[17]

Another issue between England and the United States involved the question of German ships interned in South American ports. From the outset, there was very little cooperation between the Allies and the United States over the acquisition of these ships. Each nation seemed desirous of going its own way, negotiating individually with each country without reference to the interests of its associates. France claimed privileges in negotiating with Brazil, and Hurley noted that the real interests of the Allies and the United States in working separately for an Argentinian declaration of war was explained solely by the desire of each to obtain access to the large number of confiscated German vessels in Argentina.[18]

Early in 1918, an Allied Maritime Transport Council (AMTC) was created to supervise the coordination of Allied oceanic shipping and shipping policy. Largely a creation of British thought, the London-based organization reflected a concern that many nations were holding back shipping from war participation in order to maintain nonessential foreign trade. Although the Shipping Board was represented on the AMTC by vice

16. Hurley Diary, September 28, November 1, 1917, Hurley Papers.
17. Hurley to Bainbridge Colby, November 9, 1917, U.S., State Department, *FR, Supplement 2, 1917*, 1:635; Munson to Colby, December 5, 1917, ibid., p. 643; "Summary of Memo on Neutral Tonnage Negotiations," October 17, 1918, RG 56/129, NA.
18. Hurley, *The New Merchant Marine*, p. 87.

chairman Raymond Stevens, and by George Rublee, who had just come over from the Federal Trade Commission, Wilson had been a reluctant party to the decision to send American delegates. Hurley observed à propos of Bainbridge Colby, a Shipping Board commissioner, that Wilson was "always opposed to our government maintaining a representative on any of the permanent war commissions in Europe, because he felt that it was only a question of time until the American member, being out of touch with the American situation, would be influenced by the atmosphere in which he was working and become European in his views."[19] The president once cautioned Colby not to forget his heritage when abroad. "Our men only last about six months in England when they become Anglicized," he warned.[20] Consequently, when Stevens and Rublee complained that the unwillingness of Wilson and Hurley to give fuller support to the AMTC worked contrary to an efficient military prosecution of the war, their pleas were ignored. Like United States representatives on councils among the Allies generally, Stevens and Rublee were considered suspect so long as they were overseas; they were continually frustrated and handicapped in their efforts to bring about a truly integrated shipping policy. Although the AMTC served as a valuable vehicle for the exchange of information regarding tonnage, finance, and supply, in the end it failed to achieve its original purpose; neither the United States nor the Allies would allow the council to regulate tonnage. They relied instead on cooperation, a policy that never satisfactorily buried the wariness they harbored about each other's commercial interests.[21]

Hurley's note to Baruch in late May 1918 was written not only against a background of these experiences and the important issue of raw materials but also upon the alarming news from South America that British commercial agents were actively engaged in restoring old trade ties and drumming up new business in anticipation of the end of the war. At the center of their concern was the so-called De Bunsen mission, undertaken by British military, political, and commercial personnel in April and May

---

19. "Bainbridge Colby," vignette, Hurley Papers.
20. Daniel M. Smith, *Aftermath of War*, p. 17.
21. *The Reminiscences of George Rublee*, pp. 173–74, 176, Oral History Research Project, Columbia University Library; Seth B. Tillman, *Anglo-American Relations at the Paris Peace Conference of 1919*, p. 107; Kaufman, *Efficiency and Expansion*, p. 196.

1918. As Sir Maurice De Bunsen himself expressed it privately, the mission
was "intended primarily as a visible sign of our intention to maintain and
even largely develop both politically and economically our pre-war position
in the South American continent."[22] In a form of confession that the
mission was conducted in variance with the expressed spirit of wartime
cooperation and unselfishness, the British Foreign Office dismissed courtesy
and dispatched the mission without informing the State Department of its
existence. Only when worried reports began to arrive in Washington from
United States sources in South America was the extent and purpose of the
mission comprehended. Accompanied by an admiral, a general, a member
of Parliament, and two governmental foreign trade experts, among others,
De Bunsen arrived in a British warship which proceeded to touch at ports
in Brazil, Uruguay, Argentina, Chile, Peru, Bolivia, Ecuador, Columbia,
Venezuela, and Cuba. The results poured in. Compiling a long list of complaints from American diplomatic and consular officers in South America,
the State Department's foreign trade office concluded on July 1 that Great
Britain appeared to regard commercial hostility as "perfectly consistent"
with its wartime political alliance.[23] The head of the division of Latin
American affairs surmised without humor that only by sending a "larger,
more brilliant mission, say aided by an ex-president like Taft, assisted by
a full general and a full admiral, with, say two or three ships and a picked
retinue of men able to speak Spanish," could the United States have adequately neutralized the detrimental effects of De Bunsen's mission.[24]

But the worst was yet to come. In mid-July the American naval attaché in
Rio de Janeiro gave an alarming description of what the British had been
up to. He notified the secretary of the navy, Josephus Daniels, that on the
basis of a secret proposal advanced by the British minister, the English
firm of Vickers and Armstrong would receive exclusive privileges to manufacture munitions and government and private ships, as well as sole rights
to the development of Brazilian iron and steel. These rights also included
access to water power, coal, and other necessary supplies. On this basis,

22. De Bunsen to Balfour, May 5, 1918, *Correspondence Respecting the British Mission
to South America, 1918* (London, 1919), 2, SD 033.4120/28, NA.

23. Wesley Frost, undated memorandum, circa July 1, 1918, RG 182/Munson, NA.

24. G. Stewart, memorandum, July 1, 1918, cited in Mary Klachko, "Anglo-American
Naval Competition, 1918–1922," p. 28.

there was no reason to doubt that similar clandestine propositions had been advanced in every country on De Bunsen's itinerary. Daniels notified Lansing immediately that were it to be known, or even suspected, that American war loans to the British government were being utilized to derail American commercial interests and the Monroe Doctrine in Latin America, the future would be so infused with distrust and enemy exploitation of it as to threaten with ruin the very existence of the Anglo-American war effort.[25]

For Hurley, the realization of British commercial maneuvering was unsettling, to say the least. His own predilections for trade expansion had always been Latin oriented. In addition, his advocacy of a plan to send trade missions to South America just prior to the then unknown De Bunsen mission had been vetoed by Wilson as inconsistent with the more pressing demands for war shipping and finance. Finally, ever since American entry into the war, the Shipping Board, while always maintaining its primary interest in South American trade, had been steadily forced to withdraw vessels from this area for the European war effort. Brazil, for example, a source of raw materials absolutely vital to the Allied cause, complained, directly after the British mission, that Cuba was offering better shipping service and trade facilities than the United States. But Lansing could allow only that the maritime cutback would "grow worse rather than better" as embargoes on nonessentials were increased.[26] It was a painful situation in which valuable Pan-American economic ties, cultivated successfully in large proportion during the years of neutrality but now atrophied by war diversions, were simultaneously threatened by British application of the very mechanism the Wilson administration had denied itself.

As midsummer approached, nothing transpired to alter Hurley's mind about German and English commercial plans for the "war after the war." In fact, the belligerents' activities had only strengthened his conviction that a primary means to Wilsonian ends would require outstripping them with sheer vessel weight: "My whole thought is to get a fleet of large sized ships with a tonnage of 7,500 to 15,000 d.w. so that we may be able to compete with Germany and England after the war."[27] Hurley was certain that if the

25. Daniels to Lansing, undated, circa July 17, 1918, cited in Klachko, "Anglo-American Naval Competition," p. 30; Daniels, *Cabinet Diaries,* July 19, 1918, pp. 321–22.

26. Edwin V. Morgan to Lansing, June 4, 1918, SD 611.326/49, NA; Lansing to Morgan, June 27, 1918, ibid.

27. Hurley Diary, August 14, 1918, Hurley Papers.

United States failed to obtain at least parity levels with its maritime competitors there could be little hope of eliminating international trade rivalries or bringing about a universal acceptance of the principle of the "freedom of the seas."

One of the methods Hurley employed to accomplish this goal covered ship construction in oriental yards. The Shipping and War Trade boards had contracted with Japan for forty-five cargo ships earlier in 1918. That China had not been a party to similar arrangements bothered both Hurley and the State Department. With intentions to remove all suspicion that the Japanese contracts were discriminatory, Hurley entered into negotiations with Chinese representatives in late June.[28] At first relaxed, the negotiating atmosphere became tense when news came from Peking that Vickers–Mitsubishi, an Anglo-Japanese joint enterprise, was endeavoring to block the Shipping Board's contract by securing similar working agreements before the Washington talks could be concluded. Hurley quickly wound up negotiations on July 25, thereby thwarting what was unhesitatingly interpreted as an Allied plot.[29] The American contract called for the building of four 10,000-ton freighters in the Imperial Government's Kiangnan Dock and Engineering Works in Shanghai. Totalling $30 million in value, the contract also called for options on 80,000 additional tons of ships. The necessary steel plates and shapes would be supplied by the United States. Hurley viewed the ramifications of this fortuitous contract as manyfold. Not only had it morally and economically strengthened China's hand and blocked the Anglo-Japanese countereffort, it had "opened the door on lines wider for American interests," emphasized America's "desire to cooperate and work with all foreign governments" without reference to the dollar, in addition to "showing Germany that we are awake to the necessity of going after foreign trade." When the State Department arranged for a loan of $50 million to China shortly thereafter, Hurley felt strongly that his shipping contract had paved the way.[30]

28. For a summary of this concern, see Alvey A. Adee to USSB, July 3, 1918, RG 32/618-9, NA.

29. Adee to USSB, July 12, 1918, RG 32/618-9, NA.; Hurley to Lansing, July 24, 1918, ibid.

30. Hurley Diary, July 21, 25, 1918, Hurley Papers; USSB, *Annual Report, Dec. 1, 1918*, pp. 53–54.

By this time, too, the Emergency Fleet Corporation's own shipbuilding program in the United States had finally extricated itself from the rigors of formative organization and matured into one of the most proficient factories of modern industry. Shipyards vied with each other for production marks, riveting teams claimed world records and competed for liberal bonuses, and efficiency experts labored on twenty-four-hour shifts to produce the slightest advantage for accelerated process. By summer 1918, more than 300,000 men in 158 shipyards were putting the finishing touches to the end products of a vast belt of resources that emanated from such places as the forests of the Columbia and the mines of the Mesabi. The disparate elements converged into a colossal mechanism that disgorged the greatest profusion of ships the modern world had ever seen. The corner had been turned. In many shipyards, six- to eight-thousand-ton vessels came off the ways as often as every five or six days. On one remarkable day, July 4, 1918, the EFC launched one hundred ships without holding back a single hull. Over three million tons of ships, as much as total world output in any prewar year, were launched by the end of 1918, almost all of them in the last six months. By August, the Shipping Board machine was functioning like a runaway train, fueled for a year's operation with still another year's materials already planned and under contract in extractive, productive, and fabricating industries all over the United States.[31]

With government ships finally on hand, Hurley inaugurated a massive public relations campaign in early August to propagandize the importance of the burgeoning fleet as a great peacetime commercial asset. It was time to impress the American people with the necessity of thinking in terms of ships for world trade. "The operation of these ships after the war is one of the most important matters that I have before me now and I am giving it a lot of attention," he wrote a member of the board.[32] Subsequently, in a remarkably short period Hurley wrote a series of articles for the purpose of "stimulating business thought about our new merchant marine," sponsored a symposium on the meaning of ships to government leaders,

31. USSB, *Sixth Annual Report, 1922*, p. 47; James G. Randall, "War Tasks and Accomplishments of the Shipping Board."
    32. Hurley to Raymond Stevens, August 6, 1918, Hurley Papers. See also James H. Collins memorandum for Colby, undated, Papers of Bainbridge Colby, Records of Shipping Board Commissioners and Fleet Corporation Officers, RG 32, NA.

addressed numerous groups, and sent thousands of letters to chambers of commerce nationwide asking what businessmen were doing to provide cargoes for the tremendous new fleet. The format of these inquiries emphasized Hurley's effort to inculcate a trade élan in the American public.

> The time has come for Americans everywhere to put themselves solidly behind American ships. . . . Are you taking steps to use these ships to increase your own prosperity? . . . Has your organization appointed a live committee on the Merchant Marine? Is the Chairman of this committee a man of international vision? Are you applying the new world vision to the interests represented in your organization and learning what ships can do toward widening your markets? These are your ships. It is your duty to bring them close, regard them as new railroads, spread knowledge about them through investigation, meetings, discussion.[33]

Hurley's efforts to develop a national merchant marine capable of challenging British commercial supremacy caused unending irritation in London. Inasmuch as England recognized that the most valuable American contribution to war shipping would be the mass production of merchant vessels, it was particularly galling for the British to comprehend that this same encouragement promised to have long-range ramifications decidedly detrimental to English postwar commercial considerations. British concern increased during the Anglo-American shipping talks late in 1917 when the British realized that Americans shared these views but were not inclined to thank John Bull sufficiently for having made the opportunity possible. At the same time that Hurley was recording his fear of English wartime commercial growth, Spring Rice, still British ambassador in Washington, expressed anxiety that America was convinced that the war would guarantee it "all the ships and all the gold in the world, and that the hegemony probably of the world, and certainly of the Anglo-Saxon race, will pass over the Atlantic."[34] In December, Prime Minister Lloyd George and Lord Riddell conferred over the dire threat posed to English nautical sovereignty

---

33. Copy of a letter sent to American chambers of commerce, August 28, 1918, Papers of Henry M. Robinson, Records of Shipping Board Commissioners and Fleet Corporation Officers, RG 32, NA.

34. Spring Rice to Balfour, October 25, 1917, cited in Holger H. Herwig and David F. Trask, "The Failure of Imperial Germany's Undersea Offensive against World Shipping, February 1917–October 1918."

by American maritime, commercial, and financial growth. Riddell put it bluntly: By the end of 1918, England would have lost considerably more shipping and foreign trade and fallen into extreme debt; within that same year the Americans would control world finances and have a huge merchant marine they had not previously possessed and newly opened markets on a global basis, markets developed during the years of neutrality while England was fighting. Riddell concluded that the United States resented Britain's mercantile command of the seas and that it would be imperative "to watch that in our efforts to annihilate the Germans we do not annihilate ourselves."[35] Such attitudes, speculative then, soon came to permeate thinking in British shipping circles.

When an American petition for additional British shipping for the Atlantic war supply run was made in midsummer 1918, rather than accept it as a bonafide function of war, representatives of Parliament greeted it suspiciously as an expression of commercial greed. The opposition, including members of both the British Ministry of Shipping and the War Cabinet, termed the request incongruous, claiming that if English ships were assigned to the United States other American vessels would no doubt be released to collar British service between North and South America.[36] At the same time, the embargo policies of the American War Trade and Shipping boards toward Japan were under fire from the Ministry of Shipping as an impediment to British commercial designs in the Orient.[37] Welding Ring, Hurley's director of chartering, correctly concluded that with the United States government behind shipping and guaranteeing its success, the British were justifiably "in very great fear of what this country will do after the war when we indulge in commercial business and enterprises."[38] Colonel House was informed from sources in Great Britain that there was a decided tendency "to question our purposes, and to wonder whither the American war-spirit, which from this side seems to be rolling up into a tremendous volume, will take the world."[39]

Seizing the initiative, Lloyd George and his chancellor of the exchequer,

35. George A. Riddell, *Lord Riddell's War Diary, 1914–1918*, December 9, 1917, pp. 298–99.

36. *Parliamentary Debates*, Commons, 5th series, 109:1353–54, August 7, 1918.

37. Thomas Fisher to Hurley, August 13, 1918, RG 32/618-15, NA.

38. Welding Ring to Hurley, August 2, 1918, Hurley Papers.

39. Ray Stannard Baker to Edward House, August 19, 1918, Wilson Papers.

Bonar Law, publicly addressed themselves to Britain's economic future. Both called for very harsh peace terms featuring exclusive economic alliances against the Central Powers. By implication, Lloyd George requested American agreement to the terms fashioned at the Paris Economic Conference in 1916. Law, speaking openly about what Hurley had broached quite confidentially, argued for British control over world raw materials so as to prevent "old enemies" from cornering them. Both positions were offensive to the Wilson administration which based its postwar considerations upon an international system of free trade in which a liberalized Germany would play an important part. These exasperations were compounded by the revelation that the Australian prime minister, William Hughes, contemplated an American speaking tour. Because Hughes had vociferously condemned American commercial and maritime growth during the years of neutrality and outspokenly supported the Paris resolves as a measure of retaliation against both the neutrals and Germany, Wilson angrily insisted that his visit be cancelled.[40] Although these issues did not appear to relate directly to shipping, nevertheless Hurley, McAdoo, Wilson, and others had long been on record as opposed to such tactics, unless administered by the United States. Responding much as had Redfield to Hurley the previous May, Sir Arthur Willert, owner of the London *Times,* protested his countrymen's behavior. "There is today a genuine distrust of our economic plan for 'after-the-war,' " he remarked. If things were to go wrong between the two countries, it was not outside the realm of reason "that something like 'America über alles' and especially over us might be heard at the next election."[41]

Clearly, by mid-August 1918, both the United States and England were convinced the other had its sights set on securing the inside track in the postwar race for markets. The reverberations quickly reached the Continent.

40. Fowler, *British-American Relations,* pp. 209–14. British war efforts to employ monopolies of raw materials and the discriminatory principles of the Paris Economic Conference and the serious difficulties these caused in relations among the Allies are discussed in V. H. Rothwell, *British War Aims and Peace Diplomacy, 1914–1918,* pp. 266–81.

41. Willert to Lord Reading, August 16, 1918, cited in Klatchko, "Anglo-American Naval Competition," p. 33. For a discussion of the intense American dislike of British economic policy during the war see L. W. Martin, *Peace without Victory,* pp. 112, 128–29, 176–77.

As Josephus Daniels feared earlier, the Central Powers kept close touch with the developing rift and attempted to exploit it. Hurley's ebullient speeches about growing while the growing was good were so effective in aggravating the British that Germany dropped reprints entitled "An American Peril" behind Allied lines.[42] In London there was, as one presidential observer reported, so much "loose talk along the lines of the United States sweeping British shipping from the seas, on the one hand, and English opposition and device to defeat the ultimate good success of [American] post-war shipping on the other,"[43] that on August 29 Wilson reacted and asked Hurley to refrain from further public discussion of the administration's postwar shipping plans.[44]

The president did not oppose Hurley's enthusiasm for competitive and commercial uses of America's new mercantile fleet; it was simply a question of carrying the obvious to extremes. It was clear, he remarked, that the British sought every "economic advantage within their reach," and that this was stimulated largely by their awareness "that our shipping programme will give us a very considerable advantage over them in the carrying trade, and therefore in world commerce, after the struggle is over." The Anglo-American maritime rivalry had reached a point from which it was "past hoping for that they should believe us to be fair and square." In short, what Wilson did oppose was Hurley's indiscriminate propaganda use of a fait accompli. To throw that in England's face would only exacerbate already serious commercial disputes. The tactical procedure should be to avoid giving the British even "the slightest color or provocation or excuse for what they are doing."[45]

Hurley had already anticipated Wilson's concern. Two weeks before he had confidentially noted his disappointment in the inability of the Allies to get along: "The feeling of distrust between nations is really unfortunate." More unprovidential was the Allies' failure to comprehend America's unique qualities offered to the world as "banker, adviser, and conciliator." Wilson's mission was so unlike anything that anyone had ever before encountered that most governments actually doubted its genuineness:

42. Hurley, *The Bridge to France*, pp. 125–28.
43. Samuel Blythe to Hurley, August 27, 1918, Hurley Papers.
44. Wilson to Hurley, August 29, 1918, Wilson Papers.
45. Ibid.

"They can't believe that our President is really sincere." There were, of course, those even in the United States who endorsed the old "dog eat dog" methods, but under Wilson's direction even that class was coming to appreciate "that for the benefit of government and the world generally, the President's attitude is the only one."[46]

Hurley had put these thoughts into writing and released them to the press on the twenty-third: It was expected that enemy propagandists would endeavor to use American maritime growth as a basis for causing dissention between the Allies. But America did not function that way. President Wilson had demonstrated to the world "that the people of the United States [are] not fighting for the permanency of their own liberty alone but for the liberty of civilization everywhere." It was "unthinkable" that America, tied to its Allies in combat, "should, after the war, turn its resources against them for trade conquests of the very kind which were largely instrumental in bringing on the war." American ships would be operated in the postwar period "upon principles which recognize human and national rights and equities." These principles represented Wilson's consistent aim, clarified in his public rhetoric, and documented beyond question by the history of the United States, "which [is] free from selfish aggression in either territory or trade."[47]

Hurley's response to Wilson's warning of August 29 further underlined the remarkable degree to which he viewed American policy as entirely justified on the highest plane. After having given it some thought, Hurley remarked, he did not recall having made ever any statements offensive to the British. On the contrary, all he had ever said had been "designed to show that the American merchant fleet now building would be as beneficial to the world in peace as it is intended to be in war." Britain's concerns were probably to a good degree "simulated." Englishmen, while decrying American wartime maritime growth, at the same time rather contentedly expressed satisfaction at being relieved of high war costs in ship construction. Moreover, anyone with real shipping expertise would point out that American operating costs would always be higher than English costs and that this advantage would put Great Britain back in the lead after the war. England knew absolutely that Wilson's policy was "entirely fair and generous," but

46. Hurley Diary, August 14, 1918, Hurley Papers.
47. USSB, News Release, August 23, 1918, Hurley Papers.

British businessmen who lacked international altruism were dominating the English government. In this respect, British shipping interests from the commencement of war had been advancing policy based on the needs of private enterprise first, war second. "America can afford to make sacrifices for her own ideals, but it is regrettable that interests which are identical should not have behind them an identical and single motive." Wilson could rest assured that American shipping policy would "avoid anything that might in any way lend itself to an evil interpretation of selfishness."[48] "You are certainly a brick," Wilson shot back. "It is delightful to have dealings with a man who understands perfectly the spirit of everything you say, and just the right answer to give."[49]

In order to make these views more credible, the secretary of war, Newton D. Baker, was dispatched to England to report on methods of optimizing transportational teamwork. His trip resulted in the Shipping Board's decision to give more serious consideration to ways in which the authority of the Allied Maritime Transport Council could be employed.[50] In a further effort to weaken anti-American shipping sentiments in London and working for increased commercial use of British tonnage, the Shipping and War Trade boards adopted a policy of drastic reductions in imports in order to release more ships for military purposes. On the USSB's part, this was not done with enthusiasm; Hurley recognized, as would be borne out, that America's own commercial shipping service would suffer seriously, especially to Latin America.[51]

While these gambits expressed the administration's view on the desirability of avoiding provocations between Great Britain and the United States, Wilson and Hurley did not cease to interpret British commercial policy as uncooperative and grasping. As rumours of an armistice waxed in

48. Hurley to Wilson, September 7, 1918, Wilson Papers.

49. Wilson to Hurley, September 9, 1918, Wilson Papers. Robert D. Cuff believes that Wilson's war managers "reached their administrative posts less because of their proven managerial skills than because of what Wilson . . . would call their moral reactions." See Cuff, "We Band of Brothers—Woodrow Wilson's War Managers."

50. Hurley draft, "Secretary Baker Borrows Ships From the Allied Maritime Transport Council," written for but not included in the final manuscript of *The Bridge to France*, Hurley Papers.

51. Lansing to Page, August 31, 1918, Hurley Papers. For the serious effect this had on American shipping to South America, see Welding Ring to Office of Operations, a report covering the period August 16–October 26, 1918, RG 32/Operations, NA.

late September, the Shipping Board became alarmed at the possibility that England would refuse to assist the United States in repatriating its servicemen stationed overseas, now numbering more than one million. The great majority of these men had been transported to Europe on English passenger liners, and the Wilson government did not have a sufficient number of such ships late in 1918 to bring its troops back to the United States with any speed. The withdrawal of British liners for commerce could have additional significance; American merchant vessels badly needed for the reconstitution of peacetime trade would have to be refitted and diverted. Once again, conversation revolved around the commercial "war after the war." When Hurley was unable to obtain satisfaction in this regard from British shipping representatives, he mentioned to Wilson the possibility that the British might actually hold the American army "in hostage."[52] From England, Senator Henry Hollis added fuel to these concerns. The primary goals of Lloyd George and Clemenceau, as he envisioned them, were to obtain trade advantages and preferences in the world marketplace as the result of the war. One of the means they would employ to get ahead of the United States, Hollis argued, would be to expand commercially "while we are using our ships to get our troops home to America."[53] Wilson was no less concerned. When the Shipping Board reiterated Hollis' apprehensions, the president responded that he was "keenly alive to the dangers."[54]

A flying visit to the United States by the first lord of the Admiralty, Sir Eric Geddes, did little to change the administration's strict position on England. While there were fundamental reasons for the decision to send Geddes to America, the significance of his mission was so undercut by the unheralded and coincidental opening of tentative peace negotiations between Wilson and the Central Powers that its purposes were never fully revealed. The mission apparently was conceived in late July 1918 out of the mounting British concern with American naval and mercantile shipping and shipbuilding programs. On the one hand, with the realization that its proposal would undoubtedly receive a cool reception, the British govern-

52. Hurley to Wilson, September 23, 1918, Hurley Papers.
53. Henry F. Hollis to Wilson, October 2, 1918, McAdoo Papers.
54. Sherman L. Whipple to Wilson, October 29, 1918, Wilson Papers; Wilson to Whipple, October 29, 1918, ibid.

ment desired to obtain an agreement from the United States to curtail building capital ships and concentrate upon smaller vessels badly needed for antisubmarine warfare. Second, it is clear that Geddes was very much disturbed with American mercantile growth and its postwar commercial potential, possibly more than he was with the inadequacy of American naval participation. But the mission was overwhelmed by the unexpected peace negotiations, a development Geddes had anticipated would not occur for a year. It was bad enough being forced to the side-lines, but Geddes also managed to alienate Wilson. At that time the ranking British representative in America, the first lord tactlessly criticized Wilson's negotiations as a form of appeasement and thereby earned the president's wrathful indignation. While Geddes accomplished little in the way of business, major American representatives to the talks came away feeling strongly that his mission had been devised primarily to contest American naval and maritime growth and that, for unfathomable reasons, the real intent had not been broached.[55] In London, the Ministry of Shipping and Balfour's deputy in the Foreign Office agreed that the Anglo-American shipping situation had not improved as a result of Geddes' visit—rather, it had deteriorated. Their first thought was also the carriage of American troops, for a commitment to this task would more than counterbalance the advantage coming from increased ship construction.[56] In Washington, coincident with Geddes' departure, Wilson discussed Great Britain's "selfish policy" with his war cabinet and declared: "I want to go into the Peace Conference armed with as many weapons as my pockets will hold so as to compel justice."[57]

Not unexpectedly, the signing of the Armistice released pent-up visions of unparalleled opportunities for American commerce. Talk abounded about cornering the world marketplace with the newborn American merchant marine. Wilson soon objected and reiterated his position of August twenty-ninth. He was extremely anxious to avoid publicity about foreign trade on account of the tender Anglo-American situation. England, he informed Redfield, "was very fearful that we were going to interfere with her [postwar] plan, that she was a nation that depended on ships and

55. David F. Trask, *Captains & Cabinets*, pp. 283–312; Klachko, "Anglo-American Naval Competition," pp. 37–52.

56. Trask, *Captains & Cabinets*, p. 311.

57. Daniels, *Cabinet Diaries*, October 17, 1918, p. 342.

foreign trade." To agitate for and push overseas commerce at such a short period prior to negotiations "would give England an opportunity to say that . . . America is not only in this to make this world a place worth while to live in, she is also anxious to get all the business she possibly can."[58] But Wilson's admonitions and Redfield's attempts to enforce them failed. Redfield's own assistant and the president's personal secretary spoke eagerly of sweeping the seas for "outlets for our surplus production," in the process offering the great new merchant marine as the *coup de maître*. Josephus Daniels further advocated opening the nautical floodgates. Until it got its fair share of the world's carrying trade, he declared, the United States would never stop building merchant ships.[59]

When McAdoo impatiently called for the immediate release of government ships to recapture the South American trade deemphasized during the war, Redfield's smoldering dislike for such views burst into red hot epithets. "Shall we play the hog with our feet in the trough and our eyes on the ground, or shall we play the eagle, soaring with a wide vision?" he retorted. Business sentiment, increasing in pressure by the hour, was best expressed by Miles Poindexter, senator from Washington, who rejoined that it was "time to cease this policy of international altruism and devote ourselves to self-protection and securing foreign trade if we can get it."[60] And from London the American Embassy wondered if Redfield, in his apparently commendable effort to tone commercial rivalries down in view of the peace deliberations, had not lost sight of Great Britain's determination to remain regnant in commercial affairs.[61]

Such attitudes also disturbed Hurley, for the sudden armistice had caught the Shipping Board in a state of almost complete unreadiness. Despite Hurley's rhetoric concerning the future, the board had not devised a concrete plan for the peacetime conversion and utilization of the new fleet. Hurley's basic long-range plan had always envisioned "creative" over "competitive" trade as the preferable means to expand American commerce. This involved the systematic creation and development of customers and

58. Hurley Diary, November 11, 1918, Hurley Papers.

59. *New York Times,* November 15, 16, 1918; Joseph Tumulty to Wilson, November 14, 1918, Wilson Papers.

60. *New York Times,* November 23, 24, 1918. McAdoo's views are best summarized by the assistant secretary of the treasury, L. S. Rowe, in a memorandum for Bainbridge Colby, November 27, 1918, RG 32/Operations, NA.

61. United States Embassy to Lansing, November 29, 1918, SD 611.4116/7, NA.

services on regular trade routes and included salesmanship, banking, overseas investment, and assistance to the economic growth of other nations to create markets that would add to the wealth of the whole industrialized world. Such a plan required strong central direction and could not evolve overnight. "If the shippers are given free sway," he warned Wilson, "they will ship their goods not to the points where they are most needed, but where they will get the best prices." The inevitable result would be absolute chaos.[62] Hurley also believed that at least for the immediate future the primary transportational priorities would have to be directed to areas other than the expansion of trade. When Redfield inquired about the possibility of convening a conference in regard to international shipping problems, Hurley demurred.

> Inasmuch as for months there will be practically no ship tonnage available for commercial use, because of the fact it will be needed to supply our armies overseas and to bring them home; also, that Europe must be fed and supplied with the necessary materials to permit the reconstruction of devastated areas in order that both our friends and our enemies may become self-supporting, and because of the fact that we are not ourselves now in a position to determine just what policies we should pursue, it would be unwise at this particular juncture to urge a conference for the discussion of such questions.[63]

Although he did not say so, Hurley was also undoubtedly reflecting at least some concern over the previous week's national elections. Although Wilson had rather undiplomatically asserted that a Republican victory would be interpreted as a repudiation of his leadership, the voters turned the Sixty-Sixth Congress over to the G.O.P. Inasmuch as Republican business sentiment had long been on record as strongly opposed to continued postwar government ownership of merchant shipping, Hurley and the Shipping Board would be forced carefully and tactfully to work out a peacetime commercial policy palatable to the G.O.P. but effective as an agent of foreign trade. It offered all the more reason to wait for a better reading on the matter.

62. Hurley to Wilson, November 9, 1918, Wilson Papers.
63. Hurley to Redfield, November 12, 1918, RG 32/Robinson, NA. See also the State Department's William Phillips to L. P. Sheldon, "Summary of the Effect of the Armistice on Shipping," November 24, 1918, Papers of the Supreme Economic Council (hereafter cited as SEC Papers).

Of even greater immediate importance, Wilson and Hurley shared the realization that an indiscriminate release of American ships would jeopardize one of the most powerful means Wilson had at his disposal to solicit Allied cooperation in framing the postwar peace terms. Until the treaty issues were resolved, it was agreed, the administration's maritime trump would have to be played extremely close to the vest. America's shipping strength would be used as a subtle but indispensable bargaining weapon to enable Wilson to "compel justice" at the Paris talks. The policy was roughly to persuade the Allies that United States maritime growth and competition were a permanent undertaking in three ways: by continuing a very large shipbuilding program, by extending government authority over American maritime service, and by refusing to allow the Allies use of American shipping and shipbuilding facilities, although they were badly needed by England, France, and Italy to replace their enormous wartime losses.

Hurley certified the first objective in a major mid-November press release. If there was any uncertainty about the postwar period, America's shipbuilding industry was not going to be part of it, it was here "not only to stay but to grow." Hurley predicted that within five years the nation's maritime arm would comprise a force of one million men. The United States merchant marine—less than two million tons before the war—now exceeded seven million, but this was only the beginning; the ultimate goal was more than three times that size—twenty-five million deadweight tons. The figure exceeded prewar British tonnage in foreign trade.[64]

To give government direction greater validity as well as greater effectiveness, Wilson sizably increased the power of the Shipping Board in early December by granting it authority previously reserved to the White House. The board now had the power to suspend restrictions on maximum working hours and to raise or lower freight rates and terminal charges in order to counter foreign competition.[65] While Wilson and Hurley agreed on the ultimate desirability of returning most of the ships to private enterprise, they rationalized that so long as this decision could be put off, the Allies' fear of a government-owned American shipping industry would make them more pliable at Versailles. This move also denied the Allies a pro-

64. USSB, News Release, November 16, 1918, Daniels Papers.
65. Smith and Betters, *The United States Shipping Board*, p. 18; Fayle, *The War and the Shipping Industry*, pp. 334–37.

cedural base from which to restructure their own commercial fleets for a return to private enterprise and commercial rivalry, thereby allowing the United States added time to increase its bargaining base through broadened commercial networks of its own.

Finally, Wilson ordered that Allied interests were to be denied the use of American vessels and shipyards until the peace treaty was actually signed. This was also designed to hinder British, French, and Italian maritime growth and prevent Allied orders from inhibiting United States ship-building by tying up American yards for crucial periods of time.[66] Wilson played a variation of the same theme around the efforts of the British Cunard Line to repurchase thirty-seven steamships it had sold to J. P. Morgan's IMMC in 1901. Retained in English registry by Morgan, the fleet had been requisitioned by the British government early in the war. Subsequently, within the context of England's concern over American maritime growth, the British harassed the IMMC management of the vessels to such a degree that the Morgan firm contemplated a return sale. Indignant at the prospect of losing American ownership of this valuable fleet, Wilson responded with a retaliatory plan, an effort to purchase the IMMC ships for the United States government itself. Such a proposal would also lend strength to the strategem of state control. McAdoo had additional reasons for supporting the hard line. Great Britain's real ability to purchase the Morgan ships, he complained, would be tied directly to the liberal war credit extended to England by the United States Treasury. "It would requite us in an extraordinary way," he protested to Wilson, "if Great Britain should take advantage of the strength we have imparted to her to strike this blow at America's essential ocean transportation system."[67] Collectively, these plans expressed Wilson's strategy to "permit no arrangements for any part of shipping until there had been at least a tentative agreement on a League of Nations."[68]

To that strategy, Hurley added a two-part plan that stemmed from the La Follette Seamen's Act. In the days surrounding the armistice, Andrew

66. *The Reminiscences of George Rublee*, p. 185.

67. McAdoo to Wilson, November 16, 1918, McAdoo Papers. See also Daniels to Wilson, November 18, 1918, Wilson Papers; Wilson to Bainbridge Colby, November 18, 1918, ibid.; Josephus Daniels, *The Wilson Era*, pp. 573–74; Hurley draft, "The International Mercantile Marine," written for but not included in the final manuscript of *The Bridge to France*, Hurley Papers.

68. Hurley Diary, December 9, 1918, Hurley Papers.

Furuseth and Secretary of Labor Wilson expressed alarm to the president that with the coming of peace the maritime nations of the world would undoubtedly attempt to nullify all or part of the Seamen's Act. Secretary Wilson was dead set against any compromise at all; he was especially convinced that the repeal of those sections covering wages in American ports would be a serious mistake, for these were precisely the sections that placed the United States on a competitive equality with other maritime nations. Furuseth was more explicit—the power that would attempt to defeat the act, "secretly or openly," would be Great Britain.[69]

Around November fifth, the president urged the Shipping Board to give its fullest consideration to Furuseth's views and follow the counsel of the Labor Department in all matters pertaining to the Seamen's Act.[70] Hurley responded to the White House four days later. He contended that rather than repeal or amend the law to enable the American shipping industry to compete with the much lower wage scales of its maritime competitors, the American peace delegation should endeavor to induce foreign governments to adopt the La Follette guidelines. Hurley understood perfectly the Labor Department's view of the matter; the British Embassy had been protesting since American entry into the war about the impact the wages sections were having on morale in the British merchant marine. There were recent indications that shipping authorities in London were fed up with the demands of irate British mariners for wages equal to those paid on American vessels.[71] Hurley felt that as wages were moving toward an international level it would be a goal decidedly worth fighting for.[72]

A wage war would not be sufficient in itself, Hurley argued. The United

69. W. B. Wilson to Wilson, October 16, 1918, Wilson Papers; Furuseth to Wilson, November 4, 1918, W. B. Wilson Papers; Furuseth to Wilson, November 16, 1918, Wilson Papers.

70. Wilson to Furuseth, November 5, 1918, Wilson Papers.

71. Robert P. Skinner to Lansing, October 30, 1918, RG 32/Robinson, NA; report of Robert P. Bass, Director, Marine and Dock Industrial Division, USSB, prepared by Hurley, in Bass to Wilson, November 30, 1918, Wilson Papers. Despite Hurley's and the Shipping Board's contentions, the La Follette Seamen's Act was not the primary cause for the equalization of wages during the war—war conditions themselves were more important. In the end, the act worked only when the demand for ships and seamen was optimal and seamens' unions enjoyed a fair degree of influence. When these conditions ceased after the war, the act's ability to equalize wages and working conditions also ceased. See Goldberg, *The Maritime Story*, pp. 67–71.

72. Hurley to Wilson, November 9, 1918, Wilson Papers.

States should go beyond that to demand international uniformity in freight rates and thereby free worldwide communication from the domination of any single power. Unfair advantage would thus be banished from ocean commerce: "With uniform freight rates and uniform wages to seamen, the trade would go to the efficient manufacturer, and not to the favored manufacturer." It would be identical to an application of the American Interstate Commerce Commission to the high seas. It would "solve the problem of trade wars, [and] give reality and force to the 'freedom of the seas.'" Hurley made no argument that the proposal would be gratefully received by European shipping interests, who had already expressed a reluctance to relinquish their advantages. Rather, he concluded that the humanitarian aspects of the proposal, coupled with America's new power in the realm of shipping, would carry the plan over their opposition to fulfillment as a great service to the world.[73] It was a perfect monument to Wilsonian commercialism in its liberal garb.

With all these tactics, Wilson and Hurley blended altruism and tough business talk into a plan to spring on the Paris deliberations. The position looked strong. "Never in the history of the world has fate presented a nation with such a profitable opportunity to sit tight, play a lone hand, and quietly take advantage of the grievous economic handicaps of its competitors," observed *The New Republic*.[74] Wilson formalized his plan by assigning Hurley, among others, to a European-bound commission to carry out the program under the direction of Herbert Hoover, head of the United States Food Administration. In addition to maintaining a firm grip on American shipping and shipping policy, Hurley's specific task was to obtain Germany's impounded commercial fleet "at the earliest possible moment" for repatriation, food relief, and reconstruction.[75] Above all, Hurley's goal would be to assist Wilson in achieving broad acceptance of an open and free system of international trade, stabilized on political and legal bases by a League of Nations.

73. Ibid.
74. *The New Republic*, "America and the League of Nations."
75. Wilson to Hurley, November 6, 1918, Wilson Papers; Wilson notes to Lord Balfour, M. Pichon, and Baron Sonnino, December 1, 1918, ibid.

Chapter VIII

The Paris Peace Conference
and the Commercial
"War after the War"

While Hurley harbored few illusions about the inclination of European statesmen to cooperate with the United States in Paris, he was convinced that the world's popular will would insist upon fair play and "prevent any incontinent rejection [of Wilson's proposals] by the politicians."[1] For Hurley believed firmly in the reasonableness of man and the efficacy of the bargaining process. Like most Wilsonians, he was convinced that there was nothing that could not ultimately be negotiated. Before leaving the United States in mid-November he noted optimistically that the time had come for the world's shipping interests to gather at the conference table to eliminate "suicidal competition." Harking back to his Federal Trade Commission days, he observed that "again and again . . . I saw hostile manufacturers meet in that way, and lose all their animosity for each other."[2]

Away from American soil, however, such expectations soon proved illusory. Those who thought that the nation's awesome moral, economic, and political power gave it an impregnable position from which to force a favorable peace in Europe were awakened to the rude reality of what H. G. Wells had forecast at the close of the war. His "Great Power" theory, the depiction of the European belief that "ones own state is forever in conflict and competition with other states, trying to best them and gain advantage

1. Hurley to Wilson, October 23, 1918, in *The Bridge to France*, p. 333.
2. Hurley, "Business on the Seven Seas."

on them," revealed in its very essence the environment in which Hurley had to negotiate.[3] Notwithstanding American faith in the sanctity of human reason and the contention that United States commercial and financial expansion was designed as much for the enrichment of the world as of the United States, the Allies displayed a disconcerting tendency to view the American mission's objectives as the design of a grasping national economic policy as avaricious as their own.

From the start, Hurley was forced to labor in an atmosphere rife with suspicion of America's economic intentions. He wired a description of the situation to Wilson, then aboard the *George Washington* en route to Europe.

> In all the conferences I have had on this side, I have been impressed with the fact that it is not the League of Nations, nor an International Court, or even the Freedom of the Seas that is feared by Lloyd George, Clemenceau, Orlando or their associates. What they are thinking about, as you are probably aware, is the increased power of our shipping commerce and finance. In every conversation the commercial question has come to the front. France fears that she will not be able to get the raw materials she needs at the same price as other nations. Great Britain fears that we will have a bigger merchant marine than she will be able to build, and that our government will operate it, regardless of cost, so that we can capture the best markets in the world.[4]

To Hurley, these circumstances underlined the importance of two factors. First, it appeared at that point in early December that the use of shipping to gain leverage for the League of Nations had a good opportunity of succeeding. It would work to America's advantage, he noted, for Wilson to bear in mind the power he possessed in his decision to prevent foreigners from placing orders in American yards. At the same time, Hurley was not so sanguine as to believe that the United States would not have to make some eventual concessions. On the contrary, he was coming quickly to the opinion that a policy of absolute inflexibility would only foster retaliation by the Entente.[5]

---

3. H. G. Wells, "The Core of the Trouble."
4. Hurley to Wilson, December 12, 1918, Hurley Papers. See also Hurley to House, December 4, 1918, House Papers.
5. Hurley to Wilson, December 12, 1918, Hurley Papers.

Hurley had been impressed with the seriousness of this problem in the two weeks following his arrival in Europe. In endeavoring to secure the reactivation of the German merchant and liner fleet, Hurley discovered that the Allies intended to control the relief program through either the authority of the Inter-Allied Council on War Purchases and Finance or the Allied Maritime Transport Council. Such a program would have endowed the Entente with a majority position and required, in addition to German vessels, the pooling of American ships engaged in relief, reconstruction, and repatriation. Largely representative of the Allied effort to circumscribe Herbert Hoover's intentions to control the food relief program unilaterally ("The hand that feeds Europe will control its destinies," Lord Reading had warned Hurley repeatedly), the plan would have paralleled British efforts to control raw materials and world shipping through consortiums governed by the Entente. In Hurley's opinion, it would also have removed the "chief incentive for a league of nations."[6] At the same time, Hurley received news that the British had contracted to construct half a million tons of merchant vessels for France, a move that threatened the central thrust of the leverage tactic—prohibiting foreign construction in American ship-yards.[7] On top of that, Hurley's scheme to create international uniformity in freight rates and seamen's wages and working conditions—increasing your competitor's costs, as the Allies interpreted it—was received coldly by the Entente and set aside for consideration at a later date. By the year's end, Furuseth (an unofficial American labor delegate) was perplexed; in November, everything had pointed to a real imbroglio over the Seamen's Act, but the silence was now "thunderous." Nor could any USSB officials explain the British failure to seize upon the issue. Furuseth concluded that something was fishy about this and, like Hurley, he was "keeping his eyes peeled."[8]

The development of these difficulties in Europe was compounded by domestic problems born of the worldwide transition from war to peace,

6. Hurley to Wilson, November 28, 1918, Hurley Papers. See also House to Wilson, November 27, 1918, SEC Papers. Wilson responded by virtually emasculating United States representation on Inter-Allied councils upon his arrival in Europe. See *The Reminiscences of George Rublee*, pp. 184–85. Reading's remark is recorded in John E. Barber to Hurley, December 26, 1918, Hurley Papers.

7. Hurley Diary, November 23, December 9, 1918, Hurley Papers.

8. Furuseth to Thomas A. Hanson, January 8, 1919, W. B. Wilson Papers.

especially in commercial matters. Almost simultaneously with Hurley's departure for Europe, the Shipping Board came under intense pressure from American exporters. Bound by Hurley's commitment to withhold policy considerations from public discussion, however, the board was unable to satisfy the business sector's demand for definitive information concerning the role government-constructed vessels would play in overseas trade. At issue, too, was the status of millions of tons of American ships commandeered by the USSB at the outset of American war involvement. That the USSB in time would return these vessels appeared a certainty, but when it would do so was a matter of much importance. McAdoo's impassioned call in November for a major diversion of USSB ships into Latin American trade had been embarrassing. It put a great deal of pressure on the Shipping Board to produce a statement of its own at a moment when it was endeavoring to avoid just such a commitment. Nothing was to be done precipitously and without felicitous concern for the future, the board cautioned its operations office as the result of McAdoo's outburst.[9] But that in no way halted the incessant and vociferous clamor for transoceanic shipping. Most shippers agreed wholeheartedly with the Southern Commercial Congress that the release of new and commandeered USSB vessels was imperative if the United States was to succeed in the "trade war which will come simultaneously with peace"; and they were "filled with dismay and discouragement," as the Council of Foreign Relations put it, at the administration's seeming reluctance to strike out hard for markets.[10]

In early December, the reality of ever increasing British competition intensified the administration's concern. The whole question of shipping for foreign trade was rapidly becoming an acute issue between the two nations. Even Redfield became alarmed: Two weeks after criticizing McAdoo, he came full circle and complained to Secretary of War Baker that "our commerce is being sadly damaged while British commerce is definitely and daily taking its place." In the past day, Redfield reported, four of the nation's most prominent foreign trade associations had put pressure on him to remedy the problem by providing more shipping for hemispheric trade.

9. Henry M. Robinson memorandum for John H. Rosseter, November 21, 1918, RG 32/Robinson, NA.
10. *New York Times,* December 2, 10, 1918.

Great Britain was "moving two steps to our none" he argued in an effort to persuade Baker to release military vessels for overseas commerce.[11]

Some Shipping Board personnel shied at the prospect of a commercial war. Vice Chairman Raymond Stevens and George Rublee, the USSB's chief representatives on the Allied Maritime Transport Council in London, strongly opposed an independent program of commercial competition as certain to promote pressures in England for a relaxation of shipping controls. Such a result, they argued on the eve of Hurley's departure for Europe, would precipitate international economic chaos and seriously harm innocent bystander nations less well equipped with food, raw materials, and oceanic transportation.[12] When it appeared that a majority on the board were inclined to discount such advice, Commissioner T. A. Scott notified a dissenting member that he felt strongly that England seriously doubted Hurley's ability or intention to retain effective control over the nation's merchant tonnage. On this assumption, the British appeared poised to permit their own tonnage to return to private interests who would "enter into a desperate trade fight" with the board. In Scott's opinion, however, the Shipping Board was in no position to accept the challenge: "From our own selfish point of view we cannot afford to enter into such a competitive fight for some time to come." For England unquestionably had a much greater volume of shipping to divert into overseas trade. If the board tried to compete with England, Scott maintained, the probable result would be a catastrophic trade war in which the United States would inevitably lose.[13]

As Stevens, Rublee, and Scott fully realized, however, most Shipping Board and Emergency Fleet Corporation officers did not agree with them. Upon arriving in Europe, Hurley ostracized Stevens and for all practical purposes replaced Rublee with Henry M. Robinson, a California engineer and banking executive.[14] As far as Hurley and Robinson were concerned, the Allied Maritime Transport Council was an undesirable dead end. Back in the United States, steel magnate Charles Schwab, director general of the

11. Redfield to Baker, December 12, 1918, RG 40/78137, NA.

12. Stevens memorandum for House, November 15, 1918, House Papers; Stevens and Rublee to Hurley, November 16, 1918, SD 800.88/217, NA; Stevens to Baker, November 27, 1918, Newton D. Baker Papers.

13. Scott to Charles R. Page, December 6, 1918, RG 32/618-3, NA.

14. House to Lansing, November 30, 1918, U.S., State Department, *FR, Paris Peace Conference,* 1:174; *The Reminiscences of George Rublee,* p. 186.

EFC, and P. A. S. Franklin, mustered into service as head of ship control, rejected Scott's cooperative arguments and called for the prompt release of bottoms for commercial purposes.[15] Former Shipping Board member Frank Munson warned the board that the opening of Great Britain's shipyards for cheap foreign construction would give England a tremendous edge and could well demoralize the American shipbuilding industry. It was suicidal, he protested, to prohibit the use of the finest shipbuilding facilities in the world.[16] John H. Rosseter, director of operations, and Welding Ring, director of chartering, pointed out that British lines were dropping rates and reassigning their American service to world markets so quickly (most notably to South America) that unless the United States moved speedily England would capture prime routes and prevent them from going to American operators. "We are hoping that the Shipping Board will take prompt action and not let the situation get beyond their control," Ring pleaded.[17]

Hurley assessed the problem: Ships for the nation's export trade were scarce because the primary demands upon American merchant vessels were for repatriation and food relief. The rapid production of tonnage in the United States was admittedly large, but so was the Shipping Board's return of borrowed bottoms to Great Britain. The question of returning over one million tons of neutral vessels engaged in America's South American war trade also had to be met.[18] In addition, not only were the Allies reluctantly aiding the United States in repatriation and relief shipping, they appeared determined to prejudice a favorable apportionment of the German fleet. Moreover, Germany had so far refused to agree to any shipping terms at all. Hurley was left in an extremely difficult situation; as he saw it, basically, he had two alternatives. The first was to continue to sit on the shipping lid until the league question had been settled, formal proceedings for which would not commence for several weeks. The second involved a revision of

15. *New York Times,* December 5, 1918; Franklin to C. D. Mallory, November 30, 1918, RG 32/Operations, NA.

16. Munson to USSB, December 5, 1918, SD 411.57N83/30, NA.

17. Rosseter to USSB, December 5, 1918, RG 32/618-3, NA; Welding Ring to Lester Sisler, December 13, 1918, RG 32/Robinson, NA.

18. "Statement Showing by Month Termination of Charters on Neutral Steamers," January 15, 1919, RG 32/Operations, NA. This report demonstrates the early termination of charters and the pressure being exerted by the neutrals to regain their tonnage.

the means, but not the ends, of Wilson's Paris strategy. Hurley reasoned that the creation of a universal peace backed by American economic and moral strength would be meaningless if the adoption of a holding action by the Shipping Board allowed American industry and foreign trade to wither for want of jobs and transportation. Moving quickly to the second alternative, on December 13, Hurley reassigned War Department vessels from repatriation and relief to directed use by the Shipping Board "in export trade to relieve congestion at American ports." Indecision at this time, he warned the board, would place the nation in serious straits.[19] In fact, the reassignment was minimal (800,000 tons) and hardly solved the shipping industry's problems.

One of the major difficulties was the government's general policy of war contract cancellation. Revitalized by war, the shipbuilding industry protested vehemently at the prospects of peacetime stagnation. Despite Hurley's continuation of contracts for over one thousand new vessels, the Shipping Board contemplated a cutback of up to 40 percent. Demonstrations and organized unruliness by shipyard workers immediately accompanied the announcement. Protests from shipping magnates poured in from coast to coast. Hurley feared that the unemployment would cause serious social disorder and add to an already growing domestic radicalism. Alarmed, he questioned the logic of continuing an embargo on contracts with the Allies, despite Wilson's league position. Noting that pressure from the shipyards was increasing every day, Hurley inquired of the president if his Paris plan might not be better served by reaching an immediate accommodation with French and Italian shipbuilding needs (Hurley did not take the British into consideration). To agree to contracts for both would not only decrease social pressure and benefit the shipbuilding trade in the United States but also constitute an act of international good will at a most propitious moment. Otherwise, Hurley warned, "if we keep our fist closed until they open theirs, the result may be a delay in the settlement of the larger issues."[20]

But Wilson turned Hurley down, remarking that he understood the

19. Hurley cable to Baker, Colby, Lord, Rosseter, Franklin, and McCormick, December 13, 1918, RG 32/618-3, NA.
20. Hurley to Wilson, December 20, 1918, Wilson Papers.

board's problems but that his league policy was paramount and no concessions should be made to any of the Allies until peace terms were actually
formalized. Congressional attempts to bypass the plan by legalizing open
shipyards would be met with his presidential veto.[21] Wilson then ordered
the Shipping Board to meet Allied maritime competition by lowering its
shipping rates, a policy that Hurley actually had doubts about, as it ran
counter to his philosophy that in the long run economic efficiency and
solvency were preferable to rate wars. Sensing this, Hurley's assistant,
California banker John Barber, thought it incumbent to rationalize Wilson's
decision. He reminded Hurley that no matter how one viewed England's
mercantile position, one inevitable conclusion had to be kept in mind—
Great Britain was "dealing cards from the bottom of the deck." In order
to counter this, it was important to continue to stress the Shipping Board's
willingness to "run at a loss if necessary to capture the best markets in the
world. This is one club that should not be dropped until peace is actually
signed." The Shipping Board had to remain competitive and in a position
from which it could give the British "a dose of their own medicine."[22]

    While Hurley's delegation was considerably put out by what it inter-
preted as British efforts to cripple American foreign trade and shipping,
the American naval contingent in Paris bordered on complete distraction.
Its head, navy chief of staff, Admiral William S. Benson, later USSB
chairman, painted a picture of Versailles in which English commercial
intrigue dominated the landscape. No sooner had Benson arrived in Europe
in midautumn 1918 than he claimed that Allied propaganda for a peace
favorable to the Entente posed a far greater threat to American interests
than that produced by the Germans. Unless a Wilsonian settlement was
secured, he warned Daniels, the war would have been fought in vain.[23]
Benson was soon calling for an aggressive counterthrust to British trade

    21. R. W. Bolling memorandum for Hurley, December 21, 1918, Hurley Papers; Hurley
Diary, December 23, 1918, ibid.
    22. John E. Barber to Hurley, December 26, 1918, Hurley Papers; Hurley's instructions
urging restraint were sent to Rosseter, January 1, 1919, cited in Redfield to USSB, January
22, 1919, SD 800.88/249, NA.
    23. Benson to Daniels, November 21, 1918, Naval Records Collection of the Office of
Naval Records and Library, National Archives, Record Group No. 45, Subject File,
1911–1927, Case File VP. Hereafter cited as RG 45 plus file number, NA. Benson's
antiforeign attitude is discussed in detail in Chapter 10.

expansion and arguing that the Allies were in collusion in the matter of the interned German vessels.[24] By early January, he had become so vehement over what he defined as British efforts to block American naval and mercantile growth that on one fiery occasion he very nearly exchanged blows with the first sea lord of the British Admiralty.[25] Later that month, Benson instructed the Office of Naval Operations that thenceforth its policy in regard to the national interest would be identified with that of the Shipping Board. Naval operations expressed this policy for both groups: Great Britain was "out to capture the lion's share" of the world's carrying trade. If the United States desired to get in the running at all, it would have to get its shipping organized and into competition as quickly and efficiently as possible.[26]

The Shipping Board's effort to carry out such a program was hindered seriously by the absence of Wilson and Hurley. Their departure had left the board confused and rudderless at precisely the moment the public most strongly demanded the formulation of a postwar shipping policy. But Wilson's priority was the creation of a European peace—not postwar domestic planning. As his ranking biographer observed, "for Wilson, planning for postwar reconstruction meant creating the League of Nations." In an executive vacuum, the agencies created by war either abandoned all reconstruction efforts or attempted to work out policies within very limited frameworks of authority. The consequences were often chaotic.[27]

The Shipping Board fit this pattern. With Hurley and Wilson in Paris and Stevens in London, Bainbridge Colby presided over board activities; but Colby soon discovered that his temporary authority was more theoretical than real: Decision making resided essentially with the director of operations, John H. Rosseter, formerly an executive for the Pacific Mail Steamship Company. To add to Colby's discomfort, Rosseter's functions were increased greatly when the Shipping Control Committee was dissolved on January 1, 1919. Carrying out Hurley's restrained directive, Rosseter

24. Benson, War Diary, December 4, 1918, RG 45/Box 579, NA; "Memorandum Prepared by the U.S. Naval Advisory Staff, Paris," December 17, 1918, Wilson Papers.

25. Benson memorandum, May 16, 1921, RG 45/UB, NA; Josephus Daniels to Captain Dudley W. Knox, January 29, 1937, ibid.

26. Benson to Naval Operations, January 19, 1918, RG 45/VM, NA; "Memorandum for Chief of Naval Operations," January 30, 1919, RG 45/UB, NA.

27. Link, "World War I," 2:138; Burl Noggle, *Into the Twenties,* p. 52.

lowered rates—his "bombshells," he called them—in response to British reductions, but not so much as to increase the loss of a vast shipping industry already enormously, some thought scandalously, in the red.

Rosseter drew criticism from both sides. On the one hand, Colby, who represented a small group resentful of the commercial competitiveness embodied in rate cutting, argued that the board's addiction to scoring "gratifying little victories" over Great Britain sidetracked it from the essential need, working out a sensible and permanent postwar maritime plan. Unless this was attended to at once, the board would be rendered impotent, emasculated by a public view that believed that "we do not know which way to turn and [that] these great interests are subject to our bumbling, procrastinating, uncertain touch, and that there is no expectation of results from us." Realizing the futility of his position, Colby prepared to resign.[28]

The majority, on the other hand, persistently claimed that the rate reductions were not sufficient to guarantee America a place in the world's commercial spotlight. The Commerce and Treasury departments headed the list. Arguing that a "radical difference" had developed between the Commerce Department and the Shipping Board covering maritime procedures, Redfield showed his new competitive side. He notified Hurley that the board's rates were still two or three times those of the British and that under current circumstances the country could not tolerate a policy which restricted commerce through the maintenance of artificial rates based on the USSB's need to earn profits to offset high war costs.[29] Carter Glass, McAdoo's replacement at the Treasury Department, seconded Redfield's motion and sounded a familiar theme. Glass called for an immediate reduction of freight rates to encourage export trade; it was obvious to him that "without an outlet for surplus products overproduction may quickly result which may cause closing down of industries and consequent unemployment and social unrest."[30] One of Hurley's aides in Washington summed up that the Shipping Board was "under pretty general fire from all sides." Chief

28. RG 32/Verbatim Minutes, January 13, 1919, NA; *New York Sun,* January 15, 1919. Colby publicly expressed his views in "Some Thoughts on Our Shipping Policy."

29. Redfield to Hurley, January 27, 1919, RG 56/129, NA. By the end of the month, Rosseter was in full agreement with Redfield. See Rosseter to Hurley, January 27, 1919, under August 27, 1919, SD 195.03/9, NA.

30. Glass to Hurley, January 11, 1919, Wilson Papers.

difficulties came from the operators and owners, the former insistent that they could not compete without government aid, the latter irate because their ships had not yet been returned to them. Conditions were "delicate," and there seemed to be an "uproar at every suggestion of government operation of ships." The conclusion from all hands was that Hurley was "sadly missed."[31]

Glass' commentary about the correlation between unemployment and social unrest emphasized beliefs Hurley had long honored. The Shipping Board's head had always held that idleness in the American labor force was the quickest way to economic stagnation and social upheaval. Full employment was an absolute necessity; otherwise the workers' "surplus energy would be directed towards agitation of socialism and other isms, which most always developed into extreme radicalism."[32] A week later Hurley had a lengthy conversation with the deposed Russian revolutionary leader in exile, Aleksandr Kerensky, which confirmed more than ever his apprehensions. The surplus energy of the people had to be employed, Kerensky cautioned Hurley, or the workers could be depended upon to do to Wilson in the United States as they had done to him in Russia. Hurley came away profoundly impressed. For months later he cited Kerensky's advice as among the most important he had encountered on his European assignment.[33] Hurley's subsequent management of the shipping industry and the trades dependent upon it was an obvious application of this logic.

Hurley's reactions to labor unrest in the United States, to the squabbles surrounding the Shipping Board, and to increasing commercial pressures prompted him to request permission to return to the United States in early January. But Wilson maintained that Hurley's continued presence was necessary to resolve the German ships question, due to be discussed shortly in Trier. Hurley was scheduled to preside over the preliminary negotiations concerning the disposition of Germany's commercial fleet, and Wilson was insistent he remain. The talks were conducted on January sixteenth and

31. Thomas F. Logan to Hurley, January 12, 1919, Hurley Papers.
32. Hurley Diary, December 31, 1919, Hurley Papers.
33. See, for example, Hurley's "World Shipping Data: Report on European Mission," March 1, 1919, Hurley Papers; Hurley address, "The Future of Our Foreign Trade," April 25, 1919, ibid.: Hurley interview with the press, New York Times, July 27, 1919. The two-hour conversation with Kerensky took place in Paris on January 8, 1919.

seventeenth and resulted in an agreement by the German delegates to re-convene with Allied and American representatives as soon as they had drawn up a list of all vessels, their condition, and the time at which they could be delivered for active service. While the next meeting did not take place for another two months, at this time in January an early distribution seemed imminent. Inasmuch as Hurley had also obtained a pledge from the British to provide approximately 30 percent of his shipping needs for mil-itary repatriation, he had every reason to believe that he had completed his twofold task of liberating the German ships and obtaining transportation to return American troops.[34] Hurley attributed this breakthrough with England to his efforts at avoiding misunderstanding and especially to Wilson's uncompromising position on purchasing the International Mer-cantile Marine. The British, it seemed to him, were at the moment not nearly so "independent" as in the past and had become more considerate of his delegation.[35]

All the while, calls from Washington describing the confused state of affairs at the Shipping Board continued to reach President Wilson. Glass, Daniels, Harry Garfield of the Fuel Administration, and key personnel at the Food Administration all cabled their concern on January twenty-second. A week later, the entire cabinet asked Baker to convey its desire that Hurley be allowed to return at once.[36] Wilson finally agreed. Leaving Henry Robin-son behind as his replacement, Hurley sailed for New York aboard the *Leviathan*, the former German liner, on February third.

Back at his desk ten days later, Hurley at once set about the task of restoring order in the shipyards. Unable to provide work through foreign contracts, he was forced to reduce the cancellation of government contracts and award additional contracts to well-established and old-line yards.

34. Hurley to House, January 9, 1919, House Papers; Hurley to Benson, January 9, 1919, William S. Benson Papers; Hurley to Wilson, January 20, 1919, Wilson Papers. Hurley deals with the Trier Conference in *The Bridge to France*, pp. 275–85, and *The New Merchant Marine*, pp. 108–21. See also "Agreement of 17th January, 1919, in Respect of Relief Arrangements and the Employment of German Tonnage," Benson Papers.

35. Hurley Diary, January 12, 1919, Hurley Papers. The United States ambassador to England, John W. Davis, did not share Hurley's sentiments; he felt that Hurley had weakened, not strengthened, the American position by his public statements and position on the IMMC. See Davis to Polk, January 4, 1919, Polk Papers.

36. Baker, Daniels, Garfield, Hines, Whitmarsh, and Wooley to Wilson, January 22, 1919, RG 56/129, NA; Baker to Wilson, January 29, 1919, SD 195.03/"C," NA.

Hurley did this reluctantly, knowing that in the long run continued production of ships designed primarily for war would not prove the soundest means for creating a commercially efficient peacetime merchant marine. Letting contracts for vessels that should have been either declared obsolete or substantially remodeled in size, speed, and type of power was a source of continual concern to him; but Wilson's Paris plan and White House sensitivity to Republican efforts to exploit the acute labor situation kept pressure on Hurley to continue building.[37] Several months later, Hurley would look back and admit to a ranking British shipping official that Wilson's policies fostered not only overbuilding and inefficiency but also Anglo-American friction.[38]

Under the present circumstances, however, mass production without change served as the best stopgap, and not only important construction revisions needed to create efficiency but also building reductions that might have improved diplomatic relations had to be sacrificed. In fact, so successful was his policy that within five weeks of returning from Europe, Hurley was able to report to the Shipping Board that the yards were again working at full capacity, turning over enormous profits, and taking advance orders that shattered all previous records.[39] To take pressure off export trade, Hurley increased the Shipping Board's already generous allocation of bottoms to nonrelief overseas trade routes that had been of major prewar importance. The board also pioneered new services in February, including government lines from Houston to Liverpool, New York to the western coast of Africa, and New York to previously untouched or underserviced ports in the United Kingdom.[40] At the same time, Hurley began to return USSB commandeered vessels of under 4,000 tons capacity to private control, thereby jettisoning in part the policy of feigning continued government ownership of that group of ships. Vessels in excess of this tonnage were retained, however, and those that were returned remained subject to rate controls and approval of trade through various agencies established by the board.[41] Hurley's move was intended not only to meet public demands but

37. For an example of White House political pressure on Hurley, see Joseph Tumulty to Hurley, May 2, 1919, Hurley Papers.
38. Hurley to Sir Joseph P. Maclay, July 24, 1919, Hurley Papers.
39. Hurley memorandum for the Shipping Board, March 13, 1919, RG 32/Stevens, NA.
40. USSB, *Annual Report, 1920*, pp. 54–55.
41. USSB, *Annual Report, 1919*, pp. 18–19.

also to parry Great Britain's decision to release its own requisitioned tonnage for competitive trade.

Together with lowered freight rates and Hurley's strengthening of government commercial shipping lanes, the board's ship releases helped to stimulate a mad rush for overseas trade in February and March. The push was intensified by the State and War departments' removal of almost all wartime export restrictions and by the general retooling of the industrial economy for peace. With the binders off, export products piled up on wharves as they had at the commencement of war. The strain put on Gulf and East Coast outlets increased to the point where railroad companies refused to ship products to ports. The demand for ships was so intense that on February 17, Hurley and Daniels termed the situation sufficiently serious to warrant the transfer of 500,000 tons of War Department vessels to the export trade, despite the fact that over one million American servicemen still remained in Europe. It was necessary, they maintained, because the industrial and agricultural network was tied up by its inability to obtain shipping space for its surplus. As a result, unemployment was becoming such a grave matter that returning veterans were entering an aggravated and socially disruptive situation. The surplus would have to be moved to restore economic confidence and foster a rising job market.[42]

Hurley also turned to the matter of establishing a permanent and politically agreeable peacetime maritime policy. To activate a plan, he enlisted the aid of the Council of National Defense and the conservative United States Chamber of Commerce. With the council and the Shipping Board providing the public relations work, the chamber agreed to send out to its business, civic, industrial, and labor membership a number of sample shipping programs prepared by the board in order to test public opinion. The Shipping Board proposed to consider the returns before taking a position of its own. As Hurley explained it to Wilson, his policy would attempt to bridge the chasm between the two shipping philosophies—it would avoid the "inertia and financial entanglements" that might come from government ownership, but would still provide "all safeguards that could

42. *New York Times,* February 18, 1919; War Department release, March 3, 1919, SEC Papers. See also Rosseter's address before the American Manufacturers' Export Association, March 4, 1919, RG 32/Operations, NA.

be derived from such ownership."[43] Unfortunately, this vital goal did not materialize under Hurley's leadership. One important cause was the advent of a shipping crisis brought about by the European relief program.

———————•—————

Hurley's three-pronged emphasis on enlarging commercial shipping to meet British trade competition, resolving domestic social and economic emergencies, and strengthening America's league position all at the same time severely compromised his ability to contribute to European relief and brought him into direct conflict with Herbert Hoover, whose mission Hurley originally had been assigned to complement. The episode was played out most intensely during March, April, and May and served as another means to bring Hurley's economic philosophy into clear relief.

Although Hurley and Hoover strongly endorsed the Wilsonian *Weltanschauung,* basic differences developed between them over the most preferable means to that end. To Hurley, stabilizing and strengthening America's postwar economic position meant the immediate establishment of shipping services for the complete panoply of American exports. Securing outlets for these services in new markets removed from prostrated Europe was his primary objective. Social disorder was countered by attacking it at home through continued ship construction (Hurley's contribution to full employment) and increased emphasis on commercial exportation. On the other hand, Hoover's goals were tied primarily to a single segment of the export economy, American agriculture, and to the disposition of its enormous war-induced surpluses. Ravaged Europe, not the world's open market system, offered the Food Administration its best outlet and, in terms of relief, one justified by lofty humanitarian and political requirements as well. For Hoover sensed that with food he had an extraordinary opportunity to arrest Bolshevism at the very source of international infection. The mutual association of Hoover's goals was striking. As Norman Davis, American financier and member of the peace delegation, sagaciously observed, Hoover's overriding concern for "abnormal surplus food supplies" in the United States had created a situation in which it was "difficult some times

43. Hurley to Wilson, March 14, 1919, Wilson Papers; *New York Times,* February 14, 1919; Hurley to Grosvenor B. Clarkson, February 18, 1919, RG 32/Robinson, NA.

to draw the lines between the requirements for relief and the requirements for an outlet for the surplus."[44] For Hurley, however, the important distinction of Hoover's program was its emphasis on Europe and not on those areas Hurley insisted offered the best advantages for the long-term growth of the American economy. The differences between Hurley and Hoover were exacerbated by personal antagonism. To make matters worse, both attitudes, personal and tactical, had been projected into a strong bureaucratic rivalry between their subordinates.

The rivalry commenced early in 1918 with Hurley's unwillingness to supply vessels for the Belgian relief program in numbers satisfactory to the Food Administration and simmered throughout the balance of the year.[45] Hoover and Hurley no sooner arrived in Europe in late November 1918 than they clashed over shipping authority. Hoover attempted to gain control of relief shipping by working through Colonel House. Hurley countered with the argument that ship management under a director general of relief would result in confiscatory use of vessels needed for other trade and that such use would be carried on at great loss in efficiency. The chairman's remonstrances to Wilson forced Hoover to back down and brought some discredit on House.[46] A month later, Hoover's desire for shipping drove him to another violation of Shipping Board precincts, this time in effort to have War Department tonnage assigned directly to the relief program rather than first to Hurley. Sparks flew, and Hoover was deterred again, but only temporarily.[47]

Hurley did not hold Hoover in high personal esteem. While considering him possessed of a keen mind, Hurley felt that he lacked "tact and judgment," and was propelled by an insatiable urge to "get ahead of everybody. I sometimes think that he is so impulsive and anxious to do things that he goes off half-cocked, but everyone else seems to think that it is absolute selfishness and that he is trying to do things to keep himself in the lime-

44. Davis to Albert Rathbone, January 3, 1919, Norman Davis Papers. See also Hoover to Edgar Rickard, January 5, 1919, Wilson Papers.

45. See, for example, Hoover to P. A. S. Franklin, May 11, 17, August 30, 1918, Food Administration Papers (hereafter cited as FA Papers).

46. Hurley Diary, November 27, 28, 30, December 5, 1918, Hurley Papers; Hurley to Wilson, November 28, 1919, ibid.

47. Hurley Diary, December 25, 27, 1918, January 3, 4, 1919, Hurley Papers.

light. I have heard of many prima donna's methods of doing things during my life, but he is certainly the limit." Hurley prophetically surmised that Hoover would undoubtedly "cause us more unnecessary work than any other man."[48]

Their antagonisms might have erupted more seriously had not the Allied blockade of the Central Powers, designed to maintain pressure on Germany prior to a peace settlement, diminished Hoover's immediate effectiveness and legitimate call on shipping and relegated his activity to stockpiling supplies in ports along the English Channel. In the meantime, United States shipping priorities were diverted from European relief to clearing American ports of exports. While Hoover labored to prevent ship diversions, Hurley had reassigned his vessels vigorously and with great success to the expansion of non-European shipping lanes. By early February, only 18 percent of the USSB's foreign trade tonnage was assigned to European ports, in contrast with 70 percent assigned to Latin America and the Orient.[49]

Then late in the winter of 1919, the European political and social situation deteriorated suddenly and to such an extent that Hoover's needs were increased geometrically overnight. The Allied blockade was lifted, but not before serious social and political disorder came to Germany and the countries of the former Austro-Hungarian Empire. March, in particular, was a month of blackness. Bela Kun took Hungary, invaded Czechoslovakia, and appeared poised to attack Rumania. Odessa, reckoned to be the military key to the Balkans, tottered in the face of Bolshevik attack. Indeed, if the situation could not be stabilized there appeared to be every chance that German and Russian radicalism would sweep over and dominate all of Eastern and Central Europe. Hoover emphatically argued that food and supplies transported from America could halt the red tide but that a serious lack of ships for relief undermined these possibilities. Vance McCormick corroborated Hoover's concerns. Remarking with anxiety that it appeared as though the United States was at war once again, the former head of the War Trade Board related the essentials of the difficulty to a scarcity of

48. Ibid., January 3, 4, 1919. See also Vance McCormick Diary, January 13, 1919, FA Papers; *The Reminiscences of George Rublee*, pp. 183–84.

49. "How America Has Come Back Upon the Seas," USSB News Release, March 10, 1919, Daniels Papers. See also United States, War Trade Board, *Annual Report*, June 30, 1919, pp. 137–38, 141, 144, 182, 190–91.

ships.[50] Hoover impressed his opinion upon Wilson and received his endorsement. The president cabled Hurley on March 23, emphasized the emergency, and ordered that transportation "be furnished without fall."[51]

Not surprisingly, Hurley balked at these demands, but not because he had lost sight of the long-range foreign policy objectives. He charged that the Food Administration wasted huge amounts of tonnage by failing to clear Rotterdam warehouses of food supplies and thereby causing exorbitant delays in the unloading and return of USSB vessels. Furthermore, Hoover was disposed to "continually exaggerate" European conditions in order to focus attention on his own program.[52] More important, Hoover's perspectives were out of joint, Hurley asserted. The real problems were at home, not in Europe. Not only did serious economic and social instability prevail in the United States, but the Shipping Board was burdened with the task of countering Allied foreign trade expansion as well. Ships were needed desperately to export surpluses and maintain pace with rapidly developing rival commerce, a situation so urgent Hurley would not promise to make allocations to food relief even if new tonnage became available.[53] Relief was a subsidiary necessity. Hurley had written as much to Wilson, remarking that the relief program "greatly interfered" with the Shipping Board's plan to put the county back on a commercial footing.[54] In a public statement that distressed both the British and the State Department, Hurley declared that a cutback in foreign trade tonnage would seriously damage American export–import trade and result in forfeiture of the new position the nation had gained in its fight for maritime supremacy. To wait would be to lose a great opportunity, he added: The time was especially ripe to establish trade lines while England was handcuffed by postwar domestic

50. McCormick Diary, March 19, 1919, FA Papers.

51. Wilson to Hurley and Newton D. Baker, March 24, 1919, quoted in Hoover, *An American Epic*, 2:398–99. Now also in Paris, Josephus Daniels adopted Hoover's view and urged Hurley to support relief at all costs. See Daniels to Hurley, March 31, 1919, Daniels Papers.

52. Edgar Rickard and Theodore Whitmarsh to Hoover, March 26, 1919, White House Correspondence File, FA Papers; RG 32/Verbatim Minutes, April 1, 1919, NA. Gary Dean Best takes this tack in "Food Relief as Price Support." See Lewis L. Strauss, *Men and Decisions*, p. 46, for a contrasting view emphasizing Hoover's moralistic and antisocialistic relief concerns.

53. Food Administration to Hoover, March 18, 1919, quoted in Hoover, *An American Epic*, 2:398. See also Hurley's remarks in New York, March 27, 1919, Hurley Papers.

54. Hurley to Wilson, March 3, 1919, Wilson Papers.

turmoil of its own.[55] Rosseter strongly agreed with the exploitative aspects of this view: "There has been a social revolution throughout the whole world, and England has suffered more than any one else, and while it may be selfish, it is our plain duty to take advantage of the situation."[56] Such a policy had no room for a diversion of shipping to European relief. This applied to the construction program as well: "What excuse is there in building for voyages to northern Europe, when the trade that we want to develop is the trade with Latin America?"[57]

Hurley's position was further strengthened on March 17 when the issue of the German merchant fleet was at last resolved at the Spa Conference. Pending ratification of the Versailles treaty, Germany's commercial ships were allocated to the victors on terms highly favorable to the United States. In what subsequently became known as the Wilson–Lloyd George Agreement or the Brussels Agreement, Henry Robinson arranged a settlement whereby the Allies scrapped their efforts to secure a pro rata distribution of the 700,000 tons of German ships confiscated in American ports in 1917. Virtually the only reparation claim Wilson had put forth in Europe was for retention of the German ships the United States had taken over in America after entering the war. Millions of dollars had been spent on them in repairs, and throughout the remainder of the war they served with distinction in the North Atlantic war trade. Bearing in mind the enormous reparation demands being drawn up by the Allies, Wilson considered this claim as insignificant in comparison and adamantly refused to release his German ships. Realizing this, Great Britain finally abandoned its pro rata position.[58]

Inasmuch as under this argument the British would have received 87 percent of the German vessels, the Shipping Board had good reason to

55. The *Times* (London), March 23, 1919; Lansing to Polk, March 28, 1919, SD 195.2/2073, NA. Lansing protested that Hurley's statements were "causing general and possibly far reaching complications" in Paris, and that Polk should point out prudently to him the absolute need for "discretion in such matters on account of [the] delicate international situation."

56. RG 32/Verbatim Minutes, April 1, 1919, NA.

57. Ibid.

58. "Notes of a Meeting which Took Place at President Wilson's House . . . (Paris), April 23, 1919," U.S., State Department, *FR, Paris Peace Conference*, 5:161–63. An undated copy of the Wilson–Lloyd George Agreement is located in the Wilson Papers. Actual tonnage allocations are contained in Robinson to Wilson, April 19, 1919, ibid.

jubilate over Great Britain's concession. Although the United States agreed to pay the Reparation Commission $15 million covering the evaluation of the ships, the retention of active ships was definitely worth it in American eyes, especially as the United States had stood alone in its position concerning seized enemy shipping.[59] But Robinson accomplished even more—he also arranged for the immediate, if temporary, use of 200,000 tons of Germany's finest ocean liners. Hurley was elated; he reasoned that the liners would fill both relief and repatriation requirements, thereby eliminating the need to divert American tonnage. But Hoover was quick to cut through Hurley's logic. He countered that the passenger liners were unsuitable for relief shipments because they would require extensive refitting and could not possibly be available for over a month.[60] Hurley literally worried himself into nervous exhaustion over these developments. In late March, he suffered a breakdown and was ordered by his physician to recuperate in St. Augustine. Neither this nor a relapse kept him from fretting over Hoover's position.[61] Hurley informed Robinson that there just had to be some way to use German ships, any German ships, in relief of the European situation. Hoover simply did not understand: "We have labor problems and serious conditions here just as the liberated peoples in Europe."[62] Hurley believed that the domestic situation and the need to develop trade was so critical that he was prepared to violate Armistice regulations by chartering German ships and crews: "I am willing to go the limit towards establishing ships in trades with American flags flying."[63]

One Shipping Board discussion in early April illustrated the extraordinary influence and scope of Hurley's commitment to domestic needs and their relationship to competitive nonrelief world trade. On April 1, while Hurley was ill in Florida, the board took up the question of what it could accomplish to remedy economic and social dislocation in essential American industries. Hurley's strongest supporter and constant proxy, John Rosseter, director of operations, opened the discussions. Rosseter's primary concern was with coal. The current situation was deplorable, he reported. Because

59. Robinson to Baruch, McCormick, and Lamont, April 7, 1919, Benson Papers.
60. Hoover interview with the *London Daily Telegraph,* March 17, 1919.
61. Frank B. Lord to Tumulty, April 5, 1919, Wilson Papers.
62. Hurley to Robinson, April 1, 1919, Hurley Papers.
63. Hurley to Robinson, April 11, 1919, ibid.

there was insufficient oceanic transportation to get the fruits of their labor to foreign markets, 300,000 coal miners were out of work, "living on the sale of their liberty bonds [and] existing from hand to mouth." That in itself warranted the board's most serious consideration, but it went beyond that in two essential ways. Denied external outlets, the great national coal companies were being forced into a state of fratricidal combat for internal markets, were "eating each other up," as one commissioner put it. Moreover, the huge East Coast companies were leaving their own zones for the West where they were forcing Pacific Coast and Rocky Mountain operators out of business. Rosseter argued that the problem was wholly within the board's jurisdiction, for relieving pressure on the Atlantic Coast through increased allocation of ships would refocus the East Coast coal companies' interests outward once again, thereby easing the competition and cannibalization within the country. In short, the board could put a stop to internecine commercial warfare, get men back on the payrolls and socially stable, and materially strengthen a whole industry by a simple manipulation of ships. Charles Piez, the new director general of the Emergency Fleet Corporation, envisioned these needs so strongly that he was certain the board would be held culpable if it were to do otherwise.[64] Rosseter's support from big coal was acknowledged by a spokesman for one of the larger firms in the country:

> Mr. J. H. Rosseter . . . is one of the ablest and greatest men in the nation. If Congress will appropriate the money, and the Shipping Board will give him a free hand, he will provide sufficient bottoms to take care of America's surplus of raw material and manufactured articles, at a rate that will enable the United States to compete with any nation in the world, and only in this way can we have a return to prosperity. Unless this be done, and done quickly, we are headed for mighty hard times, with hundreds of thousands of idle men anxious for work, with the resultant social unrest, and all the concomitant evils which follow when men are willing and anxious to give an honest day's work, and are unable to find employment.[65]

Rosseter was keenly aware that the opportunity to service the coal companies was enhanced at that particular moment by serious disorders in the

64. RG 32/Verbatim Minutes, April 1, 1919, NA.
65. The Archibald McNeil & Sons Co., Inc., to W. H. Stayton, February 13, 1919, RG 32/Operations, NA.

English coal industry. The return to a peacetime economy had revealed how urgently the British coal industry needed to be rationalized. Forced to compete with new fuels, notably oil, the industry was also run by conservative coal barons who gave little thought to creating necessary technological efficiency and stubbornly resisted the legitimate demands of the miners to upgrade pay and eliminate squalid working conditions. Moreover, it was becoming apparent that many mines, which had operated successfully under war prices, were having great difficulty in turning profits in peace. Large layoffs appeared imminent, and labor unrest identified with socialistic ideas pervaded the industry. It was to this situation that Rosseter and Hurley had alluded when they remarked that the time was propitious to move while Great Britain was handicapped by social difficulties of its own. Symbolically, the world viewed coal as the bellwether of England's wealth and, consequently, its national prestige and pride. As Rosseter pointed out, coal was an "outlook trade" or—as commissioner John Donald observed—the "harbinger of the general commercial trade" of a country. A nation with a well-developed coal trade would be in an excellent position to vie for markets on the most preferable bases. Rosseter was all for going ahead immediately: "Our new commerce of the world trades we are going into will be predicated very largely on the upbuilding of the coal trade." There was "tremendous pressure" on the board to assist the coal industry and an unprecedented opportunity to crack England's monopoly. As House would observe, by picking up England's former coal customers and continuing to build merchant vessels on a large scale, the United States would "be hitting at two of her [England's] most lucrative industries."[66] But so far, Rosseter agonized, "everything has been food, food, food."[67]

Hurley strongly supported Rosseter's views. Rosseter had been hired in the first place, Hurley pointed out, because he had "international vision," meaning the ability to see at a glimpse America's situation in the world marketplace and do the necessary things to enhance it. This covered not only decisions involving the assignment of vessels in terms of location, timing, and quantities, and whether goods would be exported through East, Gulf, or West Coast ports, but also what trades were to be given priority govern-

66. House to Wilson, July 30, 1919, House Papers. For a contemporary view of the British coal situation see Herbert Feis, "The Industrial Situation in Great Britain."
67. RG 32/Verbatim Minutes, April 1, May 5, 1919, NA.

ment shipping support at any given time and how and where their goods would be transported. It was as if Hurley had decided to vest the Shipping Board with the total responsibility covered by all the now defunct great government agencies of war—the War Trade Board, the War Industries Board, the Fuel Administration, etc., except that Hurley's war was being fought through global trade involvement and commercial competition not against Germany but against his very associates in war and against social disorder and economic deprivation and depression at home.

Consequently, plans were made to relieve the coal industry in the third week of April 1919 by reallocating relief vessels for the carriage of anthracite to fuel-starved Italy.[68] But Robinson cautioned the board from Paris that even though Great Britain and France had fallen badly behind their coal commitments to Italy, the situation was fraught with potential difficulties stemming from the sensitivities of the Entente. Coal could wait until July or August after the peace was signed. Moreover, Robinson noted, if American tonnage was made available for coal shipments, it was certain that pressure would be brought upon the Shipping Board to carry British coal rather than American on account of the shorter voyage.[69] When Hoover learned of the plan, he assumed that it was a further effort to neglect relief and angrily protested against it. Hurley's effort to insure "employment in the United States," he argued to Wilson, paled in importance beside his own efforts to "stem the tide of starvation in Europe."[70] Responding to the Bolshevist spectre, and in the erroneous belief that the board planned to furnish coal to Italy on an equal basis with relief, Wilson intervened for a second time within a month. On April 28 he dispatched a sharp note to Robinson criticizing the Shipping Board for placing inordinate emphasis upon commercial profits.[71] Although Robinson quickly corrected Wilson

68. Stevens to Robinson, April 19, 1919, RG 32/618-11, NA.
69. Robinson to Stevens, April 22, 1919, ibid.
70. Hoover to Wilson, April 25, 1919, SEC Papers. See also Robinson to Stevens, April 27, 1919, RG 32/618-11, NA. An exchange between Redfield and Hoover in late February illustrated Hoover's inflexible devotion to agriculture and relief. On February 17, Redfield complained with alarm to the FA that its price control system was intensifying a serious unemployment situation and "playing directly into the hands of a real revolutionary party." Hoover replied that the FA's promise to maintain agricultural controls constituted a "moral obligation" considerably more important than the American unemployment situation. See Redfield to T. F. Whitmarsh, February 17, 1919, Commerce Department Files, FA Papers; Hoover to Redfield, February 21, 1919, ibid.
71. Wilson to Robinson, April 28, 1919, Wilson Papers.

and insisted that Hoover was actually being oversupplied with ships, the incident put a stop to the scheme to export coal. Not until late May did the board dare take up the coal plan again.[72]

While Hurley's antagonism for Hoover and his relief program was often expressed in harsh terms, their differences did not deter Hurley from satisfying the needs of both the Shipping Board and the relief programs. While Hurley continued to construct ships and expand trade, he also reallocated vast numbers of ships to fill relief requirements. In fact, Hurley's reassignment of ships to Hoover actually broke the back of the European crisis. As Rosseter had alleged, by early May it was apparent that with two million tons of USSB ships to provide supplies, European economic and political stabilization had been satisfactorily achieved and Bolshevism adequately contained. In the same period between February and May, Hurley actually augmented the nonrelief national foreign trade fleet by 900,000 tons. That figure was achieved despite the fact that hundreds of thousands of tons of vessels requisitioned for the war were returned to private owners, domestic and foreign. Many of these ships were also involved in overseas trade. Hurley's feat was accomplished largely through mass production in shipyards operating under government contract, which had twice as many launching ways and produced more tonnage than all other nations combined.[73]

If Hoover recognized Hurley's ultimate contribution to the European relief program, he did not acknowledge it. Instead he emphasized the Shipping Board's commercialism and insisted upon placing a moral onus on Hurley for failing to respond with the alacrity the Food Administration demanded. When the FA secretly admitted in May that it had overemphasized its transportation needs and was placed "in the embarrassing position of having to return ships," J. P. Cotton, a ranking Hoover aide, immediately threw up a self-righteous shield of defense: "We can throw the entire blame back on Hurley, as we can explain that failure to provide certain countries with food at a given time cannot be rectified by supplying

72. Robinson to Hurley, Stevens, and Rosseter, April 30, 1919, RG 32/Operations, NA. See also RG 32/Verbatim Minutes, May 5, 1919, NA.
73. USSB, *Second Annual Report, 1919*, pp. 10–11, 15, 18–19; "Report of the War Trade Board," June 30, 1919, p. 182.

the same food a month later after the need has passed."[74] Hoover adopted Cotton's tack. To his death, he regarded Hurley's emphasis on non-European carrying trade as virtually traitorous. "Our deficits in deliveries to starving people were caused by the Shipping Board," he moralized acidly. "The pressure on [Hurley] by the export trades proved too strong."[75]

In the final record, the controversy between Hurley and Hoover clouded the similarity of their objectives. This was not a collision between willful and obtuse men; rather it represented a serious debate by two dedicated administrators over the most preferable means to protect, strengthen, and maximize American power in the postwar world. While bureaucratic, professional, and personal jealousies certainly played their part, Hurley and Hoover did not clash philosophically, but expressed in similar ways the major theme in Wilsonian thought: both agreed that the requirements of America's expanding capitalism coincidentally necessitated a universal obligation to the creation of a humane and, above all, orderly world system.

———•———

Woodrow Wilson's three-part nautical power play at Versailles had mixed results. Although toned down, the USSB's postarmistice shipbuilding program continued at a scale sufficient to demonstrate the administration's resolve to build a competitive peacetime mercantile fleet. All the while, Hurley assigned ships to foreign trade in order to prevent Great Britain from reasserting itself too strongly in the mainstream of world commerce. To guarantee the exclusive use of American shipyards for the construction of American vessels, Wilson never budged on the prohibition against foreign contracts.[76] Although France and Italy were given the opportunity

74. Cotton to Hoover, May 20, 1919, SEC Papers.

75. Hoover, *An American Epic*, 2:400–401. It should be pointed out that Hoover's accounts were written in the anticommunist Cold War environment of the 1950's. In early May 1919, while scolding Hurley for overemphasizing export trade, Hoover congratulated himself and the FA for having successfully cleared up the American pork, cereal flour, rye, and wheat surplus situation through the relief program. See Hoover to Julius Barnes, May 7, 1919, in *Organization of American Food Relief in Europe, 1918–1919,* ed. Suda L. Bane and Ralph H. Lutz, p. 470.

76. While Hurley defended Wilson's prohibitions in public, in private he continued to oppose them as a policy conceived with insufficient reference to the domestic labor situation. See Hurley to Robinson, May 24, 1919, SD 195/239a, NA.

to purchase USSB ships, they refused to take up this offer on the apparent grounds that the rates quoted were prohibitive and that the vessels marked for sale tended toward obsolescence. Wilson's additional effort to feign a policy of permanent state control over shipping was recognized by the Entente as a ploy. Public discussion in the United States had left little doubt in Europe that while official rhetoric professed one thing, in reality the Shipping Board intended to turn the government fleet over to private enterprise. Consequently, against USSB hopes, Great Britain had begun to release vessels and lower freight rates at the outset of the New Year. This move forced the Shipping Board to change course and compete on England's terms before it desired to do so. In January, the board began to refix its rates. A month later, it followed England's suit and returned neutral shipping. It then released to American owners vessels of less than 4,000 tons capacity. However, Wilson did not authorize the board to return all requisitioned vessels until peace was actually finalized. Until the distribution of Germany's vessels was determined, Wilson also continued a tough line on the ships of the IMMC.[77]

With respect to those conference results Americans considered positive, Wilson's shipping leaders were convinced that the United States had scored a substantial victory. Realizing that Wilson would not release the seized German ships, Great Britain backed down on its campaign to apply pro rata formulas, and 700,000 tons of enemy vessels were retained at a cost per ton just one-tenth of what the USSB was demanding on the world market for its own surplus ships. The board had also secured the temporary use of 200,000 tons of German liners for military repatriation. Hurley's successor expressed the Shipping Board's view when he described the Wilson–Lloyd George Agreement as a British "defeat, [and] greatest material achievement of the Conference."[78] In an apparent concession that the peace conference shipping accord had substantially benefited the United States, in early April the State Department informed the IMMC that it was with-

77. Sensitivity to British feelings and knotty questions over legal procedures convinced Hurley and the State Department in late January that it would be inadvisable to purchase the vessels. However, in order to maintain leverage in Paris, the administration purposefully withheld this decision from the British for over two months. See Hurley draft, "The International Mercantile Marine," Hurley Papers; John W. Davis to Lansing, February 3, 1919, SD 811.85/9, NA.

78. John Barton Payne statement to the press, *New York Sun*, September 12, 1919.

drawing its plan to purchase the company's vessels—nor would it prohibit their sale to the British. The timing of the announcement indicated that it was no doubt another of those many tradeoffs that marked the political road to a final peace.[79]

Other aspects of the American maritime policy failed to have the positive and salutary effect desired. A principal concern of the American shipping group late in 1918 had been to obtain the immediate use of Germany's impounded merchant fleet, but American negotiators were unable to bring about the actual sailing of those vessels for nearly six months. Nor was Wilson able to persuade the Allies to allow Germany the active use of its own merchant fleet to reintegrate its economy more readily into the commercial commonwealth of nations he sought. Furthermore, in the final reckoning, the principle of the "freedom of the seas," originally considered by many to be one of Wilson's primary peace goals, was abandoned. Bitterly opposed by the British, it suffered the same fate as most other neutrality issues in Wilson's overriding quest for a league.

Hurley's hopes to create a universal uniformity in seamen's conditions were eventually addressed in a special conference on labor legislation associated with the peace negotiations. The American delegation was led by Henry Robinson, Samuel Gompers, president of the American Federation of Labor, and Andrew Furuseth, who attended the conference as an observer and voluntary adviser. From the outset, the American group faired poorly. Conservative shipping interests, most notably from Great Britain, dominated the conference. Their fervent desire was to create an international labor principle that would make the seaman "subject at all times and places to the law of the flag under which he serves." If the United States endorsed a league with this principle embodied in it, those sections of the La Follette Seamen's Act aimed at creating universal equalization in seamen's conditions would fail of their purpose. Furuseth attempted to undercut these forces by enlisting the major European seafarer's organizations in the American cause, but they could not be moved. The British Seamen's Union presented such a case. Its officials admitted that as laborers they admired the Seamen's Act, but declined to endorse it officially on account of their government's hostility toward it and because they feared that its demonstrated ability to equalize seamen's conditions would also sap the competitive strength of the British merchant marine. Consequently, Furuseth acknowledged that the American delegation was isolated and that other than having brought about some permanent global improvements, the Seamen's Act and its benefits would have to be enjoyed largely by American mariners alone.[80]

American maritime interests were also frustrated in matters concerning transoceanic cable communication. Cables were considered maritime subjects, for they passed through the seas. At the outset of the war, the Allies had seized Germany's extensive cable system. Inasmuch as the German cables connected the continent with areas deemed vital to American commercial interests, such as South America, the American shipping delegation strongly opposed any arrangement that would leave these cables in the permanent possession of the Allies. Henry Robinson, with a rich background of telephonic engineering experience, warned Hurley of the commercial hazards involved in these seizures as early as November 1918.[81] Although from the Allies' standpoint there were distinct parallels between Wilson's seizure of German ships and the Entente's seizure of German cables, the American delegation chose not to equate the two. Instead, Robinson and Admiral Benson fought to prevent the peace conference from permanently assigning these cables to Great Britain and France as reparations for war damages. The verdict went against the United States, however, and Great Britain was left with close to 90 percent of the world's undersea cable network. Moreover, Germany and England were the sole producers of deep sea cable, and Great Britain controlled the world's entire output of gutta percha, a vital source of insulation. Summarizing, an American delegate complained that instead of establishing a "communication system free from special privilege and putting every part of the world in immediate contact with every other part," the peace conference's decision demonstrated that "selfish and chauvinistic special interests [were] seeking to extend their control over the

80. Furuseth to Hanson, March 7, 1919, W. B. Wilson Papers; Furuseth memorandum, "On the Constitution of the Conference on Labor Legislation in Relation to the Seamen's Act of America," March 20, 1919, ibid.; Robinson to Wilson, March 24, 1919, Wilson Papers; Furuseth to Wilson, March 26, 1919, ibid.; Furuseth to Hanson, May 7, 1919, W. B. Wilson Papers.

81. Robinson to Hurley, November 20, 1918, RG 32/Robinson, NA.

world's means of quick communication."[82] While the principal Allied and Associated powers agreed to arrange for an early international congress to consider the matter further, Benson concluded that the immediate results simply confirmed "that every phase of the treaty of peace while in the making has exposed the commercial ambitions of our Allies."[83]

All things considered, it was a disappointed shipping delegation that returned to the United States in the late spring of 1919. To American maritime proponents, the peace settlement did not reflect a basic interest in the creation of a moral, cooperative, and stable internationalism but expressed in the main the avaricious economic aims of the Allies. "It is evident," Admiral Benson complained to Wilson, "that commercial interest is underlying every factor under consideration by the various nations, except ourselves." Great Britain was the ringleader: As a nation that had systematically crushed maritime competition for centuries, it now prepared to add America to the list of the fallen. It was a situation requiring extraordinary vigilance and the utmost in safeguards.[84] A week later, the admiral actually warned Daniels of the possibility of war with Great Britain and urged him to keep the American fleet fully manned, "and in every respect ready for action."[85] While few others desired to go to such extremes, by late spring 1919 no one in important government shipping circles cared to express American nautical policy in the old utopian terms. Even Edward Hurley, who in late May had decided to resign, refrained for the time from describing the nation's shipping role as an international benevolency. The concept of American maritime growth conceived as a benefit for the whole world was tarnished considerably during the armistice period, and the ensuing bitterness was reflected in much of the remaining twenty months of the Wilson administration.

82. Walter S. Rogers to Wilson, May 27, 1919, Benson Papers. See also Benson to Daniels, May 2, 1919, ibid.
83. Benson to Daniels, May 29, 1919, Benson Papers.
84. Benson to Wilson, April 28, 1919, Daniels Papers.
85. Benson to Daniels, May 6, 1919, Daniels Papers.

Chapter IX

The Case of the *Imperator:*
The Shipping
Dispute Intensified

Effective August 6, 1919, Woodrow Wilson put the Shipping Board under the chairmanship of John Barton Payne, a well-known Chicago lawyer and erstwhile magistrate, from which very limited latter experience he had acquired the sobriquet "Judge." As one of the largest contributors to Wilson's 1912 campaign war chest, Payne had been offered but declined the post of solicitor general. But the administration did not forget him. In 1917, the Shipping Board hired him to arbitrate several West Coast shipyard strikes. On that basis, Payne shortly thereafter became counsel to the Emergency Fleet Corporation. He then employed his legal talents for the United States Railroad Administration. Consequently, the new shipping czar came into office combining practical knowledge in government direction in two major transportation fields.

While Payne's tenure in office lasted only seven months, it was sufficiently long to encompass a major shipping dispute born of the intensified Anglo-American commercial rivalry. The altercation involved the disposition of a major portion of Germany's oil tanker and passenger liner fleets, including in the latter category the world's largest ship, the *Imperator.* Enmeshed in the case were fundamental maritime rivalries among the great powers, including the control of world oil supplies, unresolved shipping controversies inherited from Versailles, and the paralysis of presidential authority arising from Wilson's serious illness in the fall of 1919.

Central was the concern over oil. The Great War underlined the crucial importance of petroleum as a vital propellant and lubricant and as a resource critical to the security and economic welfare of the industrial world. The main protagonists, Great Britain and the United States, had particular reason to be concerned about acquiring influence over oil. England, with virtually no petroleum at all in the British Isles, lacked sufficient oil reserves elsewhere in its empire. Although the United States had once been the world's wealthiest nation in known deposits, theoreticians had begun predicting that American petroleum production had reached its zenith. The only other source of oil available to the United States, and then only through private control, was in revolutionary Mexico. The self-interests of both nations were intensified by their increasing reliance upon foreign trade and its protection through naval growth. Still mistress of the seas, and determined to maintain that position, England was faced by a nation openly committed to obtaining naval and mercantile parity, if not superiority. Practically and technologically, oil would make those naval and mercantile ambitions possible.

The Shipping Board's first oil alarm was sounded by Henry Robinson who represented the United States on the Supreme Economic Council. In April 1919, Robinson expressed concern that the nation's inferior competitive position for the world's oil supply was bound to have serious negative effects upon the future of the American navy and merchant marine. Robinson was particularly concerned with British efforts at creating oil monopolies in the liberated countries, at the expulsion of the Standard Oil Company from its prewar Rumanian holdings, and at the efforts of the British to exclude American oil interests from Asia Minor. The possibility that England would corner oil in the Middle East worried him; already American naval and merchant vessels were being forced to pay usurous rates at Port Said. Inasmuch as Robinson believed petroleum to be the maritime fuel of the future, he concluded that the successful operation of the American merchant marine could well become "entirely contingent upon the oil supply." It was high time to attend to the rights of the United States in the matter.[1] Later Robinson reiterated his concerns to Hurley. A government attitude compelling an open door in the world's oil-bearing

1. Robinson to House, April 14, 1919, House Papers.

districts had to be obtained if the nation hoped to maintain its merchant fleet and navy in competition with commercial rivals, particularly Great Britain. Robinson pointed out that this concern had been presented to Wilson on numerous occasions but hoped Hurley would also lend his influence to the cause.[2]

Hurley's final report as shipping chairman summarized this position. Of all the international problems facing the nation, he informed Wilson on July 31, nothing was "more essential [than] the protection of the American Merchant Marine and the United States Navy in the matter of fuel oil supply." Already the merchant fleet's use of petroleum had exceeded its use of coal, conversions were taking place rapidly, and the development of diesel power promised to add additional pressure. The latest reports from the Bureau of Mines indicated that while the range of ships bunkered with oil was greater than that of those bunkered with coal, the nation would be subject to the discrimination of foreign suppliers in about two-thirds of the world. Great Britain had already taken full stock of this and controlled a great number of oil fields with tremendous capacity and potential. Working through the Royal Dutch Shell Company, England held producing fields in all the important oil regions of the United States, in Mexico, in the Persian Gulf, and in various parts of Europe, including Rumania and Russia. Its holdings dwarfed America's possessions in the continental United States and Mexico. Arguing that the matter "lies close to the heart of the successful operation of our merchant marine," Hurley called for a plan to project American interests abroad on a more competitive oil-seeking basis.[3]

Payne thus had the Shipping Board's view of the matter clarified for him when he took hold of maritime matters a week later. He also had the State Department's stiffening attitude to take into consideration. By the mid-summer of 1919, the State Department had discarded its earlier cautiousness for a hardened position on British oil maneuvering in the Middle East. With the Standard Oil Company regularly reporting British discrimination against claims the company held in that area, the department determined to protect those vital American interests. In addition, England's blocking of Standard Oil's claims in Palestine and Mesopotamia had serious bearing on

2. Robinson to Hurley, July 2, 1919, RG 32/Robinson, NA.
3. Hurley to Wilson, July 31, 1919, Wilson Papers.

Wilson's league position: Both areas were slated for assignment as mandates to Great Britain. Under the American interpretation of the mandate system, which Wilson felt had been agreed upon by the Entente, the mandatary was obligated to administer the areas within the framework of the Open Door policy. Great Britain's hostility toward American oilmen was in direct violation of these principles.[4]

Such was the environment when Wilson advised Payne on August 11 that he expected American shipping development to continue "independent" of foreign interests.[5] When a controversy arose almost immediately concerning the Standard Oil Company's claim that it held title to nine German tankers impounded in European ports by the Allied Naval Armistice Commission (ANAC), the new shipping head moved quickly to enforce the president's policy. The dispute involved the legality of the company's wartime sale of the ships, which had been registered under the German flag through a subsidiary, the Deutsch Amerikanische Petroleum Gesellschaft (DAPG). These vessels had been turned over to dissimilar German shipping interests shortly after the United States declared war in order to avoid their confiscation by the German government. The company argued that the sale was invalid because of a technicality and that the vessels should therefore be returned to American ownership; the Allies maintained that Standard Oil no longer rightfully owned the tankers and that they would be distributed by the Reparation Commission on the now familiar pro rata basis.[6] That the tankers in contention were under actual Allied naval control and on the verge of being moved to British waters for safe keeping (ostensibly as a security measure in response to Germany's scuttling of its naval fleet in Scapa Flow on June 21), did not strengthen the American position. The company's fear of losing the vessels was augmented by continual reports from Europe indicating that a verdict had already been reached out of court on a basis unfavorable to the United States. The French, in particular, had been stating since March that the tankers would

4. John DeNovo, "The Movement for an Aggressive American Oil Policy Abroad, 1918–1920"; idem, *American Interests and Policies in the Middle East, 1900–1939*, pp. 167–74.

5. Wilson to Payne, August 11, 1919, Wilson Papers.

6. B. W. Palmer to Kirk, June 5, 1919, SD 862.85/78, NA.

be claimed as part of France's individual indemnity. In July, France publicly commenced to link these vessels with plans for a state oil monopoly.[7]

Yet, the shipping question was a two-sided coin. Great Britain, for example, was demonstrably irked over the manner in which the United States had employed its own confiscated German ships since 1917. For while the Allies were deadlocked in debate throughout the spring and summer of 1919 arguing over procedures covering allocations and title transfers of German vessels tied up in European ports, the Shipping Board was profitably utilizing its own German ships in competitive commercial trade. Robinson put his finger on a source of Britain's irritation in late May. Attempting to allay American fears that the Allies would renege on the Wilson–Lloyd George Agreement, he reminded House that the British had actually been exceedingly generous in their agreement with the president. The decision, in fact, had been criticized in England as a giveaway. Consequently, America's competitive and aggressive use of these ships placed British maritime authorities in an awkward spot.[8] An additional exacerbation stemmed from the fact that the United States already possessed seventeen commandeered tankers, or more than half the former German oil tankers still operative after the war. These tankers had been utilized in trade for over two years, and, should Standard Oil obtain title to the additional nine it claimed, twenty-six out of thirty-two tankers would fall into American hands, leaving only six for the remaining Allied claimants. Considering that Great Britain was already distressed by the traumatic transition of world financial leadership to the United States, the American effort to match British mercantile and naval strength, and the more immediate international oil rivalry, the situation was weighted heavily against Standard Oil.

Exasperated by the continuing Anglo-American commercial antagonism, Raymond Stevens arranged with an associate to write a critical article which appeared on August 17 in the *New York Times* under the headline "For

7. Standard Oil Company (New Jersey) to Lansing, August 8, 1919, Polk Papers; Lansing to Polk, August 13, 1919, SD 862.85/89, NA.

8. Robinson memorandum to House, May 28, 1919, House Papers. For American concerns see Hurley to Robinson, May 24, 1919, Daniels Papers; Daniels to Hurley, June 2, 1919, ibid.

Shipping Co-operation." The article maintained that there had been in reality no cooperation at all, but rather "a disposition, on both sides, to overlook the tremendous issues involved, in a continuous series of petty scrambles for single ships or cargoes." Wittingly or unwittingly, the board had given the impression that the United States was deliberately attempting to take advantage of Great Britain by depriving it of its legitimate prewar commerce. These declarations had been accepted literally by British citizens and officials alike, who contrived a retaliatory policy. It was as if the two countries "were hostile American trusts of the olden days, one bent upon eliminating the other from competition by driving it into bankruptcy." The only solution was an Anglo-American agreement upon shipbuilding programs and the designation of trade routes "so as not to increase the supply of tonnage beyond the proper figure, in a helter-skelter scramble for business."[9]

But Payne and the White House were unmoved by Stevens' indirect appeal. When Lansing inquired about the accuracy of the article, Payne responded that it had always been the board's earnest desire to pursue a policy of friendly competition, but that regretably this did "not seem to be the policy pursued by the British."[10] Wilson interpreted Allied behavior in much the same way: He revealed to Lansing that he was so completely put out by Allied selfishness that he was "almost inclined to refuse to permit the country to be a member of the League of Nations."[11]

In September, these attitudes were intensified by new developments. The tanker issue had importance beyond the gratification of American commercial interests because it affected Wilson's plan to reintegrate Germany as quickly as possible into the European commonwealth of states he so fervently desired. On that basis, whether Standard Oil or its Allied competitors ultimately gained custody of the tankers was immaterial, the State Department observed, for Germany desparately needed petroleum. Idle tankers counteracted the Wilson effort to stabilize and strengthen the German economy to enable it to satisfy not only immediate domestic needs

9. Charles S. Haight, "The United States Vs. Great Britain," carbon copy in RG 32/Stevens, NA. The article was retitled upon publication. See also Haight to Stevens, June 27, 1919, ibid.

10. Alvey A. Adee to USSB, August 25, 1919, SD 195.03/8a, NA; Payne to Lansing, August 29, 1919, SD 195.03/9, NA.

11. "The President's Feelings as to the Present European Situation," August 20, 1919, Robert Lansing Papers.

but also the awesome reparations demands sure to be required by the Allies. Mindful of the Supreme Council's prior pledge to allow Germany "freedom of commercial intercourse," the State Department urged its European mission in mid-September to press vigorously for a decision that would allow the use of the tankers for the carriage of oil from the United States to Germany pending the final disposition of the vessels in conformity with treaty provisions.[12]

But this plea at once ran into an Allied roadblock. In fact, measures had already been taken to prevent such a possibility. All the tankers in question had been declared eligible for trade by the Wilson–Lloyd George Agreement. Yet, when Germany expressed a desire in midsummer to use these vessels to transport American oil, the president of the Allied Naval Armistice Commission, a British admiral, cancelled the exemption on the basis of what the United States naval advisor, Admiral H. S. Knapp, termed an "arbitrary assumption of power."[13] No tangible justification for the cancellation order was offered. The ANAC's decision was quickly endorsed by the Allied Maritime Transport Executive, the next office in the Peace Commission's chain of command. Then, at a hastily called meeting in Brussels on September 20, notice of which apparently did not reach the Paris-based American delegation in time, the Supreme Economic Council (SEC) voted to uphold the cancellation order. Although the United States did not have official representation on the SEC (Wilson had skeletonized the American Delegation across the board in July), proceeding without notifying the American delegation violated patterns previously employed and raised suspicions among the mission's membership. The American delegation also claimed that such decision making did not belong to the SEC, which had exceeded its authority, but was the special province of the ultimate voice on the Peace Commission, the Supreme Council, to which Frank L. Polk, undersecretary of state and America's ranking representative in Europe, was officially assigned. The situation worsened when news was received that the SEC had ordered the immediate removal of the tankers from their Hamburg berths to the Firth of Forth.[14] While this action

12. Phillips to Polk, September 16, 1919, SD 862.85/95, NA.
13. Admiral H. S. Knapp memorandum to American Commission to Negotiate Peace, September 18, 1919, Polk Papers.
14. Norman Armour to Polk, September 21, 1919, SD 862.85/102, NA; Ellis Loring Dresel to Polk, September 23, 1919, Polk Papers.

appeared as much the result of Allied concern to avoid another Scapa Flow as a reflection of British desire to gain an advantage over Standard Oil, Wilson's administrators believed that the United States had been dealt a crooked hand and labored in late September to reverse the decision.[15]

In the waning days of the month, John Barton Payne and his supporters on the Shipping Board seized the initiative. Two factors enabled Payne to put into effect a plan designed to defeat the Allied position. The first involved the disposition of the eight German passenger liners obtained on temporary assignment by the United States as a result of the Wilson–Lloyd George Agreement. These ships, including the *Imperator,* at 52,117 deadweight tons the largest vessel afloat, had just terminated their assigned tasks of repatriating American servicemen for the Army Department. In late September, they were being reconditioned for turnover to the British, in whose custody the Allied Reparation Commission had just determined they would permanently reside as compensation for war losses. Payne had initially denied that the USSB had any role in the transfer of these ships from the army to Great Britain, but he suddenly changed his mind when he apparently sensed that so long as the liners remained in American hands he had a powerful means by which to pressure the Allies into releasing the tankers to Standard Oil, or at least to obtain a favorable settlement.[16] The second factor enabling Payne to move came when Wilson suffered his famous nervous and physical breakdown on September 25, 1919 in Pueblo, Colorado while campaigning for the League. Profiting from the shock and confusion caused by the president's serious illness and the subsequent collapse of lines of authority and communication, on September 27, with Rosseter's strong support, Payne arbitrarily refused to release the liners to British shipping authorities.[17]

Responding to Assistant Secretary of State William Phillips' request for

15. Phillips to Polk, September 23, 1919, SD 862.85/107, NA; Phillips to Polk, September 25, 1919, SD 862.85/108, NA. Polk acknowledged that the scuttling of the German naval fleet at Scapa Flow had played a role in the decision. See Polk's memorandum, undated (circa October 15, 1919), Polk Papers.

16. R. S. Crenshaw memorandum, September 9, 1919, RG 45/VE, NA; Memorandum of a phone conversation between Commander Ghormely and General Hines, September 27, 1919, ibid.

17. This was not the only effort to take advantage of the president's illness to benefit petroleum interests. See Clifford W. Trow, "Woodrow Wilson and the Mexican Interventionist Movement of 1919."

a statement explaining Payne's move, Rosseter painted the board's usual dark picture of Allied commercial machinations. In the process he listed all the grievances that had accumulated over the past two months and in every case took a position in support of the Standard Oil Company's interests. Rosseter first cited the decision of the British president of the ANAC in overriding the company's claim as arbitrary, precipitant, and uncalled-for behavior. He noted "the exceptional speed of action" that seemed to govern Allied moves, implying that the British intended to rush this form of discrimination through before the United States could adequately respond. Payne and the board, Rosseter pointed out, believed that the whole purpose in Britain's action was "to obstruct American–German oil business." He also argued that rumours suggested that the French and British had already arranged for the disposition of the tankers on the basis of secret agreements that would support French plans to further a government petroleum monopoly. Rosseter concluded that inasmuch as it would furnish a significant precedent in determining the future of ships sailing under the German flag but equitably owned by the United States, "a strong position in this case [is] very important."[18]

Lansing interpreted these justifications in a dispatch to Polk on September thirtieth. To Lansing, the entire question appeared to involve the rivalry between Standard Oil and Royal Dutch Shell. He believed that in order to protect Standard Oil's German oil market it would be essential to prevent the company's tankers from falling into the hands of its chief foreign competitors. Unless his instructions were followed carefully there was a danger that an unfortunate precedent would be established. Lansing then ordered Polk to press for a reconsideration by the Supreme Council with a goal of either allowing the tankers to proceed to sea on business designated by Standard Oil or allocating all of them provisionally to the United States. The Allies should be made to understand that such action was by no means intended to prejudice any solutions ultimately reached by the Associated Powers. Above all, Polk had to prevent the tankers from being put into British or French service, or there would be great difficulty in retrieving them for the company.[19]

18. Rosseter memorandum for Lansing, September 28, 1919, RG 32/555-8, NA. See also Robinson to Payne, October 1, 1919, ibid. Robinson had already resigned.
19. Lansing to Polk, September 30, 1919, SD 862.85/110, NA.

Despite Lansing's support, Payne's decision to embargo the *Imperator* group of ships was assailed immediately from many sides. Although most board members appeared to agree with the chairman, Stevens, ever the adversary, protested strongly that the Shipping Board's action in retaining the *Imperator* and announcing that it would put the German ships into service seriously violated the Brussels Agreement.[20] In the State Department, Lansing found that the majority agreed with Stevens.

Polk's reaction was absolutely vitriolic. His initial response was to blaim the board's action on Rosseter's Anglophobia, for he could perceive no legal grounds whatsoever justifying the decision. In every case, the move was sure to widen the chasm in Anglo-American relations. Irritation in England was immense. Not only were the British aware of the blatant illegality of Payne's act and the fact that the United States already retained the majority of Germany's tankers, they still bitterly resented the concession Wilson had wrangled from Lloyd George. The matter was one of a most "delicate character" with any new aggravation certain to magnify old grievances: "My experience with the Shipping Board leads me to believe that they insist on rights which do not exist and that Rossiter [*sic*] was frequently influenced by the individual interests of American corporations rather than the just claims of the United States Government."[21] John Foster Dulles, now an advisor to the State Department and quondam American representative to the Interim Reparations Committee, prepared a memorandum that spelled out Polk's protests in depth. The Wilson–Lloyd George Agreement, Dulles argued, had conceded to the United States shipping twice as great as American losses during the war and given the nation "a tremendous advantage," whereas the Allies would have only a small fraction of their war losses replaced. Against that fact, holding the *Imperator* group was an inexcusable breach of faith. The Shipping Board had adopted a "drastic retaliatory action, of a gravity entirely disproportionate to the importance of the tankers."[22]

While they did not express it, Polk and Dulles were also aware that the British had sent more than a thousand crewmen and officers to New York to sail the liners back across the Atlantic. Without employment and dis-

---

20. Stevens to Payne, September 29, 1919, RG 32/555-8, NA.
21. Polk to Lansing, September 30, 1919, SD 862.85/109C, NA.
22. Dulles memorandum for Lansing, "In Re German Ships," undated (circa October 1–2, 1919), RG 32/555-8, NA.

gruntled at being put up on Ellis Island like common immigrants, the men were "running the streets" and "getting out of hand" in the metropolitan area and forcing the British government to pay royally and begrudgingly for their upkeep. In addition, it was painfully clear to the British, and a blow to their nautical pride, that the United States now possessed the two largest vessels in the world, for the Shipping Board had confiscated the *Leviathan,* sister ship to the *Imperator,* at the time of American entry into the war. Moreover, Englishmen did not forget the loss of the *Lusitania,* Britain's second largest liner, to a German submarine.[23]

The British Embassy raised most of those issues in a meeting with the State Department on October sixth. Sir Edward Grey, still British ambassador to the United States, regarded the action of the Shipping Board as inexplicable, unless it was caused by friction over the tankers. Although England was only one of five major powers expressing interest in the tankers, the board's action appeared to lay the entire blame on Great Britain. In addition, Grey pointed out, the question of quartering the British seamen sent over to man the ships was causing his country great embarrassment. Lansing, however, did not commiserate with Grey but perceived a good opportunity to explain the American position. While refusing to endorse the Shipping Board's action, he nevertheless indicated that many of his colleagues felt that the United States had been treated shabbily in regard to the tankers. He noted that "the confusion and difficulty had arisen on account of the arbitrary action and obstructive tactics" of the British president of the ANAC and that the weight placed on these matters by the strength of American public opinion could not be overemphasized. Arguing that there was at least a theoretical connection between the two questions, he suggested that if Great Britain would support the American position, the tankers question could be readily settled. Convinced that he had impressed the British with the validity of the American argument, Lansing urged Polk to continue to pressure the British and, until the matter was again considered by the Supreme Council, do his utmost to keep the tankers berthed in Hamburg.[24]

23. See, for instance, John R. Ditmars, Jr. to Anthony Caminetti (commissioner general of immigration), October 5, 1919, RG 32/1091 5023, NA; and a verbatim conversation between E. M. Raeburn of the British Embassy and a reporter for the Associated Press, undated, ibid.

24. Lansing to Polk, October 6, 1919, SD 862.85/117, NA.

Payne made it clear, however, that he was not about to acquiesce on the ship issue except on terms clearly favorable to the United States. Lansing reported that it was becoming increasingly difficult even to communicate with the board, a matter made worse by Wilson's inability to exert a coordinating influence. To Lansing, the board had combined not two, but five, questions, on none of which it would compromise. They included (1) a determination to put a stop to arbitrary acts by the British Admiralty and British Shipping Ministry and (2) to obtain favorable solutions to the tanker issue, (3) the *Imperator* case, (4) controversies with the French over ships confiscated in 1917, and (5) Allied requests for the supply and transportation of coal. The shipping issue, as Lansing saw it, could well be deadlocked for some time.[25] Payne emphasized the inflexibility of his attitude in a note sent pointedly to the British Shipping Ministry's Sir Joseph Maclay. The United States would not release the *Imperator* group "until Great Britain turned over the tankers to the United States flag." Payne went on to imply that he was not bluffing, for the Shipping Board's requirements for passenger service dictated the importance of securing a "sensible proportion" of Germany's liner class ships, either afloat or building. Rosseter had already announced publicly that the division of operations was proceeding with plans to put the *Imperator* group into service as passenger and freight liners, perhaps as early as April 1920.[26]

Though Lansing had initially been inclined to see value in Payne's position, Polk's constant protest and Payne's utter intractability had their effect upon him. Polk pointed out repeatedly that he disagreed with Lansing's "theoretical" coupling of the tankers and *Imperator* group issues. Payne's handling of the affair was a clear case of blackmail, would never stand up in court, and would possibly provoke the British into an impossible position on the tankers issue. He was convinced that the State Department had accomplished everything for which the Standard Oil Company was "reasonably entitled to ask" and he hesitated to fight further for its claims. Lansing's suggestion that the tankers be allowed to proceed on such business as their owners desired, Polk maintained, actually prejudged the whole question, as true ownership had not been determined by the Repara-

25. Lansing to Polk, October 10, 1919, SD 862.85/125, NA.
26. Payne to Sir Joseph Maclay, October 14, 1919, RG 32/555-8, NA; *New York Times*, October 4, 16, 1919.

tion Commission. Moreover, Polk felt that the Standard Oil Company was acting in bad faith itself: In his opinion, the company had done "all it could to divest itself from its legal title in order to prevent seizure by Germany [during the war]."[27] Perhaps the best solution, Polk said in an aside to John Davis, the American ambassador to London, would be for Lansing to "take John Barton Payne and chuck him into the river."[28]

By mid-October, Lansing was wavering. The linking of the *Imperator* and the tankers by the Shipping Board was a clear case of expediency, he admitted to Polk. But the secretary could not communicate with Payne and was unable to obtain an audience with the bedridden president, who had the final authority to veto Payne's decision. The president's increasing personal antagonism to Lansing, which grew out of differences over the League, complicated the State Department's position. Mrs. Wilson, the president's intermediary throughout the period, shared her husband's animus. Testimony before the Senate Foreign Relations Committee in mid-September had charged Lansing with disloyalty on the League issue. Lansing had chosen to ignore the allegations, which Wilson considered treasonous, and would probably have been cashiered had not the Western trip and the president's collapse intervened.[29] Compromised as well by increasing Anglophobia in the domestic political environment, Lansing could do little more than express his disapproval to those who would listen.[30]

Payne took full advantage of the situation. On October 21, Lansing held a long cabinet meeting to explain his opposition to the Shipping Board's position. Most of the cabinet appeared to agree that Payne had no right to hold the *Imperator* and that the affair was causing considerable distress in England. Daniels urged that Payne be invited to come to the meeting to present the board's side of the affair. Lansing opened the questioning by asking Payne if his action was not in fact specifically designed to benefit the Standard Oil Company. "That is an impertinence," Payne responded. To Lansing's second question he replied identically. Attorney General A. Mitchell Palmer then salvaged a tense situation by asking tactful questions.

27. Polk to Lansing, October 10, 13, 1919, SD 862.85/110 and 123, NA.
28. Polk to Davis, October 19, 1919, Polk Papers.
29. See, for instance, Joseph Tumulty, *Woodrow Wilson as I Know Him,* pp. 441–45; Daniel M. Smith, "Robert Lansing and the Wilson Interregnum, 1919–1920."
30. Lansing to Polk, October 16, 1919, SD 862.85/126, NA.

Payne thereupon justified his action upon the grounds that Great Britain had embarked upon a policy to obstruct American maritime growth and expansion. Except by direction of the president he would not change his position.[31] After the meeting Payne informed Davis in London that no settlement would be forthcoming until Wilson was "sufficiently recovered to give the matter his personal attention."[32] In a highly appropriate analogy, a member of the State Department remarked later that as Wilson had always dominated American diplomacy, his disability had so paralyzed foreign policy that one got the feeling of a "ship at sea with engines stopped."[33] Since no solution was better than a compromise as far as Payne was concerned, Wilson's illness had become a refuge of considerable and efficacious importance. As Polk expressed it, Wilson's incapacitation "was responsible for the whole difficulty."[34]

At this point, Polk tried to provide the State Department with a workable policy. His position was unexpectedly made easier by German shipping authorities in Hamburg who (apparently at the behest of Standard Oil officials) were able to detain the tankers in late October by instigating a "sympathetic strike."[35] Given this breathing space, Polk emphasized to the British that their position on the tankers was having such an unfavorable effect on American efforts to ratify the Treaty of Versailles that the State Department could in no way consent to any settlement that would be "at the expense of long vested American interests."[36] Turning to Lansing, he impressed upon the secretary the need to alter tactics: The problem was now clearly not so much a concern for oil for Germany but "a straight out and out fight for the Standard Oil Company." Consequently, Polk urged Lansing to recognize that because the oil company's claim was a purely legal one, the Supreme Council, as a politically motivated body, would more than likely be unwilling to sit as a court. The Reparation Commission, however, could be expected to act judiciously according to its delegated

31. Daniels, *Cabinet Diaries*, October 21, 1919, p. 451.

32. Payne to Davis, in Payne to Tumulty, October 23, 1919, Wilson Papers.

33. J. V. A. MacMurray to Roland Morris, February 7, 1920, Morris Papers.

34. Polk Diary, October 28, 1919, Polk Papers.

35. "Memorandum submitted to the SC by the British Delegation, October 23, 1919," in *Documents on British Foreign Policy, 1919–1939*, ed. E. L. Woodward and R. Butler, 2:111; "Notes of a meeting of the heads of Delegations of the Five Great Powers held in Paris, Nov. 14, 1919," SD 180.03501/92, NA.

36. Polk memorandum to Sir Eyre Crowe, October 25, 1919, Polk Papers.

authority. In the meantime, he would avoid comment on the Shipping Board's action, which he deplored, and stress instead the complications that had arisen as the result of Wilson's incapacitation and the American political situation.[37]

To get a clearer line on the reality of events and attitudes in the United States, Polk sent home a member of his European delegation, Lester H. Woolsey, a solicitor to the State Department. Woolsey investigated for two weeks and outlined the situation to Polk on November fourth: With one major exception, Polk's views were pretty much agreed to. The exception was the tankers case, but that did not surprise Woolsey as the Standard Oil Company and the Shipping Board had been "sitting on the bedpost" of the department ever since the case had opened and been "filling the ears of everyone with their own side of the case." As a result of this incessant clamor, the department had taken the position that the Supreme Council should decide the legal question of the tankers' ownership. After a warm discussion with John Bassett Moore, the company's attorney on the case, Woolsey was convinced that Standard Oil wanted the decision made by the Supreme Council because its verdicts had to be unanimous. In the Reparation Commission, simple majorities prevailed. As the case appeared to be clearly weighted against the company, Standard Oil was anxious to have the question decided on the council, because one negative vote (meaning Polk's) would enable the State Department to hold up a decision for an indeterminate period. Woolsey had been working assiduously and with apparent success to convince the department to discard the Supreme Council policy for a sensible decision by the Reparation Commission, once the United States had ratified the treaty and named a commissioner to it.[38]

On the following day, Lansing acknowledged that he had been influenced by Woolsey and Polk: Although the department had formerly thought it wise to support a decision-making role for the Supreme Council as the surest means of safeguarding American rights out of fear that an adverse decision by the Reparation Commission, based upon European political and economic requirements rather than upon judicial principles, would strengthen the position of the senators who opposed the League, a positive League

37. Polk to Lansing, October 27, 1919, SD 862.85/130, NA. See also Polk's much more frank note to Phillips, October 27, 1919, Polk Papers.

38. Woolsey to Polk, November 4, 1919, Polk Papers.

position could now best be served by avoiding any sort of decision by the council. Inasmuch as the Reparation Commission would not adjudicate the question until at least two months after the treaty came into force, it would be best to employ this avenue so that a verdict would not prejudice the Senate as it concluded its deliberations over the treaty. Lansing did not say why he had not thought of this tactic before, as the delayed decision-making authority of the Reparation Commission was established in the Wilson–Lloyd George Agreement. Nevertheless, it seemed inadvisable to maintain as hard a line on the tanker question.[39] Elaborating upon the concerns of Davis in London, Lansing then wrote to Payne, pointing out that indiscriminate statements to the press by Shipping Board members were seriously fraying British nerves. Unless properly leashed, the secretary warned, Payne's uncompromising attitudes would complicate the economic and political relations of the two countries at a moment when cooperation and understanding were absolutely essential.[40]

In late October, Polk and Lansing attempted to put pressure on the British by taking advantage of France's desperate need for tonnage. On November 2, André Tardieu, the French minister of shipping, communicated with Polk about France's crying requirements for coal. Although arrangements for large quantities had already been made in the United States, the coal could not be shipped because of the lack of vessels. Tardieu confided that Premier Georges Clemenceau personally desired to request shipping aid from the United States but could not do so himself for fear of losing political face if he were refused. In response, Polk suggested that the Shipping Board could assuredly be persuaded to supply the necessary tonnage provided the French "would compromise on the tank ships."[41] Payne's response, however, was short and vague. His only concrete offer was a proposal to sell tonnage sufficient to meet the emergency. Polk hastily called for a more definitive statement, for time was of the essense; he felt that it was only a matter of hours before the tankers would be forceably moved to British waters. The board responded by expressing a willingness to accept a reasonable proposal from the French for ships to relieve the coal shortage, but insisted that it would not take action until the French specified

---

39. Lansing to Polk, November 5, 1919, Polk Papers.
40. Lansing to Payne, November 5, 1919, SD 195.03/9, NA.
41. Polk to Lansing, November 2, 1919, SD 862.85/133A, NA.

their needs. The board was also willing to sell tonnage, but only after receiving an initial offer. The implication was that such a move on its own initiative would weaken the board's intransigent position on the tankers.[42]

Polk subsequently noted that the French appeared to have taken a conciliatory position on the tankers as a result of these negotiations.[43] But on November 14 in the Supreme Council a fiery discussion of the whole question refirmed hardened lines and largely nullified Polk's efforts at compromise. Sir Eyre Crowe represented British views. Remarking on the "notorious fact" that unending difficulties arose whenever the question of oil was broached, Crowe took a tack that an American delegate felt had already been seriously overworked, "usually to the disadvantage of the United States." Crowe maintained that Standard Oil and its German affiliates were playing both sides for fools. Aided and abetted by the company, the Germans were working for time and counting on dissension between the Allied and Associated Powers. The ability to retain the tankers in Hamburg was ostensibly aiding the United States, but Polk was to go under advisement that no compromise would ever be extended by Great Britain until the tankers were moved. The question had "become one of the honor and prestige of the Allied and Associated Powers in the eyes of the Germans." The holding of the *Imperator* group by the Shipping Board would in no way effect the outcome—the tankers had to be sailed to the Firth of Forth. The French and Italian representatives readily concurred.[44] Polk informed Lansing that the discussion had gone badly for the United States. To Davis he was even more explicit. His unsuccessful fight for the Standard Oil Company had left him in a "murderous mood. If the Government is going to have me represent the Standard Oil, I think they should at least allow me to charge the usual legal rate of corporation lawyers."[45] Unable to rationalize doing otherwise, Polk acceded to the Allied position and voted with the Supreme Council to have the Allied Naval Armistice

42. Payne to Lansing, November 7, 1919, RG 32/Operations, NA; Lansing to Polk, November 12, 1919, SD 862.85/139, NA.

43. Polk to Lansing, November 12, 1919, SD 862.85/139A, NA.

44. N. A. McCully to Polk, October 24, 1919, Polk Papers; "Notes of a meeting of the heads of Delegations of the Five Great Powers held in Paris, Nov. 14, 1919," SD 180.03501/92, NA.

45. Polk to Lansing, November 14, 1919, SD 862.85/140A, NA; Polk to Davis, November 15, 1919, Polk Papers.

Commission remove all fourteen tankers from German waters. The nine tankers claimed by Standard Oil were to be retained in the Firth of Forth pending further discussion by the council.[46]

New developments at that point both strengthened and weakened Payne's position. Lansing's view of the shipping question appeared to have finally breached the security set up around the president by his wife and physician. Moreover, the department's legal counsel had discussed the issue in great depth with Joseph Tumulty, Wilson's personal secretary. After being excluded from the president's quarters for more than a month, Tumulty was now allowed limited contact with the chief executive. Lansing hoped that these contacts would result in Wilson authorizing Tumulty to have the Shipping Board transfer the liners to the British at once. A reply was expected from Wilson momentarily. In addition, various representatives of the Shipping Board were concerned that the job of maintaining the *Imperator* group was becoming a grave financial burden and causing serious complications regarding crews and docking facilities. "Except for the position of the Chairman who apparently will not listen to argument," Lansing pointed out, "it would seem that the Board for their own protection would be forced to hand over the *Imperator* group regardless of the decision of the President."[47]

Both developments materialized quickly, but not as Lansing would have wished. On the seventeenth of November, the White House informed the secretary that Wilson did not have sufficient strength to consider the *Imperator* affair.[48] Clearly, what vitality Wilson did have was going into his final unsuccessful effort to save the League, at that moment only hours from defeat. On the same day, Payne was forced to make a distasteful decision: The *Imperator* would be released. Payne confronted the board with the problem: Daniels had formally demanded that all the American seamen (over 1,000) manning the ships be relieved no later than November 25. Most of these men had been drafted and were due for discharge. Because there was little likelihood that any compromise arrangements could be

46. "Notes of a meeting of the heads of Delegations of the Five Great Powers held in Paris, Nov. 17, 1919," SD 180.03501/94, NA.

47. Lansing to Polk, November 15, 1919, SD 862.85/141, NA.

48. Phillips to Polk, November 17, 1919, Polk Papers; Lansing to Polk, November 19, 1919, SD 862.85/146, NA.

made with England prior to that date, the board faced two alternatives: It could man the ships with its own crews and place them in commercial service, or it could release the vessels, all of them, to the British without a quid pro quo.[49] As it turned out, Payne actually adopted a third alternative offered by Newton Baker; shortly after the board meeting, he decided to transfer only the *Imperator,* recognizing it for the white elephant it was in so many respects.[50] But the remaining seven liners would not be delivered until the United States had secured the tankers, which Payne was convinced legally belonged to the Standard Oil Company, despite evidence to the contrary.[51] Payne then responded to charges the State Department had made over the previous weeks. He protested strongly that the board had always adhered to a "passive policy" in its relations with Great Britain. Rate cutting had been the British forte, not the Shipping Board's. All the board asked was "free and fair competition." As for irresponsible publicity, Payne doubted whether anything the board might have said could have favorably influenced British maritime opinion without correspondingly weakening the confidence of American shipping interests. Admittedly, there had been a great deal of needless irritation on both sides of the Atlantic, but much of it had been virtually uncontrollable. The board was prepared to meet England halfway on any plan designed to eliminate ruinous competition between their merchant marines, but its current position would not allow it to take an initial step. Great Britain would have to make the first compromise move.[52]

For four weeks, the Shipping Board sat tight. When Lord Curzon, the new British foreign secretary, requested information from Davis in London about the position the board could be expected to take, Payne did not reply.

49. Payne to Donald, Scott, Rosseter, and Cushing, November 17, 1919, RG 32/555-8, NA. There is no evidence that Daniels did this to embarrass Payne.

50. Baker to Tumulty, November 14, 1919, Wilson Papers. See also *New York Times,* November 22, 1919, for the New York shipping community's observations on the *Imperator's* costliness. By comparison, the next largest liner, the *Kaiserin Augusta Victoria,* at 24,581 deadweight tons, was less than half its size. Fittingly, Payne got in a parting shot by holding up the *Imperator's* departure for several days by charging that without authorization British officials had overloaded the vessel with coal. See *New York Times,* December 8–11, 1919.

51. Payne to Lansing, November 19, 1919, in Lansing to Polk, November 19, 1919, SD 862.85/146, NA; RG 32/Minutes of Proceedings of the USSB, November 20, 1919, NA.

52. Payne to Lansing, November 21, 1919, RG 32/Operations, NA.

On the twelfth of December, Payne was reminded by the State Department that Curzon's request had urgent importance and required an early response.[53] Payne replied four days later that the situation had not changed. Once the Allies turned over the tankers to the Standard Oil Company, the board would deliver the remaining vessels of the *Imperator* group to the British crews and officials waiting in New York. Until this was agreed upon or until Wilson himself finally assumed overriding authority, Payne could be expected to do nothing.[54] On the instructions of Curzon, the British Embassy retorted in now familiar terms: The two questions were entirely distinct and could not legitimately be connected with each other. Until the Shipping Board separated the issue, the tankers would remain in British custody.[55] Close to three months had now passed, and neither side had even come close to breaking the stalemate.

Absolutely fed up, Lansing responded to Payne's latest refusal to compromise by writing him a scorching letter four days before Christmas, first sending it to the president. Lansing believed the British Embassy's position was correct: There was no relationship between the two maritime matters, and the Shipping Board's seizure of the *Imperator* group as a reprisal against Allied decisions on the tankers had "embarrassed action of our diplomatic representatives in the settlement of certain matters of interest to the United States and Great Britain [and] become the most effective obstacle to a solution of the tanker controversy itself." Such unwarranted action had also placed a large financial burden on the British government by forcing it to maintain crews in New York. In Lansing's opinion, the United States would have to admit to the legitimacy of the claim and pay it in its entirety (the final bill came to $720,000). Arguing that all the major questions that could have been resolved concerning the tankers had been dealt with a month before, Lansing insisted that Payne release the vessels in accordance with the British government's demands.[56]

Lansing's note drew the long awaited White House decision. Edith Bolling Wilson informed Payne that her husband "much to his regret, [had found] no ground for differing from the Sec[retary] of State's judg-

53. Lord Curzon to Davis, November 26, 1919, SD 862.85/149, NA; Adee to Payne, December 12, 1919, RG 32/555-8, NA.

54. Payne to Adee, December 16, 1919, RG 32/555-8, NA.

55. Sir Auckland Geddes to Lansing, December 19, 1919, RG 32/555-8, NA.

56. Lansing to Payne, undated and routed via Wilson to Payne on December 21, 1919, RG 32/555-8, NA.

ment in this important matter."[57] Payne forthwith released the liners to the British. Severed from their relationship to the *Imperator* group, the tankers were held in the Firth of Forth for another half year, at which point the Reparation Commission allocated them to the Standard Oil Company on a provisional basis pending continued study. Not until the Calvin Coolidge administration was the issue resolved. On August 5, 1925, an arbitration tribunal voted two to one that Standard Oil had not made good its claim to the tankers. The tankers, their proceeds, and the proceeds of three tankers sold by agreement in the interim period, would have to be turned over to the Reparation Commission for subsequent distribution among the Allies. With minor reservations, the State Department agreed, and Standard Oil was compelled to comply.[58]

Precisely why it took so long for the White House to take action on the *Imperator* question will probably remain one of those historical enigmas connected with Wilson's illness. As there is no evidence Wilson ever considered the matter prior to the twenty-first of December, it is possible that he had not been apprised of it and that Mrs. Wilson had pigeonholed the matter as comparatively unimportant, a tactic she employed freely. What was meant by the phrase "much to his regret" also remains unclear. If this remark was genuinely Wilson's sentiment, three factors bearing on this episode might account for it: first, Wilson's deepseated antagonism toward the Allies and what he interpreted as their tendency toward selfish commercialism; second, the personal falling-out with Lansing; third, his longstanding support for the American merchant marine. In short, Wilson, singly or collectively, regretted having to give in to the British, loathed having to reach an accomodation with Lansing, or reluctantly sanctioned a measure that in effect defeated and embarrassed the Shipping Board's position. As nothing further came from either the president or his wife interpreting the expression, these appear to offer the most plausible explanation.

57. Edith Bolling Wilson to Payne, December 23, 1919 [should have been dated December 21], RG 32/555-8, NA; Payne to Lansing, December 21, 1919, ibid.

58. For the legal background to the tanker case, see "Majority Award in the Case of the Tankers of Standard Oil Company," in Ralph W. S. Hill to Charles Evans Hughes, August 13, 1926, U.S., State Department, *FR, 1926*, 2:166–95. For the final American agreement, see Frank Kellogg to Myron Herrick, November 17, 1926, ibid., pp. 198–99.

Chapter X

The Merchant Marine
Act of 1920

Wilson's acquiescence in the *Imperator* case did not signal in any way a diminution of his resolve to strengthen the nation's maritime position and hence its international commercial role. The president reemphasized these directions in his annual message of December 2, 1919. "The provincial standards and policies of the past, which have held American business as if in a straight-jacket, must yield and give way to the needs and exigencies of the new day in which we live," he remarked. The recent war had terminated the insular character of the American economy. The nation's productivity, accelerated beyond all expectation, required an outlet for its exports. The government's ships, his message implied, had not been built for a nation intent upon commercial isolation.[1]

One of the first congressional orders of business to come up in late 1919 concerned how Wilson's huge merchant fleet would be employed in peacetime commerce. To the vast majority of the Sixty-sixth Congress, conditions warranting continued federal construction and control simply no longer existed. Large numbers of Democrats, as well as Republicans, shared this sentiment. Returning to the prewar business view that it would not be desirable for government to retain ownership of the fleet, and to the stipulations of the Shipping Act of 1916 that government was to relinquish its shipping business within five years after the war, Congress determined to repeal the emergency measures and reform the organizations that had

1. U.S., State Department, *FR, 1919*, 1:x–xi.

carried them out. On November 8, 1919, the House voted overwhelmingly (240 to 8) to annul emergency provisions and prevent the Shipping Board from letting additional building contracts. The measure then went to the Senate Committee on Commerce. Under the leadership of Washington senator Wesley Jones, the committee reflected House attitudes by determining that the time was propitious for legislation that would promote an American merchant marine operated by private ownership yet provide for a strong program of government initiatives and supports.[2]

Jones opened hearings on a new shipping bill in January 1920. Archetypical of the men who had become involved in the maritime program, Jones was obsessed with concerns about trade rivalries and foreign discrimination and had already established himself as a member of the growing congressional lobby supporting protectionist and retaliatory policies. Maintaining that the effort to create a "shipping mentality" and a lasting and effective American merchant marine would have to be accomplished "in the face of the most determined opposition and the fiercest competition," Jones insisted upon reading into the record a pair of recent statements relating to the situation. One expressed the American view, the other the British. The American statement came appropriately from John Rosseter, now back in private West Coast shipping circles after resigning from the Shipping Board in December. On January 6, 1920, Rosseter gave the San Francisco *Examiner* an interview. He compared the world shipping business with something like an athletic contest, a "big and stiff game," as he called it. In the competitive arena, training and teamwork spelled the difference between victory and defeat. At the moment, however, America was still at the novice stage while the other teams in the league were "skillful, determined, aggressive, [and] trained to play us for our lives." The competition gloated over America's predicament, laying long odds against the possibility that the United States could make a decent showing. These odds were based upon an appraisal of the American maritime effort from two viewpoints, as an "all-Government team, or as an assorted commercial team. [The former] would show up very hefty, but with a lot of weak spots," while America's opponents would figure to beat the commercial team by picking off its members "one by one." Obviously Rosseter's point, which Jones

2. Zeis, *American Shipping Policy*, p. 115.

hoped to emphasize, was that in order to beat the odds America would have to combine its two teams and "meet all comers with a united front."[3]

To make this need doubly clear, Jones then introduced an article from a recent issue of the British shipping organ, *Fairplay*. Published at the height of the *Imperator* struggle, it suggested to Jones an example of the hostile environment in which, if the British had their way, the American maritime program would have to compete.

> Thanks to vigorous instruction from President Wilson and Mr. Hurley [we know] that our friends on the other side have this common with ourselves that they never put their hand to the plow without the fullest intention of driving the furrow to the bitter end, regardless of what may happen to interfering competitors. . . . When it has been a question of the survival of the fittest, we have invariably done our level best to crush or mold opposition, and, as regards America's new merchant marine, we shall go on doing it, and expect her to do the same to us.[4]

Thereafter Jones carried this article with him constantly, pulling it out and playing it to its hilt when the occasion warranted.

While Jones and his committee continued their hearings, Wilson named John Barton Payne secretary of the interior, effective March 15, following the resignation of Franklin K. Lane. Payne accepted the new job reluctantly—his heart was in the shipping business, he remarked. Jones and other members of the Commerce Committee were much disturbed. "To take him away at this time cannot help but lead to delay and disorganization," they protested to the president. In view of the fact that Congress would probably pass shipping legislation in the next two or three months, such a change seemed incongruous to them.[5] While Wilson did not explain the reasons for the switch, he no doubt felt that Payne's recent experiences in shipping and oil, the latter the special province of the Interior Department, made him the most qualified candidate. At that time, the administration was extremely agitated over the international oil situation and what it

---

3. U.S., Congress, Senate, Committee on Commerce, Remarks before the committee, January 21, 1920, *The Establishment of an American Merchant Marine*, 66th Cong., 2d sess., pp. 323, 336.

4. Ibid., pp. 397–409.

5. Fletcher, Jones, McFurnald, and McNam to Wilson, February 16, 1920, Wilson Papers.

interpreted as Great Britain's efforts to buy up oil and oil concessions everywhere in the expectation of controlling world commerce and shipping.[6] British commercial policy so distressed Wilson that he remarked to Polk on March 4 that it was "evident to me that we are on the eve of a commercial war of the severest sort, and I am afraid that Great Britain will prove capable of as great commercial savagery as Germany has displayed for so many years in her competitive methods."[7]

Wilson's reassignment of Payne takes on added interest when one considers that the cabinet was filling up with shipping men. Joshua Alexander, former chairman of the House Committee on Merchant Marine and Fisheries and the foremost House proponent of the Shipping Act of 1916, was appointed Secretary of Commerce pursuant to Redfield's resignation. After Lansing's forced departure in early February, the State Department went to a former Shipping Board commissioner, Bainbridge Colby. Colby also had some oil experience, having served as a legal counsel for the Standard Oil Company during the *Imperator* episode. Naval affairs were still presided over by Josephus Daniels, who had always linked national prosperity with foreign trade and an enlarged American merchant marine.[8]

Payne's move to the Interior Department actually made it possible for Wilson to head up the Shipping Board with a man unparalleled in his desire to live up to the *Fairplay* game plan: former chief of naval operations, Admiral William S. Benson, mandatorily retired from the navy in late September 1919. A Georgian by birth, Benson had caught Daniels' eye early in the Wilson administration. In an extraordinary move, Daniels bypassed five senior captains and twenty-six admirals and named him to be the first chief of naval operations and the ranking senior naval officer.[9] In Paris during the peace negotiations, Benson was an outspoken opponent of British efforts to slow down American naval and maritime growth programs. He had already achieved notoriety for insisting upon the so-called

6. Daniels, *Cabinet Diaries*, March 1, 1920, p. 502.

7. Wilson to Polk, March 4, 1920, Wilson Papers. British feelings were mutual. See Wiseman's remarks as recorded in Polk's Diary, April 12, 1920, Polk Papers.

8. Daniels' most recent pronouncement, "The Navy's Need of a Merchant Marine," was released through the Office of Naval Operations, December 13, 1919, Daniels Papers.

9. Daniels, *Cabinet Diaries*, p. 384, n.; *Dictionary of American Biography*, Supp. 1, s.v. "Benson, William Shepherd."

"Blue Plan," a naval contingency plan for war with England.[10] Subsequently, he had serious scraps with British naval personnel and completely identified with the administration's effort to stem British commercialism. Toward the close of his stay in Europe, he complained to Wilson that those six months had convinced him that "American interests, the American viewpoint, American aims and ideals were entirely foreign to those of the other powers and that in practically all important cases the representatives of the other powers have agreed with the representatives of Great Britain."[11]

Reflecting an age highly sympathetic toward the concept of America for Americans (immigration restriction was just around the corner), Benson intensely disliked and distrusted anything of foreign origin. After attempting to persuade Benson to adopt Raymond Stevens' more conciliatory attitude toward neutral claims arising from the war, Polk found the new chairman already "prejudiced" by the intransigent antiforeign views of his predecessor.[12] A major ingredient in Benson's determination to take a strong stand emanated from his economic and political philosophy. Like so many other Wilsonians, Benson was convinced that the prosperity of the country was contingent upon the successful disposal of its exportable surpluses and that America's ability to compete in the world market was predicated on the delivery of its commodities in first-class condition in the shortest time at the lowest prices. Benson felt that oceanic transportation was an indispensable link in this economic chain and that the nation would be at a decided disadvantage unless it owned and controlled its own shipping. So long as the United States continued to be a great industrial and producing nation, he believed, it would have to maintain a persevering effort at securing outlets for its foreign trade and unyieldingly hold its ground against competitor nations desiring to prejudice the outcome of that mission.[13]

Benson's chairmanship also had certain unique aspects. Wilson's failure to keep the Shipping Board at full strength left Benson with almost dicta-

10. I am obliged to Robert Greenhalgh Albion for a description of the "Blue Plan."
11. Benson to Wilson, May 5, 1919, Daniels Papers.
12. Polk Diary, March 16, 1920, Polk Papers.
13. See, for example, Benson, "Sea Power and its Relation to National Prosperity," undated, Benson Papers; USSB, *Annual Report, 1920*, p. 9; Benson, "Our New Merchant Marine."

torial powers. The Shipping Act of 1916 had authorized a five-man board which stabilized with American entry into the war and remained constant throughout the conflict. With the war's end, however, the board's membership was depleted by Colby's resignation in March 1919 and Charles R. Page's soon after. Thomas A. Scott replaced Colby, and Page's slot was filled by Henry Robinson. But Robinson resigned a few months later, coincident with Wilson's illness and the subsequent paralysis of the executive appointment process. Payne then became Secretary of the Interior, and Benson was appointed Shipping Board chairman. Scott, John A. Donald, and Raymond Stevens remained on the board. Donald had always been a staunch supporter of a combative maritime program, and when Stevens and Scott resigned only weeks after Payne's departure, the Board entirely lost any opposition to Benson's antiforeign, discriminatory policy. In fact, Benson for all extensive purposes became not only chairman but the board itself and operated in this unanticipated manner throughout the remaining months of the Wilson administration.

Benson had his work cut out for him. Hurley and Payne had accomplished virtually nothing during their terms in office toward achieving maritime reorganization. Hurley had been extremely serious about creating a national maritime policy that would provide for private operation and ownership within a system of strong government controls and supervision. Hurley's plans to create such a compromise between conservative and liberal reasoning began to take form in the winter of 1918–1919. These were sidetracked, however, by personal workloads borne of the European mission, by his sickness in the spring of 1919, and by the enormous demands placed upon him and the Shipping Board by the relief and foreign trade programs. Although there was a wave of disappointed protest that a permanent policy could not be attained without his leadership, Hurley had determined for the sake of his family, physician, and business interests to resign.

Payne had also failed to work up a policy, having been distracted completely by the struggle over the *Imperator,* the Standard Oil case, and Wilson's illness. In March 1920, at the penultimate board meeting over which he presided Payne admitted: "We have nothing but ships. We have no organization. We have nothing but ships. So far as the operation of ships is concerned, we are infants." If the Shipping Board did not quickly find a way to make the whole operation pay, it would be "only a question of time before the Congress refuse[s] to appropriate for the deficiencies, and the merchant marine go[es] into the ash heap."[14]

Benson sought to remedy the difficulties by building bigger and better discrimination into the legislation before the Jones Committee. In doing so, he was not breaking new ground, since the movement toward discrimination and preference was rampant throughout the world. He was, however, prepared to go to far greater lengths in this respect than any of his predecessors on the Shipping Board. This was especially true of the manner in which he expressed his interest in upgrading the merchant marine. While Hurley and Payne had not minced words concerning foreign competition, neither had built his rhetorical platform for an American merchant fleet on xenophobia. Benson never ceased to characterize the opposition as alien. Nor was their room in Benson's mind for neutralism. One enthusiastically supported the board's plans or one did not. Those who did not were suspected of having come under alien influence in one of two ways—either they had selfish economic reason to support foreign interests or they had wittingly or unwittingly come under the influence of enemy propaganda. "We must always be on our guard against insidious and falsifying propaganda," Benson warned the National Marine League on April twelfth. It was sufficiently bad that foreign competition had sought to cripple the American merchant marine in the three basic areas of shipping, fuel, and communication, but the most serious obstacle was the foreign "art of propaganda, [employed] to tear down what we are bent on making permanent—an American merchant marine made up of ships built by Americans, owned by American capital, sailing under the American flag, and carrying the products of this country to all parts of the world."[15]

Benson pushed Jones to produce as tough a measure as possible. While the Commerce Committee was already building discrimination into the bill, Benson wanted it to go considerably further. If the Congress truly desired to insure the success of the American merchant marine, he pointed out to Jones, it would have to provide strong subsidies. Benson was considering the European example; although he always strove for 100 percent Amer-

14. RG 32/Verbatim Minutes, March 11, 1920, NA.
15. *New York Times*, April 12, 13, 1920.

ican involvement in all shipping matters, he was not adverse to employing foreign methods. In fact, he considered the prewar commercial system of Germany as the ideal model from which to fashion an American maritime policy. Germany had secured 60 percent of its exports and 50 percent of its imports in German vessels by the use of preferential rail rates. By the same policy, Japan had forced American shippers to employ Japanese ships. Only by adopting identical methods, could the United States hope to maintain its own fleet in world competition.[16] R. A. Dean, the board's general counsel, underlined Benson's concern. The United States had to adopt the restrictive policies of Germany for its own protection. It was the only road to success. The operation would either "result in the greatest commercial enterprise in the world or be a most colossal failure." The decision was up to Congress.[17]

Benson's push for strong federal initiatives was exemplified by a conference he held with Daniels and Newton D. Baker, secretary of war, in mid-May 1920. Baker described the meeting to the president: Benson insisted upon placing all ships then in government service, including those operated by the army, in new commercial and privately controlled trade. He then demanded control over all government harbor facilities and water terminals in the United States. His insistence did not derive simply from a desire for administrative efficiency, but resulted primarily from his obsession with a world view that envisioned the problem as "one of fierce and final competition between the British mercantile marine and the American mercantile marine."[18]

No sooner had Baker's message gone to the White House than Benson called for new lines to Antwerp, Panama, and points in the Pacific. If the Shipping Board did not establish them, he informed the War Department, the nation's competitors would. Benson charged that Baker was hampering his effort by retaining vessels that could be turned over for the Shipping Board's development of needed lines. Daniels felt much the same way; unless service was expanded and consolidated at once, other countries would service those connections and the United States would have to return to the prewar dependency upon foreign transportation.[19]

16. Benson to Jones, April 19, 1920, RG 56/Box 131, NA.
17. Dean to Jones, April 27, 1920, RG 56/Box 131, NA.
18. Baker to Wilson, May 13, 1920, Baker Papers.
19. Benson to Baker, May 13, 1920, Baker Papers; Daniels to Baker, May 14, 1920, RG 45/SP, NA.

Working overtime, Jones cleared a final bill through both houses that reached the president only thirty minutes before the close of the legislative session. The bill was almost solely the product of Benson and the Commerce Committee; there had been virtually no congressional debate, and it was passed without a recorded vote. Benson described the bill on Wilson's desk as one intended "to meet and offset the countless discriminations by other nations against American shipping with which Shipping Board ships and privately owned vessels of the United States have had to contend."[20] Wilson reviewed the pros and cons of the bill with his cabinet on June 1 and sided with the Shipping Board. The president reiterated his old proclivity for "freedom of the seas" but admitted that his concern with British commercial selfishness and his desire to see the American flag floating over a strong merchant marine took precedence.[21] In adopting this shipping policy, Wilson seemed to have completely rejected his disavowal of discrimination in the earlier years of his administration. The president signed the bill into law on June fifth.

The passage of the Merchant Marine Act of 1920, the Jones Act, accomplished two administrative objectives. First, it completed the government's general economic demobilization following the war. Whereas such agencies as the War Industries Board, Food Administration, War Trade Board, and Fuel Administration had been terminated with celerity, in railroads and shipping the administration followed a different tack. The wartime experience had made it clear that major improvements in transportation were necessary and that these could be obtained from federal rationalization, a direction that American transportation interests were leaning toward even before the conflict. Although Congress was not willing to embark upon a full program of public operation, it agreed that government regulation and encouragement in rails and ships should be retained, strengthened, and expanded. Wilson had already dealt with the railroads. As of March first, the Transportation Act of 1920 left operations and liberal profits in corporate hands, but vested the Interstate Commerce Commission with stronger powers, among which were complete control over rates and the ability to recapture excess profits to strengthen weaker lines. Although the Shipping Board had built many of its own vessels while a system of rentals

20. Benson to W. T. Christensen, July 21, 1920, RG 32/618-4, NA.
21. Daniels, *Cabinet Diaries,* June 1, 1920, p. 536.

from private companies prevailed with the railroads, the Merchant Marine Act of 1920 followed the Transportation Act by arranging ways in which the Shipping Board could turn its fleet over to private business and support and regulate its operation and growth. In this light, provisions authorized the board to provide funds to American shipping companies for the construction of new vessels and arranged for the systematic sale of government ships at almost ludicrously low rates—200 wooden ships were sold for the price of one, for example. Sales to aliens, however, were strictly monitored: Only vessels absolutely "unnecessary to the growth and maintenance of an efficient American merchant marine" were eligible. The Jones Act also exempted American shipping companies from corporate income and excess profits taxes, provided the money saved was employed in the construction of new vessels in American shipyards.[22]

These and other provisions were intended to satisfy the second objective—a major strengthening of the foreign trade apparatus of American commerce. The measure resulted in the landmark creation of an "essential trade routes" plan, and directed the Shipping Board to devise means by which to maintain those selected sealanes. If private enterprise was unable to provide service, the Shipping Board was authorized to operate ships in them until it was. Overall, this was designed to encourage American shippers and shipowners to undertake permanent trade with foreign markets deemed necessary by the government for various economic and political reasons. It was also intended to prove the economic feasibility of doing it, and employing private businessmen in the management of public lines would help pave the way for an efficient transition to eventual private ownership. The board was also placed in the business of developing ports and transportation facilities needed for overseas commerce. Additional clauses extended the regulatory principles of the Shipping Act of 1916, giving the USSB authority to supervise the rules and regulations of all government departments, boards, bureaus, or agencies directly or indirectly involved with shipping matters in foreign trade. Further, the act improved the American competitive position by banning from United States ports all

---

22. Cook, *History of the United States Shipping Board*, pp. 10–13; Zeis, *American Shipping Policy*, pp. 116–19; Burl Noggle, *Into the Twenties*, pp. 58–59, 82–83; David A. Shannon, *Twentieth Century America: The Twenties and Thirties*, pp. 50–52.

lines and vessels resorting to deferred rebates, rate cutting (the "fighting ship" tactic), blacklisting, or discrimination.[23]

An important provision circumvented the maritime insurance monopoly of Lloyd's of London by improving American insurance conditions and allowing American marine insurance companies waivers from the antitrust laws. This provision received enthusiastic private and public applause. For years, shipping hearings had convincingly demonstrated that America's foremost maritime competitors employed their maritime insurance programs as powerful commercial weapons. America's weakness stemmed not from lack of capital, but from the independent and nonintegrated manner in which its insurance companies operated. Consequently, the financial base needed to compete with Lloyd's and other major foreign insurance firms could not materialize. Before the war, over two-thirds of the policies issued on American vessels had been foreign. McAdoo's War Risk Insurance program and Hurley's support of a new American Bureau of Shipping created to classify ships during the war had met emergency needs.[24] Now the Jones Act established permanent bases for these advantages. It created a format based upon the recently adopted Webb-Pomerene and Edge acts, measures that encouraged American manufacturers to combine for foreign trade without penalty of prosecution under the Sherman and Clayton antitrust acts.[25] Benson implemented this program on June 30, 1920 by announcing an epoch-making event for American maritime insurance underwriters—the formation of the American Marine Insurance Syndicate. The syndicate was composed of three syndicates in all, two wholly American and one that allowed one-third interest to foreign firms with branches in the United States. For the first time, American underwriters had the ability to cover American hulls at a liability rivaling Lloyd's. Also for the first time, the Jones Act organized American companies to create a comprehensive American service plan for maintenance inspections and shipping surveys, services that such companies as Lloyd's had previously conducted, often at

---

23. Ibid.

24. See Hurley's "Final Report," July 31, 1919, Wilson Papers; Hurley remarks, July 9, 1919, U.S., Congress, House, *Hearings before the Subcommittee on the Merchant Marine and Fisheries*, 66th Cong., 1st sess., pp. 8–11.

25. William F. Notz and Richard S. Harvey, *American Foreign Trade as Promoted by the Webb–Pomerene and Edge Acts;* Kaufman, *Efficiency and Expansion*, pp. 247–48.

great disadvantage to the United States. Fittingly, the first syndicate to be formed, the so-called "A" Syndicate, was headed by Charles R. Page, Shipping Board commissioner under Hurley and recently vice president of the Clyde and Mallory Steamship Company. It is significant that concerned observers in London noted that the USSB's new system paralleled in striking ways the prewar insurance methods and structures of Germany, a nation that had created its own systems for successfully avoiding British underwriters.[26]

Important as these contributions were, they were overshadowed throughout the summer of 1920 by controversy that seethed around three other major provisions of the Merchant Marine Act, all of which were highly discriminatory. One clause extended the coastal monopoly to the Philippines and other remote American insular possessions. A more important clause (Section 28, which was personally inserted by Benson) granted preferential inland rail rates to American cargoes carried in American vessels, provided there was a plethora of American tonnage to handle a port's foreign trade. A final clause (Section 34) instructed the president to abrogate all treaties in conflict with the right of the United States to impose discrimination. As Jones described the new measure, "They say it will drive foreign shipping from our ports. Granted; I want it to do it."[27] Congressional sentiment warmly endorsed this position. And characteristically, as tough as the bill was, Benson complained that the measure was still not tough enough; it did not stipulate that in all ways concerning ownership and personnel United States ships would be 100 percent American. He hoped that the next Congress would correct the deficiency.[28] As it turned out, such an inclusion might have only exacerbated difficulties, for the bill at once ran into serious legal problems.

Controversy focused primarily on one major point, which Section 34 was intended to remedy. The discriminatory provisions of Section 28 violated no fewer than thirty-two foreign treaties. The State Department had already expressed concern. Colby's solicitor predicted that if enacted the bill would in all probability result in retaliation: in "the withdrawal from American citizens engaged in the shipping enterprise and other activities in foreign

26. *New York Times*, July 1, 1920.
27. Cited in C. J. France to Benson, August 19, 1920, RG 32/618-4, NA.
28. Benson to Wilson, June 5, 1920, RG 32/Benson, NA.

countries, of the protection and benefits of favorable treaty provisions, subjecting them and their business to such treatment as the foreign governments see fit to accord them."[29] The postmaster general, Albert S. Burleson, and David F. Houston, secretary of agriculture, opposed the bill on similar grounds, and Payne shortly joined them for the same reasons. Complaints on this point from domestic and foreign sources reached such proportions that Benson was forced to declare a moratorium on the enforcement of Section 28 only four days after the act was passed. For a ninety-day period this section was set aside in order to permit further discussion and study. On July 24, the moratorium was extended to January 1, 1921.

The resistance of Pacific Northwest shipping interests clarified the nature of the problem. Without waiting for official expression from the Imperial government, Japanese shipping interests reacted to Section 28 by threatening to boycott American ports in that area and transferring their trade to Vancouver or even Gulf and Atlantic ports in order to avoid the possibility of rail rate differentials. Largely dependent upon oriental trade, northwest port authorities and shippers protested that the Japanese reactions would prostrate commerce along the entire Pacific Coast. Benson reacted angrily. In one particularly vituperative note that he released to the press, he raked the commissioner of the Port of Seattle for failing to support the new act: The Shipping Board had determined only after the most careful inquiries that in order to protect precisely such ports as Seattle it would be necessary to apply the preferential methods used by foreign competitors. The new legislation was predicated upon the fact that a preferential rail rate, which had been utilized by Germany before the war, was one of the most effective discriminations ever employed. The Shipping Board was simply doing for American shippers and ports what foreigners had done for their own.[30] But W. T. Christensen, the Seattle port commissioner, was not impressed: The Jones Act, rather than solving any problems, only promised to bring about counterretaliations of the most severe sort. In fact, the German method of preferential rates had "antagonized the whole shipping world and was one of the factors which led up to the World War."[31] The National Foreign Trade Council endorsed this attitude: Its secretary in-

29. State Department memorandum, May 31, 1920, Wilson Papers.
30. Benson to W. T. Christensen, July 21, 1920, RG 32/618-4, NA.
31. Christensen to Benson, August 7, 1920, RG 32/618-4, NA.

formed Benson that the council had always favored empowering the government to use retaliation when necessary, but the Jones Act seemed "to take an important step beyond that by initiating discriminations."[32] From Australia, an American attaché expressed alarm over the impact the Jones Act promised to have on Anglo-American shipping relations:

> We would be unwise to ignore the fact that shipping and overseas trade constitute the very life-blood of British commerce and that it would not be unnatural for them to desire, and even to encourage, the failure of our plans for a permanent and efficient merchant marine. . . . Notwithstanding our repeated assurances that the American merchant marine is not to be built up at the expense of that of any other country, with the possible exception of Germany, every man connected with the British shipping industry, from the builder to the operator and agent, feels that this statement is not true and that the whole industry will soon face the bitterest competition of its history. It is the nature of the Briton to meet such competition by fair means if he can; but instances in the history of British commerce show that he is not above utilizing questionable methods if driven to it.[33]

Benson was given a good idea of the developing impasse by the results of an international shipping rate conference held at Kobe, Japan in early August. Benson endeavored to deal with the Pacific shipping problem by sending an American representative to the conference, but none of the participants (Great Britain, Japan, France, and the Netherlands) could be moved by his power play—an attempt to use the latent power of Section 28 to force them into an agreement on a fixed freight rate for Pacific Ocean traffic. The consensus was that they would wait until they had a better bearing on whether the Wilson administration would indeed enforce the discriminatory clauses of the Jones Act.[34]

The clause favoring an extension of the coastal monopoly was also strongly opposed. Jones had unsuccessfully sponsored a bill the previous summer extending that monopoly to the Philippine Islands. Lansing had remarked that the measure would be justifiable if it were devised to counter foreign discrimination. But the Jones bill appeared to be an initiation of

32. O. K. Davis to Benson, July 28, 1920, RG 32/618-4, NA.
33. Henry P. Starrett to Bainbridge Colby, July 29, 1920, SD 800.88/826, NA.
34. *New York Times,* August 9, 1920.

discrimination rather than a response. If Japan were to employ the same reasoning, Lansing argued, the loss to American shipping would exceed the advantages to be gained from the measure. In addition, Great Britain and other nations with vested interests in Pacific trade could be expected to adopt similar retaliation. Lansing could see no reason for supporting the measure as proposed.[35] While that particular bill did not receive congressional favor, Jones nevertheless ignored Lansing's warnings and incorporated his old bill into the new Merchant Marine Act. Protest against the provision extending the coastal monopoly was almost as intense as that directed against Section 28. An important source of objection was the Philippine administration itself. Manuel L. Quezon, president of the Philippine Senate, spoke for many of the islands' commercial leaders when he rejected the clause with the argument that Manila would be abandoned by foreign maritime service. The loss of foreign shipping would dull the competitive edge and be followed by an inevitable deterioration of service. Thus Manila's effectiveness as a center for American Far Eastern commerce would be seriously damaged. Under such conditions, "the dream of making Manila another Hong Kong [would] become a nightmare."[36] Remonstrations such as Quezon's forced Benson to shelve this clause as he had Section 28.

Concerns such as these gave Benson fits throughout the summer of 1920. The office of naval operations, he noted in late June, had been a much more gratifying position.[37] The major question confronting the Wilson administration was whether the Jones Act would cause serious international diplomatic difficulties. The moratorium on Section 28 dampened protest from abroad, but the State Department continued to receive numerous inquiries from embassies and legations as to its disposition in the matter. Colby's policy was to refuse comment. Probably out of courtesy, no nation officially threatened to employ retaliation until deep into the summer. Nevertheless, it was becoming increasingly apparent that Wilson was hesitant to translate Section 28 into policy by abrogating treaties in ninety days as directed by Section 34. Benson and Jones toiled throughout July and August in effort to persuade the president to use this prerogative, but

35. Lansing to Jones, August 20, 1919, SD 800.88/438, NA.
36. *New York Times,* July 22, 1920.
37. Benson to A. F. Carter, June 29, 1920, RG 32/Benson, NA.

Wilson's conspicuous silence was foreboding. Daniels outlined the administration's dilemma after a cabinet discussion on August 26: Foreign nations were protesting that a treaty was "not a scrap of paper" and could not be abrogated except by "mutual consent." Moreover, Congress appeared to have usurped executive privilege by impairing the terms of treaties when it wrote abrogation rights into the Merchant Marine Act. Daniels observed that Colby was caught between the nation's treaty obligations and congressional dictates. Wilson insisted that Congress could not assume executive functions, but cabinet members pointed out that by signing the bill he had literally given away that authority. The cabinet then approached a tentative policy by which Colby would notify countries of the new law and ask them to consent. If they refused, the administration would take the matter up with the new Congress that would convene in early December. The Jones Act, in short, had become a "troublesome question."[38]

With increased protest from abroad, John Barton Payne himself abandoned the Shipping Board's position a few days after the cabinet meeting. He announced to the United States Chamber of Commerce that he felt the international situation sufficiently serious to disapprove of Section 28. He was especially fearful of the retaliation that the abrogation of the nation's commercial treaties would surely precipitate.[39] As if to emphasize Payne's concerns, the premiers of Norway, Sweden, and Denmark announced on September 4 that they had concurrently agreed to institute a program of retaliation if the Merchant Marine Act harmed Scandinavian commerce.[40] Only Benson and Jones seemed unmoved. Benson notified the White House that the Shipping Board still believed that Section 28 should be retained in the act as a "long step forward in the development of our Merchant Marine."[41] And Jones continued to campaign in support of his measure.

Wilson and Colby ignored these protests. Denying that Congress had the power to issue such directives as were embodied in Section 34, Wilson authorized Colby on September 24 to announce that his endorsement of that section would have been "wholly irreconcilable with the historical respect

38. Daniels, *Cabinet Diaries*, August 26, 1920, p. 552. See also Bainbridge Colby, *The Close of Woodrow Wilson's Administration and the Final Years*, pp. 18–21.

39. *New York Times*, August 31, 1920.

40. Ibid., September 5, 1920.

41. Benson to Tumulty, September 10, 1920, Wilson Papers.

which the United States has shown for its international engagements and would falsify every profession of our belief in the binding force and the reciprocal obligations of treaties in general." Wilson signed the bill in June under pressure of time, Colby argued, and in the belief that his subsequent refusal to carry out the discriminatory mandate of Congress would not effect the overall validity and operation of the measure which contained a great many "sound and enlightened provisions."[42] Responding a week later to congressional rumblings of impeachment, Colby insisted that the chief executive's resolve to build up the merchant marine had not diminished in the least. The action had been intended primarily to relieve tension in international commercial and shipping circles. Colby and Wilson both believed that Section 34 had been interpreted throughout the world as a challenge to one of the greatest economic conflicts the world had ever known. Wilson, Colby asserted, had taken a position "that will stand out as one of the most valuable acts of his administration for the people of this nation."[43]

Colby's remarks in this respect were important because they made clear a reshifting in Wilson's attitude toward foreign affairs. In 1919, Wilson's reactions to Allied diplomatic maneuverings and to the debate over the League at home had left him bitter, but Colby helped forge a new reasonableness into the presidential position that Lansing had probably hindered by hanging on long after he had ceased to be a trusted confidant in the White House.[44] By September 1920, Wilson had come a great distance from his hostile, anti-Allied position of only months before. One of his staunchest supporters had seen the Jones Act as a crucial test of the nation's foreign policy. In a note embracing his apprehension that Benson's position represented the absolute antithesis of what he championed as the liberal dimension of Wilson's world view, William S. Culbertson, a tariff expert and former Hurley associate on the FTC, outlined the situation.

Today is a time of easy sledding for the politicians who want to set American interests against foreign interests—who advocate a purely selfish,

42. *New York Times,* September 25, 1920.
43. Ibid., September 30, 1920.
44. See Daniel M. Smith, *Aftermath of War.* Smith does not discuss maritime policy or maritime diplomacy.

narrow, little-America policy. Some may even want to revert to the harsh, commercial policy of over a century ago and their arguments will seem plausible. We should not, however, be led astray. Now is a good time to "keep our shirts on." Our commercial policy should be firm but constructive and generous. We have great economic power and it should be used to further the best ideals in international affairs. Note that I say "used." A positive statement of a liberal policy by the United States at the present time would do wonders toward checking the movement towards discriminations and the exclusive designs which are rampant in some countries. I feel sure that a shortsighted policy adopted now will be embarrassing to those who in the near future will be called upon to assist in rebuilding the world along liberal lines.[45]

On theoretical bases, Benson could agree with Culbertson's ends. "While the many quotations apparently coming from me in the press would indicate a contrary feeling," he wrote a British admiral in late August, in actuality his objectives were an international understanding accepting the world's oceans as a "free field. I really believe the peace of the world and the success of the League of Nations could be most readily insured if all the countries largely interested in shipping and commerce would . . . agree to harmonize their differences, and carefully avoid all occasions—such as rate-cutting, rate wars and discriminating rules and practices that so easily irritate and eventually bring trouble."[46] Nevertheless, in practice Benson was not an idealist. Despite these protestations, major differences had evolved between him and the White House. Initially exasperated with foreign discriminations, both Benson and Wilson had sought in June 1920 to give America's competitors a dose of their own medicine. The acceptance of a free world marketplace system would come when the world was forced to recognize the folly of its position. By late summer 1920, however, Wilson had determined to reject those methods, employing reasoning advanced by those who thought as William Culbertson did. Generosity and constructive policy were in order once again. The president put it in his

45. William S. Culbertson to William Allen White, June 1, 1920, William S. Culbertson Papers. Culbertson's relieved reaction to Wilson's decision to limit the scope of the Jones Act is indicated in Culbertson, *International Economic Policies*, p. 444. See also Richard J. Snyder, "William Culbertson and the Formation of Modern American Commercial Policy, 1917–1925." Culbertson ghost-wrote Hurley's *The New Merchant Marine*.

46. Benson to Vice-Admiral Sir Walter Hugh M. Browning, August 24, 1920, RG 32/Benson, NA.

own perspective shortly thereafter. There were two ways in which the nation could assist in fostering a spiritual and pure world democracy—by applying equality of treatment in domestic legislation, and by "standing for right and justice as towards individual nations."[47]

---•---

While Benson's hopes to force reason into world commerce through discrimination were thus dashed by Wilson's change of mind, other matters continued to occupy the board's time. One was its effort to secure for private American shipping interests the prewar trade and commercial facilities of the great German Hamburg-American Line (HAL), which had extensive port and marketing facilities but had lost most of its fleet to postwar impoundment. The final transactions in this effort took place during Benson's chairmanship, but the initial attempt began with Edward Hurley's specific policy of establishing American ships in important foreign trade. Mindful of the enormity of the HAL's operation—a vast network of sixty world trade routes serviced by a tremendous investment in the finest harbor and port facilities and boasting enormously valuable long-term shipping experience—Hurley devised a way, long before the peace treaty was signed, to edge out the Allies and gain control of this shipping bonanza. In early April 1919, he sent J. W. Burchard, a vice president of the General Electric Company and intimate associate of German commercial leaders, to Europe as a special commissioner for the Shipping Board. Hurley's tactic was to have Burchard and Henry Robinson make a dash into Germany with the signing of peace in order to "do something in connection with our ship routes to Hamburg and other plans in connection with our export and import trades." Predicting a "great scramble" to establish trade ties with Germany the minute peace was signed, Hurley emphasized that Burchard had been chosen precisely because he did *not* have direct shipping connections. In that manner, Hurley reasoned, Burchard would "be able to do things in a quiet way that shipping men who would be more or less checked up by our friends in England could not do."[48]

Hurley's ploy turned out to be overly optimistic, as a number of Amer-

---

47. U.S., State Department, *FR, 1920*, 1:vii–xii. This was Wilson's annual message, December 7, 1920.
48. Hurley to Robinson, April 9, 1919, Hurley Papers.

ica's foreign competitors arranged to make similar contacts. Ultimately, however, only the Shipping Board was willing to take the risk of assuming such a vast responsibility. Consequently, Hurley's persistence paid off. A second agent, W. G. Sickel, American director of the HAL before the war, came away with firm commitments. In November 1919, Sickel returned to the United States. After a conference with board members he agreed to arrange a form of contract enabling the Shipping Board to take over all of the German line's facilities at Hamburg.[49] Almost four months transpired before the Board resumed serious discussions. Two of Payne's last three board meetings covered the matter extensively. On March 4, the board resolved to contact private companies in the United States on the question of their negotiating with the HAL. At this time, only two companies were considered sufficiently large to undertake the operation—the IMMC, and the American Ship and Commerce Corporation (ASCC). On March 11, the board met with a familiar representative of the first, P. A. S. Franklin, head of the USSB's ship control committee during the war and now elevated to the presidency of the IMMC. Franklin did not please the Board. He argued that while the immediate benefits from such an arrangement would be great, in the long run his company would be put at a great financial disadvantage. He cited, among other things, the costs involved in giving up the IMMC's own long-established port facilities to take over those of the German line.[50] Franklin made one point, however, that the board took to heart. His opposition to the Shipping Board going into partnership in the operation was so strong that Payne at once announced that the government would disengage itself from any direct negotiations between the HAL and private American interests. In the future, the USSB would limit itself to supplying the ships, approving the contract, and cooperating in every way.[51] Benson followed that directive closely.

In early May, the young New York financier, W. Averell Harriman, bought the American Ship and Commerce Corporation. Combined with

---

49. RG 32/Minutes of the Board, November 20, 1919, NA. See also Dr. Wilhelm Cuno to W. G. Sickel, undated, cited in the board's minutes, March 4, 1920, ibid.

50. RG 32/Minutes of the Board, March 4, 1920, NA; RG 32/Verbatim Minutes, March 11, 1920, NA.

51. *New York Times,* March 14, 1920. See also Benson's reiteration of this position to Sickel, April 21, 1920, RG 32/Minutes, NA. Payne revealed the negotiations for the first time to the Senate Committee on Commerce.

Harriman's already impressive holdings in ship construction, operation, ownership, and marine finance and insurance, the acquisition made the 29-year-old America's foremost maritime magnate.[52] The move also guaranteed Harriman the inside track in the Hamburg-American Line's dormant operations. Even before the purchase of the ASCC, Harriman had spent time in Germany anticipating such a deal. Then the director general of the HAL, Dr. Wilhelm Cuno, followed Harriman to New York to discuss the possibilities of a merger further. Although the results were not officially announced until August 1920, it became evident that they had been consummated on a mutually agreeable basis when Cuno received a hero's welcome upon his return to Germany in late May.

The Shipping Board regarded Harriman's mercantile credentials as impeccable. Besides possessing one of the nation's most complete ship systems, Harriman had been building cargo ships for the government since 1917 and operating USSB charters since the end of the war. Believing that no one had a better chance of securing the merger, Benson supported Harriman's negotiations with vigor. After carefully screening and revising the draft contract so that it would not, in his judgment, overly favor the Germans, he released the formal twenty-year agreement on August 16, 1920.[53]

Benson considered the Harriman–HAL contract one of the most important ocean traffic developments ever concluded. Not only would American ships and American seamen now share in servicing the old HAL passenger and freight routes on an extensive and farflung basis, a major portion of the American shipping industry would also profit from association with what was globally recognized before 1914 as one of the world's premium steamship companies and the absolute epitome of commercial organization and business efficiency applied to oceanic services. Association with the company's methods, personnel, and experience, Benson reasoned, would inestimably benefit American shipping commerce. In addition, Benson reveled over the financial base of the arrangement—100 percent American money. So that Harriman would not have to disrupt his own ongoing shipping operations, the vessels for the new organization would be provided by the Shipping Board. Finally, the transaction prompted Harriman to reor-

52. Larry Irvin Bland, "W. Averell Harriman," pp. 32–34. See also W. Averell Harriman, "What Shipowners Are Up Against."

53. See Benson to Harriman, July 3, 1920, RG 32/Benson, NA.

ganize his own American shipping holdings into one massive company, the United American Line (UAL), which operated eighty-six vessels totalling over 600,000 deadweight tons. While this figure included 200,000 tons under government charters, the gross tonnage made Harriman's fleet the largest ever assembled by a private citizen under the American flag.[54] For the Shipping Board, which equated corporate integration with business efficiency and considered it an important prerequisite for achieving a competitive position, it was a gratifying development. With the Merchant Marine Act of 1920, the Harriman pact with the Hamburg-American Line was the crowning achievement of Benson's chairmanship of the United States Shipping Board.[55]

Inevitably, important American shipping interests expressed strong dissatisfaction with the agreement. The essential objection seemed to come from competitors of the Harriman firm who disagreed with Benson on the grounds that the Shipping Board had sanctioned a deal that benefitted the German merchant marine substantially more than it did that of the United States. Considerable protest also came from within Harriman's own ranks. Claiming that they would have nothing to do with any arrangement that was not 100 percent American, ranking officials of what had been the Kerr Navigation Line (part of ACSS), now part of the United American Line, resigned from the new corporation. Benson was incensed with their position, a counteremployment of one of his own tactics. He urged Harriman to release the full text of the agreement, charged that the opposition had succumbed to "foreign propaganda," and praised Harriman as a true "full blooded American citizen" who should be acknowledged for his ardent nationalism and willingness to undertake risks no other American shipowners were prepared to assume.[56]

At first glance it appeared that opponents of Harriman and Benson had powerful weapons on their side. The agreement between Harriman and Cuno initially specified the utilization of Shipping Board vessels—certainly Benson had so believed when appraising the original contract. But on this basis, there appeared to be a serious roadblock. The Jones Act decreed that

54. Bland, "Harriman," p. 37.
55. Details of the agreement are covered in the New York Times, August 17, 1920. See also New York Times, September 16, 1920.
56. Ibid., October 2, 6, 1920.

no major undertakings could go into operation until officially approved by the new seven-man board authorized by the act. But this board simply did not exist—Wilson had made no appointments. Benson and Donald remained the only commissioners. It appeared unlikely that Wilson would appoint a new board just to rectify the problem, and there was serious concern in early October that the operation might not be launched at all. Then Harriman provided the solution: To Benson's relief he announced that he would transfer United American Line ships into the new German-American trade. Within a week, Harriman's vessels were taking bookings for the old HAL service. Harriman described the already functioning trade on October 14 before the American Manufacturers' Export Association: Although Germany had been given a new lease on maritime life, America was the real winner because it had been afforded an unparalleled opportunity to profit from association with a firm world renowned for its shipping expertise and savvy. The new arrangements would give the United States merchant marine a big boost and the nation "a foothold in trade" that it could have gotten on no other basis.[57] In later months, Harriman's operation would falter and he would fall out with the board, but the spadework and vital concern to expand American trade and shipping on the part of Hurley, Payne, and Benson initially made it possible.[58]

———————— •◆• ————————

Though almost half a year remained in Wilson's administration, the Jones Act and the Harriman deal represented the Shipping Board's last significant contributions to the development of American foreign trade. From November 1920 to March 1921, the board was largely a one-man holding action pending the transition of political control to the Harding Administration. The reasons were threefold: First, there was little that

57. Ibid., October 7, 15, 1920.
58. Benson to Harriman, February 9, 1921, Benson Papers; Harriman to Benson, February 14, 1921, ibid. Harriman's operation shortly fell into bad times. This was caused by the completion of his USSB shipbuilding contract, the setting in of the recession of 1921, the institution of high tariffs, and the curtailment of passenger revenue through immigration controls. He had also overanticipated government aid and underestimated British determination to retain world maritime dominance. See Bland, "Harriman," pp. 38–48.

could be done because of the board's situation. The Jones Act provided for a new seven-man board, but it left to Congress the detail of appropriating commissioners' salaries. Since Congress adjourned the very day it gave Wilson the bill and would not reconvene until December 5, any board members appointed in the interim would have to serve without pay. They would also face the hazardous possibility that their recess appointments would not be confirmed. Confronted by these difficulties, Wilson moved slowly in making appointments. On November 19, he finally announced a board composed of four Democrats and three Republicans, even though Warren G. Harding and the G.O.P. had been given an overwhelming popular mandate in the national elections only hours before. The appointments were clearly temporary, and one new board member resigned for better things almost as soon as he joined. His decision was wise; Congress never confirmed the interim appointments. In the meantime, Benson did his best to keep shipping operations running and the ship construction project moving toward completion.

Nor did Benson neglect his crusade against foreign discrimination. He carried on nit-picking feuds with the British and argued to the end, although Section 28 was again indefinitely suspended on December 10, that the preferential sections of the Merchant Marine Act provided the sole means by which a fair share of world trade could be obtained for American ships.[59] Benson's assignment as an American representative to the International Conference on Communications, which had been promised at the Paris Peace Conference and finally met in Washington, D.C. between November and March 1920–1921, only intensified his hostility toward Great Britain for what he interpreted as its domination of the minor

59. Benson to Colby, December 1, 1920, RG 32/618-4, NA; Benson to Senator Arthur Capper, December 23, 1920, ibid. At the same time, Benson carried on a heated controversy with the British Ministry of Shipping concerning claims made against Great Britain by the USSB for payment on oil transported to England for English use in American bottoms during the war. Great Britain had paid a portion upon receipt, but the rest was to be paid upon later negotiations. As war oil prices had dropped by a half in late 1920, England offered to pay the rate difference based on the going market. Benson demanded full war price or "he would make it a diplomatic issue," despite his operations department's statement that the British case was beyond arguing. See Captain Paul Foley to Benson, December 28, 1920, RG 32/580-712, NA; Benson to Raeburn, March 11, 1921, ibid.; Benson to Charles Evans Hughes, April 5, 1921, ibid.

powers and its efforts to manipulate them in ways inimical to American interests.[60]

A second factor that seriously limited the effectiveness of the board's work in the waning months of the Wilson administration entailed an irritating and drawn out special House committee investigation of alleged corruption and criminal waste in the board's wartime shipbuilding and shipping programs. Featuring lengthy testimony from practically all of the board's former ranking administrators—including Denman, Hurley, Payne, Schwab, and Rosseter—and many of the board's most inveterate enemies, the sessions dragged on continuously from October through early March, ending only days before Wilson relinquished office. Always intense with charges and countercharges, and often sensational—as when Schwab wept on the witness stand or Denman revealed "secret" British efforts in 1917 to discriminate against China—the proceedings caused an emotional and psychological drain on all involved.[61]

A third factor which had serious long-range effects on the Shipping Board and upon international ocean transportation was the onset of a worldwide recession in 1920. Despite the destruction of huge amounts of shipping during the war, the armistice found the maritime nations in possession of the greatest surplus of merchant ships ever known. As the result of its own herculean efforts, the United States possessed most of the world's surplus. For a period directly after the war of approximately one and a half years, however, the surplus was less than evident, largely because of the impact of continued government spending on the foreign trade economy. The Shipping Board also endeavored to sell off its ships to existing private companies and promote the foundation of new companies. At the same time, the board continued to operate vessels over as many as forty-one separate ocean trade routes. The general plan also featured an appeal to patriotic sentiment, employed enthusiastically by Hurley during the war and with nativistic gusto by Admiral Benson after it. In the long run, none of

60. Notes on this conference are contained in Benson's memorandum, "Notes Relating to the International Conference on the Limitation of Armaments," September 26, 1921, RG 45/UB/Benson, NA.

61. *New York Times*, December 16–18, 24, 1920, February 18, 1921. British parties denied knowledge of Denman's allegations.

these efforts was highly successful. Only a third of the new companies the board endeavored to establish were ultimately formed, and throughout this period USSB ships often sailed with partial loads. By the beginning of 1920, postwar government spending tapered off considerably, and for the first time since early 1917 Treasury receipts surpassed expenditures. In addition, Treasury increases on rediscount rates to curb inflation, the revival of European production, and increased foreign competition in trade and in the shipment of American and non-American goods brought about a serious economic decline in which the United States maritime industry was hit badly.[62] Beginning in midsummer 1920, reports began drifting in that commercial tonnage around the globe was having difficulty in obtaining cargoes. The bottom fell out in December. By January 1, 1921, for lack of adequate business, the Shipping Board had tied up 468 of its approximately 1,600 vessels. A month later, the figure rose to 513. By March 1, close to 35 percent of the board's ships were lying idle in American ports, and eventually this figure would rise to 70 percent.[63] The crisis was not confined to the United States; Great Britain also suffered and Japan possibly more. Whereas ship tonnage had surpassed prewar levels, the aftermath of the war caused a decrease in oceangoing cargoes. For the time being, the board admitted in early March 1921, there were "too many ships for the business," a luxury costing United States taxpayers, New Jersey Senator Walter Edge estimated, $750,000 a day. To add insult to injury, the special House committee, while exonerating the wartime board of wrongdoing, called for its abolition and urged the creation of a centralized one-man executive authority.[64]

In an economically debilitating and politically hostile environment, even Warren Harding, rejecting the House committee's recommendations to reorganize the USSB, had difficulty in putting together a Shipping Board. Three candidates for the chairmanship failed to materialize. Harding's first choice, James Farrell, president of U.S. Steel, declined. Congressional senti-

---

62. USSB, *Annual Report, 1921*, pp. 79–80, 118; John D. Hicks, *Rehearsal for Disaster*, pp. 24–27.

63. Benson, *The Merchant Marine*, p. 116; *New York Times*, March 3, 1921. Shipping conditions were reported periodically to the State Department by American consuls stationed worldwide. For this period, see SD 641.1112/40-200, NA.

64. *New York Times*, March 3, 1921.

ment clearly did not favor P. A. S. Franklin, president of the IMMC. And Walter Teagle, president of Standard Oil, turned it down when an important family member of the business became ill, requiring Teagle to assume unexpected responsibilities.[65] Harding finally settled on Albert D. Lasker, a Chicago Republican of advertising fame. Benson, whom Harding had asked to continue as chairman while the new president assembled a board, was appointed a member—the sole retainee from the Wilson administration.

65. *The Reminiscences of Albert D. Lasker,* Oral History Research Project, Columbia University Library, p. 141.

Chapter XI
Conclusion

In looking back, members of the Wilson administration could view their maritime accomplishments with considerable pride. In 1917, at the outset of American involvement in World War I, the Shipping Board requisitioned, commandeered, or levered into its wartime service over a thousand oceangoing vessels. It marshalled men and equipment to the European front and carried on vital worldwide trade for the materials required to prosecute the war. These accomplishments helped to shorten the conflict and required considerable cost and sacrifice. Had the conflict lasted longer, however, the contribution would have been overshadowed by the EFC's massive shipbuilding program. Although the program unfortunately fell disappointingly short of expectations for war use because of the unanticipated formative difficulties and the sudden cessation of hostilities, no one could dispute that the administration had put tremendous effort into it. In 1921, a special House committee acknowledged that "considering the program as a whole, the accomplishments in the number of ships constructed, the tonnage secured, and the time within which the ships were completed and delivered, constitute the most remarkable achievement in shipbuilding that the world has ever seen."[1]

The real extent of the building program was made evident in the immediate postwar period. In the last months of 1918, the EFC produced over three million tons of oceangoing cargo ships and continued at near that rate into the ensuing year. Wilson contemplated two immediate government uses for the vessels during the armistice period. He not only envisioned

1. *New York Times,* March 3, 1921.

employing their commercial and military potential as a means of forcing a preferable peace but also actively utilized them in a major effort to stabilize the staggering political economies of a number of European nations. In the first attempt, he failed utterly. The prodigious growth of the American merchant marine, rather than commanding respect and adherence to the Wilson plan for a liberal peace, catalyzed barely submerged wartime rivalries into intense commercial and political difficulties. Nevertheless, American aid, sent to Europe in American ships, did stem anarchy and social radicalism and strengthen Western capitalist economies. Furthermore, from the standpoint of the American economy, the vessels served invaluably. With the war's close and the commencement of an unusual eighteen-month period of prosperity, the world's maritime nations began a great scramble to employ their tonnage for their own peacetime needs. Had it not possessed its own ships constructed during the war and after, the United States would have suffered as it had in 1914—beset by huge surpluses but lacking the means to transport them abroad. Ownership of the tonnage also enabled the Shipping Board to save vast sums on freight costs and fostered the establishment of permanent and lucrative trade on a world-wide basis. Even the Harding administration could look back at this aspect of government control and operation as "an act of courage and vision."[2]

Once the boom reached its end, however, the strength of the government fleet was revealed as in many respects illusory. The haste with which the American ships had been built manifested itself in poor performance; the wooden ship program was disastrous, and most of them could not be utilized after the war; and the transition from coal to oil and then to diesel fuel antiquated many vessels even before they left the ways. Most of the fleet should have been scrapped at once, but it would have been hard, if not impossible, to justify such a policy on political, no less than commercial or financial, terms in the immediate postwar period. The plethora of American ships added to an already troublesome world surplus and caused a serious depreciation in rates, stagnation, insolvency, and general economic distress in the maritime industries. In the meantime, wages and operating expenses were greatly inflated. The Merchant Marine Act of 1920 was

2. Statement of Albert D. Lasker, U.S., Congress, House and Senate, *To Amend Merchant Marine Act of 1920,* Joint Hearings before the Committee on Commerce and Committee on Merchant Marine and Fisheries, 67th Cong., 2d sess., 1:9.

marketed as a solution to the nation's shipping problems, but it did not prove highly successful. In the hurried effort to construct a strong maritime alternative to foreign competition and meet congressional deadlines, the measure was designed without sufficient notice of the impending depression, signs of which were already visible at the time. Such features as the construction loan fund and exemptions from excess profits taxes were anachronisms—of little value in the crash that shook the shipping industry at the time of the bill's passage. Between 1920 and 1926, the proportion of American foreign trade transported in American ships declined to less than 25 percent.[3]

Although the Jones Act did not halt the slump in American shipping in the early 1920's, in important ways it was the culmination of Wilson's eight-year campaign to strengthen the nation's economy through government leadership in promoting and integrating foreign trade. Under the act, it was the duty of the Shipping Board not only to establish an American merchant marine, "but to make it render efficient service—to keep American industry moving, and make American progress sure."[4] Always implicit in such reasoning was the belief that without a national merchant fleet the American way of life would be threatened. "If it is the desire of the American people to maintain their present high standards of living and to retain even approximately their present position in finance and trade," Benson summarized at the end of 1920, "our annual surplus must be sold in foreign markets; and in order to do this it is necessary to have a merchant marine owned and controlled by American citizens."[5] That the work of Wilson's Shipping Board had lasting significance is evidenced in the fact that the provisions and aims of the Jones Act provide the fundamental principles upon which current maritime policy is based.[6]

Always in the background of this effort to create an efficient overseas transportation network in order to build up the domestic economy was the equally important consideration Wilsonians gave to world politics. Al-

3. Ibid., pp. 5–9; Saugstad, *Shipping and Shipbuilding Subsidies*, p. 30; Abraham Berglund, "The War and the World's Mercantile Marine"; E. S. Gregg, "Failure of the Merchant Marine Act of 1920."
4. Cook, *History of the United States Shipping Board*, p. 7.
5. USSB, *Annual Report, 1920*, p. 9.
6. Lawrence, *United States Merchant Shipping*, p. 41.

though his ardor was dampened at times, Wilson never abandoned the notion that the triumph of a world liberalism was possible only if the United States assumed a portion of leadership, and leadership could be obtained only on the basis of national power and prestige. From this perspective, shipping growth increased the national power by giving the economy greater flexibility, freeing it from commercial dependency and increasing the national wealth through the expansion of foreign trade. Most important, it provided the United States with another means by which to assist in constructing the just and stable world capitalism Wilson sought through American participation in and direction of international commerce.

The liberal view was ably summarized by Edward Hurley, who offered a fitting testimonial to Wilsonian maritime policy in 1920. "The resources of the world," he wrote in *The New Merchant Marine*, "are distributed on an entirely different basis, and their distribution in conformity with the requirements of nations is the chief occupation of mankind." The growth of the American merchant marine constituted a long step toward that fulfillment, servicing not only American needs, but of all humanity. "With the aid of American ships, American producers can dispose of their surplus goods by helping to restock the empty shelves and to fill the empty larders of four continents and many archipelagos." But none of these accomplishments could be realized unless foreign trade was vigorously sought and sustained. Otherwise the result in America would be "over-production, unemployment, and liquidation." If this occurred, it stood to reason that the United States could do little to assist in world reconstruction through the development of international trade. Insofar as opportunities for America and the world were concerned, the question would be resolved only by a basic principle: What was good for America was good for the world.[7]

In the final analysis, no one could rightly claim that Woodrow Wilson had solved all of the nation's overseas shipping problems, but as Colby expressed it, "no man [had] done more in recent years for the development and upbuilding of the American merchant marine."[8] That Wilson's accomplishments proceeded not only from his conception of the need for a stable domestic political economy based upon a vigorous and efficient

7. Hurley, *The New Merchant Marine*, pp. xiii, xxiv, 272-73.
8. *New York Times*, September 30, 1920.

foreign trade but also from the requirements of his world view and the calling of its diplomacy, distinguished it beyond all other considerations. This was best articulated by Benson: In his last days as Shipping Board chairman, he anxiously attempted to assist the incoming Harding administration "in its efforts to build up an American merchant marine and in carrying out a strong foreign policy."[9] To Wilsonians the two were inseparables.

9. Benson memorandum, May 16, 1921, RG 45/UB/Benson, NA.

Bibliography

Manuscript Sources

Cambridge, Mass. Harvard University Library. William Phillips Papers.
Chapel Hill. University of North Carolina Library, Southern Historical Collection. George J. Baldwin Papers, Claude Kitchin Papers, Daniel Augustus Tompkins Papers.
Concord. New Hampshire Historical Society. Jacob H. Gallinger Papers.
Madison. State Historical Society of Wisconsin. Paul Reinsch Papers.
New Haven, Conn. Yale University Library. Edward M. House Papers, Frank Polk Papers, Sir William Wiseman Papers.
New York City. Columbia University Library. Frank A. Vanderlip Papers.
New York City. Columbia University Library, Oral History Research Project. Albert D. Lasker Reminiscences, George Rublee Reminiscences.
Notre Dame, Ind. Notre Dame University Library. Edward N. Hurley Papers.
Philadelphia. Pennsylvania Historical Society. William B. Wilson Papers.
Princeton, N.J. Princeton University Library. Bernard Baruch Papers.
Stanford, Cal. Hoover Institution on War, Revolution, and Peace. Supreme Economic Council Papers, United States Food Administration Papers.
Washington, D.C. Library of Congress. Newton D. Baker Papers, William S. Benson Papers, Bainbridge Colby Papers, William S. Culbertson Papers, Josephus Daniels Papers, Norman Davis Papers, General George Goethals Papers, Robert Lansing Papers, Breckinridge Long Papers, William G. McAdoo Papers, Roland S. Morris Papers, Daniel Augustus Tompkins Papers, Woodrow Wilson Papers.
Washington, D.C. National Archives. Record Group 32, United States Shipping Board Files; Record Group 40, Department of Commerce Files; Record Group 41, Bureau of Navigation Files; Record Group 45, Department of Navy Files; Record Group 56, Department of the Treasury Files; Record

Group 59, State Department Files; Record Group 182, War Trade Board Files; Record Group 280, Federal Mediation and Conciliation Service Files.

Printed Sources

Albion, Robert G., and Pope, Jennie Barnes. *Sea Lanes in Wartime: The American Experience, 1775–1945.* 2d enl. ed. Hamden, Conn.: Archon Books, 1968.

Albion, Robert G.; Baker, William A.; and Labaree, Benjamin W. *New England and the Sea.* Middletown, Conn.: Wesleyan University Press, 1973.

Allin, Lawrence C. "Ill-Timed Initiative: The Ship Purchase Bill of 1915." *American Neptune* 33(July 1973):178–98.

Auerbach, Jerold S. "Progressives at Sea: The La Follette Seamen's Act." *Labor History* 2(Fall 1961):344–60.

Bailey, Thomas A. *The Policy of the United States towards the Neutrals, 1917–1918.* Baltimore: The Johns Hopkins Press, 1942.

Baker, Ray Stannard. *Woodrow Wilson: Life and Letters.* 8 vols. Garden City, N.Y.: Doubleday, Doran & Company, 1927–39.

Bane, Suda L., and Lutz, Ralph H., eds. *The Organization of American Relief in Europe, 1918–1919.* Stanford, Cal.: Stanford University Press, 1943.

Bartlett, Ruhl J., ed. *The Record of American Diplomacy.* New York: Alfred A. Knopf, 1959.

Bates, William W. *American Navigation: The Political History of its Rise and Ruin and the Proper Means for its Encouragement.* Boston and New York: Houghton Mifflin Company, 1902.

Beers, Burton F. *Vain Endeavor, Robert Lansing's Attempt to End the American–Japanese Rivalry.* Durham, N.C.: Duke University Press, 1962.

Bell, Sidney. *Righteous Conquest: Woodrow Wilson and the Evolution of the New Diplomacy.* Port Washington, N.Y.: Kennikat Press, 1972.

Benson, Rear Admiral William Shepherd. "Our New Merchant Marine." *United States Naval Institute Proceedings* 52(October 1926):23–32.

Benson, Rear Admiral William Shepherd. *The New Merchant Marine.* New York: The Macmillan Company, 1923.

Bentinck–Smith, Joan. "The Forcing Period: A Study of the American Merchant Marine, 1914–1917." Ph.D. dissertation, Radcliffe College, 1958.

Berglund, Abraham. "The War and Trans-Pacific Shipping." *American Economic Review* 7(September 1917):553–68.

Berglund, Abraham. "The War and the World's Mercantile Marine." *American Economic Review* 10(June 1920):227–58.

Best, Gary Dean. "Food Relief as Price Support: Hoover and American Pork, January–March, 1919." *Agricultural History* 45(April 1971):79–84.

Birdsall, Paul. "Neutrality and Economic Pressures, 1914–1917." *Science and Society* 3(Spring 1939):217–28.

Bland, Larry Irvin. "W. Averell Harriman: Businessman and Diplomat, 1898–1946." Ph.D. dissertation, University of Wisconsin, 1972.

Broesamle, John T. *William Gibbs McAdoo: A Passion for Change, 1863–1917.* Port Washington, N.Y.: Kennikat Press, 1973.

Calvert, Peter. *The Mexican Revolution, 1910–1914: The Diplomacy of Anglo-American Conflict.* Cambridge: At the University Press, 1968.

Clémentel, Étienne. *La France et la politique économique interalliée.* Paris: Presses Universitaires de France, 1931.

Coker, William S. "The Panama Canal Tolls Controversy: A Different Perspective." *Journal of American History* 55(December 1968):555–64.

Colby, Bainbridge. *The Close of Woodrow Wilson's Administration and the Final Years.* New York: Kennerley, 1930.

Colby, Bainbridge. "Some Thoughts on Our Shipping Policy." *Annals of the Academy of Political and Social Science* 82(March 1919):338–41.

Cook, Arthur E., ed. *A History of the United States Shipping Board and Merchant Fleet Corporation.* Baltimore: Day Printing Company, 1927.

Cooper, John Milton. "The British Response to the House–Grey Memorandum: New Evidence and New Questions." *Journal of American History* 59(March 1973):958–71.

Cuff, Robert D. "We Band of Brothers—Woodrow Wilson's War Managers." *Canadian Review of American Studies* 5(Fall 1974):135–48.

Culbertson, William S. *Commercial Policy in War Times and After: A Study of the Application of Democratic Ideas to International Commercial Relations.* New York: D. Appleton Company, 1919.

Culbertson, William S. *International Economic Policies: A Survey of the Economics of Diplomacy.* New York: D. Appleton Company, 1925.

Daniels, Josephus. *The Cabinet Diaries of Josephus Daniels, 1913–1920.* Edited by E. David Cronin. Lincoln: University of Nebraska Press, 1963.

Daniels, Josephus. *The Wilson Era: Years of War and After, 1917–1923.* Chapel Hill: University of North Carolina Press, 1946.

DeNovo, John A. *American Interests and Policies in the Middle East, 1900–1939.* Minneapolis: University of Minnesota Press, 1963.

DeNovo, John A. "The Movement for an Aggressive American Oil Policy Abroad, 1918–1920." *American Historical Review* 61(July 1956):854–76.

Diamond, William. *The Economic Thought of Woodrow Wilson.* Baltimore: The Johns Hopkins Press, 1943.

Dignan, Don. "New Perspectives on British Far Eastern Policy, 1913–1919." *University of Queensland Papers* 5(January 31, 1969): 263–302.

Dudden, Arthur, ed. *Woodrow Wilson and the World of Today*. Philadelphia: University of Pennsylvania Press, 1957.

Fayle, Charles Ernest. *The War and the Shipping Industry*. London: Humphrey Milford, Oxford University Press, 1927.

Feis, Herbert. "The Industrial Situation in Great Britain: From the Armistice to the Beginning of 1921." *American Economic Review* 11(June 1921): 252–67.

Fowler, Wilton B. *British-American Relations, 1917–1918: The Role of Sir William Wiseman*. Princeton: Princeton University Press, 1969.

Furness, Sir Christopher. *The American Invasion*. London: Simpkin, Marshall & Company, 1902.

Garraty, John A. *Henry Cabot Lodge: A Biography*. New York: Alfred A. Knopf, 1953.

Ginger, Ray. *Age of Excess: The United States from 1877 to 1914*. New York: The Macmillan Company, 1965.

Goldberg, Joseph P. *The Maritime Story: A Study in Labor–Management Relations*. Cambridge, Mass.: Harvard University Press, 1958.

Great Britain. *Parliamentary Debates*. House of Commons, 5th ser., (1916–19). London, 1916–19.

Great Britain. *Documents on British Foreign Policy, 1919–1939, First Series*. Edited by E. L. Woodward and R. Butler. 16 vols. London, 1947–58.

Gregg, E. S. "Failure of the Merchant Marine Act of 1920." *American Economic Review* 11(December 1921):610–15.

Gregory, Ross. "A New Look at the Case of the Dacia." *Journal of American History* 55(September 1968):292–96.

Grey, Edward. *Twenty-Five Years, 1892–1916*. 2 vols. New York: Frederick A. Stokes Company, 1925.

Griswold, A. Whitney. *The Far Eastern Policy of the United States*. New York: Harcourt, Brace & World, 1938.

Hankey, Maurice. *The Supreme Command, 1914–1918*. 2 vols. London: George Allen & Unwin, 1961.

Harbough, William Henry. *The Life and Times of Theodore Roosevelt*. New York: Collier, 1963.

Harriman, W. Averell. "What Shipowners Are Up Against." *Nation's Business* 9(April 1921):23–24.

Hays, Samuel P. *The Response to Industrialism, 1885–1914*. Chicago: University of Chicago Press, 1957.

Hendrick, Burton J. *The Life and Letters of Walter H. Page*. 3 vols. Garden City, N.Y.: Doubleday, Page & Company, 1925–26.

Herwig, Holger H., and Trask, David F. "The Failure of Imperial Germany's

Undersea Offensive against World Shipping, February 1917–October 1918." *The Historian* 33(August 1971):611–36.

Hicks, John D. *Rehearsal for Disaster: The Boom and Collapse of 1919–1920*. Jacksonville: University of Florida Press, 1961.

Hoover, Herbert. *An American Epic*. 2 vols. Chicago: Henry Regnery Company, 1960.

Hornbeck, Stanley K. "Trade Concessions, Investments, Conflict and Policy in the Far East." *Proceedings of the Academy of Political Science* 7(1917–1918):604–22.

House, Colonel Edward. *The Intimate Papers of Colonel House*. Edited by Charles Seymour. 4 vols. Boston and New York: Houghton Mifflin Company, 1926–28.

Houston, David F. *Eight Years with Wilson's Cabinet, 1913–1920*. 2 vols. Garden City, N.Y.: Doubleday, Page & Company, 1926.

Hurley, Edward N. "American Ships on the Pacific." *Asia* 18(November 1918): 907–10.

Hurley, Edward N. *Awakening of Business*. Garden City, N.Y.: Doubleday, Page & Company, 1917.

Hurley, Edward N. *The Bridge to France*. Philadelphia: J. B. Lippincott Company, 1927.

Hurley, Edward N. "Business on the Seven Seas." *System* 34(December 1918): 810–12.

Hurley, Edward N. "How Our New Merchant Marine is Aiding Farm and Stockyard." *United States Shipping Board* (March 9, 1919).

Hurley, Edward N. *The New Merchant Marine*. New York: The Century Company, 1920.

Hurley, Edward N. "Ships for the War—And After." *Bulletin of the Pan-American Union* 47(September 18, 1918):385–94.

Hurley, Edward N. "What America's New Merchant Marine Means to the World." *Annals of the American Academy of Political and Social Science* 83(May 1919):141–44.

Hutchins, John G. B. *The American Maritime Industries and Public Policy, 1789–1914*. Cambridge, Mass.: Harvard University Press, 1941.

Hutchins, John G. B. "The American Shipping Industry Since 1914." *Business History Review* 27(June 1954):105–27.

Israel, Jerry. *Progressivism and the Open Door: American and China, 1905–1921*. Pittsburgh: University of Pittsburgh Press, 1971.

Kaplan, Edward S. "William Jennings Bryan and the Panama Canal Tolls Controversy." *Mid-America* 56(April 1974):100–108.

Karsten, Peter. *The Naval Aristocracy: The Golden Age of Annapolis and the*

Emergence of Modern American Navalism. New York: The Free Press, 1972.

Kasson, John A. "The Monroe Doctrine in 1881." *North American Review* 133(December 1881):523–33.

Kaufman, Burton I. *Efficiency and Expansion: Foreign Trade Organization in the Wilson Administration, 1913–1921.* Westport, Conn.: Greenwood Press, 1974.

Kaufman, Burton I. "United States Trade and Latin America: The Wilson Years." *Journal of American History* 58(September 1971):342–63.

Klachko, Mary. "Anglo-American Naval Competition, 1918–1922." Ph.D dissertation, Columbia University, 1962.

LaFeber, Walter. *The New Empire: An Interpretation of American Expansion, 1860–1898.* Ithaca, N.Y.: Cornell University Press, 1963.

Lamont, Thomas W. *Across World Frontiers.* New York: Harcourt, Brace, & World, 1950.

Lansing, Robert. *War Memoirs of Robert Lansing.* Indianapolis and New York: The Bobbs-Merrill Company, 1935.

Laut, Agnes C. "Will the Shipping Bill Help or Hurt Our Commerce?" *Outlook* 109(February 3, 1915):289–93.

Laut, Agnes C. "The Tremendous Boom in American Shipping." *Current Opinion* 60(April 1916):287–89.

Lawrence, Samuel A. *United States Merchant Shipping Policies and Politics.* Washington, D.C.: The Brookings Institution, 1966.

Levin, N. Gordon, Jr. *Woodrow Wilson and World Politics: America's Response to War and Revolution.* New York: Oxford University Press, 1968.

Link, Arthur S. *Woodrow Wilson and the Progressive Era, 1910–1917.* New York: Harper & Row, 1954.

Link, Arthur S. *Wilson: The Road to the White House.* Princeton, N.J.: Princeton University Press, 1947.

Link, Arthur S. *Wilson: The New Freedom.* Princeton, N.J.: Princeton University Press, 1956.

Link, Arthur S. *Wilson: The Struggle for Neutrality, 1914–1915* Princeton, N.J.: Princeton University Press, 1960.

Link, Arthur S. *Wilson: Confusions and Crises, 1915–1916.* Princeton, N.J.: Princeton University Press, 1964.

Link, Arthur S. *Wilson: Campaigns for Progressivism and Peace, 1916–1917.* Princeton, N.J.: Princeton University Press, 1965.

Link, Arthur S. "World War I." In *Interpreting American History: Conversations with Historians,* edited by John A. Garraty, 2:121–44. 2 vols. New York: The Macmillan Company, 1970.

McAdoo, William G. *Crowded Years: The Reminiscences of William G. McAdoo.* Boston and New York: Houghton Mifflin Company, 1931.

McAdoo, William G. *Opposing Views of William G. McAdoo and Theodore Burton on the Ship Purchase Bill*. Washington, D.C.: United States Chamber of Commerce, 1915.

McAdoo, William G. "The Pan American Financial Conference." *World's Work* 30(August 1915):393–96.

McCormick, Thomas J. *China Market: America's Quest for Informal Empire, 1893–1901*. Chicago: Quadrangle Books, 1967.

Mahan, Alfred Thayer. *The Influence of Sea Power upon History, 1660–1783*. Boston: Little, Brown & Company, 1897.

Mahan, Alfred Thayer. *The Interest of America in Sea Power: Present and Future*. Boston: Little, Brown & Company, 1897.

Mahan, Alfred Thayer. "The United States Looking Outward." *Atlantic Monthly* 66(December 1890):816–24.

Martin, L. W. *Peace without Victory*. New Haven, Conn.: Yale University Press, 1958.

Marvin, Winthrop L. *The American Merchant Marine: Its History and Romance from 1620 to 1902*. New York: Charles Scribner's Sons, 1902.

Marx, Daniel, Jr. *International Shipping Cartels: A Study of Industrial Self-Regulation by Shipping Conferences*. Princeton, N.J.: Princeton University Press, 1953.

May, Ernest R. *The World War and American Isolation, 1914–1917*. Cambridge, Mass.: Harvard University Press, 1959.

Meeker, Royal. *History of Shipping Subsidies*. New York: The Macmillan Company, 1905.

Muchnic, Charles. "Relation of Investments to South American Trade." *Proceedings of the Academy of Political Science* 6(1915–16):138–46.

Muller, Louis. "Our Tariff in its Relations to the Grain Trade." *Annals of the American Academy of Political and Social Science* 29(May 1907):528–36.

National Foreign Trade Council. *Convention Proceedings* (1914–20). New York: National Foreign Trade Council, 1914–20.

National Foreign Trade Council. *Effect of the War upon American Foreign Commerce*. New York: National Foreign Trade Council, September 23, 1915.

National Foreign Trade Council. *European Economic Alliances: A Compilation of Information on International Commercial Policies after the European War and Their Effect upon the Foreign Trade of the United States*. New York: National Foreign Trade Council, 1916.

New Republic. "America and the League of Nations." 17(November 30, 1918): 116–18.

Nixon, Lewis. "Panama Canal Tolls." *Independent* 72(April 18, 1912):838–40.

Noggle, Burl. *Into the Twenties: The United States from Armistice to Normalcy*. Urbana: University of Illinois Press, 1974.

North, S. N. D. "The Industrial Commission." *North American Review* 168(January 1899):708–19.

Notter, Harley. *The Origins of the Foreign Policy of Woodrow Wilson.* Baltimore: The Johns Hopkins Press, 1937.

Notz, William F., and Harvey, Richard S. *American Foreign Trade as Promoted by the Webb–Pomerene and Edge Acts: With Historical References to the Origin and Enforcement of the Anti-Trust Laws.* Indianapolis: The Bobbs-Merrill Company, 1921.

Noyes, Alexander D. *Forty Years of American Finance.* New York: G. P. Putnam's Sons, 1909.

Noyes, Alexander D. *War Period of American Finance, 1908–1925.* New York: G. P. Putnam's Sons, 1926.

Outlook. "What Foreigners Think of our New Tariff." 105(October 18, 1913): 353–55.

Parrini, Carl. *Heir to Empire: United States Economic Diplomacy, 1916–1923.* Pittsburgh: University of Pittsburgh Press, 1969.

Parvin, Emerson E. "The Workings of the Seamen's Act." *Proceedings of the Academy of Political Science* 6(1915–16):113–25.

Plesur, Milton. *America's Outward Thrust: Approaches to Foreign Affairs, 1865–1890.* DeKalb: Northern Illinois University Press, 1971.

Plesur, Milton. "Rumblings Beneath the Surface: America's Outward Thrust, 1865–1890." In *The Gilded Age: A Reappraisal,* edited by H. Wayne Morgan, pp. 140–68. Syracuse: Syracuse University Press, 1963.

Pletcher, David M. *The Awkward Years: American Foreign Relations under Garfield and Arthur.* Columbia: University of Missouri Press, 1971.

Pratt, Edward E. "Commercial America and the War: Present and Future Effects of the European War on our Industries and Foreign Trade." *Scientific American* 114(March 4, 1916):241, 260–63.

Pringle, Henry F. *The Life and Times of William Howard Taft.* 2 vols. New York: Farrar and Rinehart, 1939.

Pugach, Noel. "American Shipping Promoters and the Shipping Crisis of 1914–1916: The Pacific & Eastern Steamship Company." *American Neptune* 35(July 1975):166–82.

Randall, James G. "War Tasks and Accomplishments of the Shipping Board." *Historical Outlook* 10(June 1919):315–20.

Redfield, William C. *The New Industrial Day.* New York: The Century Company, 1912.

Reinsch, Paul S. *An American Diplomat in China.* New York: Doubleday, Page & Company, 1922.

Reinsch, Paul S. "The Merchant Marine of the World." *Chautauquan* 34(January 1902):375–80.

Richardson, James D., ed. *A Compilation of the Messages and Papers of the Presidents, 1787–1897*. Washington, D.C.: United States Government Printing Office, 1898.

Richardson, James D., ed. *A Supplement to a Compilation of the Messages and Papers of the Presidents*. Washington, D.C.: United States Government Printing Office, 1902.

Riddell, George A. *Lord Riddell's War Diary, 1914–1918*. New York: Reynal & Hitchcock, 1934.

Roach, John. *The American Carrying-Trade*. New York: H. B. Grose & Company, 1881.

Rosenthal, Benjamin J. *The Need of the Hour: An American Merchant Marine*. Chicago: Privately Printed, 1915.

Rothwell, V. H. *British War Aims and Peace Diplomacy, 1914–1918*. Oxford: Clarendon Press, 1971.

Saliers, Earl A. "Some Financial Aspects of the International Mercantile Marine Company." *Journal of Political Economy* 23(November 1915):910–25.

Salter, Sir Arthur. *Allied Shipping Control: An Experiment in International Administration*. Oxford: At the University Press, 1921.

Sanders, Alvin. "Reciprocity with Continental Europe." *Annals of the American Academy of Political and Social Science* 29(May 1907):528–36.

Savage, Carlton, ed. *Policy of the United States toward Maritime Commerce in War*. 2 vols. Washington, D.C.: United States Government Printing Office, 1936.

Schonberger, Howard R. *Transportation to the Seaboard: The "Communications Revolution" and American Foreign Policy, 1860–1900*. Westport, Conn.: Greenwood Press, 1971.

Seager, Robert, II. "The Progressives and American Foreign Policy, 1898–1917: An Analysis of the Attitudes of the Leaders of the Progressive Movement toward External Affairs." Ph.D. dissertation, Ohio State University, 1957.

Sklar, Martin J. "Woodrow Wilson and the Political Economy of Modern United States Liberalism." *Studies on the Left* 1(Fall 1960):17–47.

Smith, Daniel M. *Aftermath of War: Bainbridge Colby and Wilsonian Diplomacy, 1920–1921*. Philadelphia: American Philosophical Society, 1970.

Smith, Daniel M. *The Great Departure: The United States and World War I, 1914–1920*. New York: John Wiley & Sons, 1965.

Smith, Daniel M. "Robert Lansing and the Wilson Interregnum, 1919–1920." *The Historian* 21(February 1959):135–61.

Smith, Darrell Hevener, and Betters, Paul B. *The United States Shipping Board:*

Its History, Activities and Organization. Washington, D.C.: The Brookings Institution, 1931.

Smith, J. Russell. *Influence of the Great War on Shipping.* New York: Oxford University Press, 1919.

Snyder, Richard J. "William Culbertson and the Formation of Modern American Commercial Policy, 1917–1925." *Kansas Historical Quarterly* 35(Winter 1969):396–410.

Spinks, Charles Nelson. "Japan's Entrance into the World War." *Pacific Historical Review* 5(December 1936):297–311.

Sprout, Harold, and Sprout, Margaret. *The Rise of American Naval Power, 1776–1918.* Princeton: Princeton University Press, 1939.

Stead, William T. *The Americanization of the World, or the Trend of the Twentieth Century.* New York: H. Markley, 1901.

Strauss, Lewis. *Men and Decisions.* New York: Doubleday & Company, 1962.

Synon, Mary. *McAdoo: The Man and His Times: A Panorama in Democracy.* Indianapolis: The Bobbs-Merrill Company, 1924.

Taussig, Frank W. *The Tariff History of the United States.* New York: G. P. Putnam's Sons, 1923.

Tillman, Seth B. *Anglo-American Relations at the Paris Peace Conference of 1919.* Princeton: Princeton University Press, 1961.

Tompkins, Daniel A. *American Commerce, Its Expansion: A Collection of Addresses and Pamphlets Relating to the Extension of Foreign Markets for American Manufacturers.* Charlotte, N.C.: Privately Printed, 1900.

Trask, David F. *Captains & Cabinets: Anglo-American Naval Relations, 1917–1918.* Columbia: University of Missouri Press, 1972.

Trow, Clifford W. "Woodrow Wilson and the Mexican Interventionist Movement of 1919." *Journal of American History* 58(June 1971):46–72.

Tumulty, Joseph P. *Woodrow Wilson As I Know Him.* Garden City, N.Y.: Doubleday, Page & Company, 1921.

Tyler, David Budlong. *Steam Conquers the Atlantic.* New York and London: D. Appleton-Century Company, 1939.

Underwood, Oscar W. "High Tariff and American Trade Abroad." *Century* 84(May 1912):22–24.

United States, Commerce Department, Commissioner of Navigation. *Annual Reports* (1894–1922). Washington, D.C., 1894–1922.

United States, Commerce Department [Jesse A. Saugstad]. *Report on Shipping and Shipbuilding Subsidies: A Study of State Aid to the Shipping and Shipbuilding Industries in Various Countries of the World.* Trade Promotion Series 129, 1932. Washington, D.C., 1932.

United States, Congress. *Congressional Record* (1909–21). Washington, D.C., 1909–21.

United States, Congress, House. *Addresses of President Wilson, January 27– February 3, 1916.* 64th Cong., 1st sess., H. Doc. 803.

United States, Congress, House. *American Merchant Marine in the Foreign Trade.* 51st Cong., 1st sess., H. Rept. 1210.

United States, Congress, House. *American Shipping.* 47th Cong., 2d sess., H. Rept. 1827.

United States, Congress, House. *Creating a Shipping Board, Naval Auxiliary, and Merchant Marine.* 64th Cong., 1st sess., Hearings before the House Committee on Merchant Marine and Fisheries. Washington, D.C., 1916.

United States, Congress, House. *Creating a Shipping Board, a Naval Auxiliary, a Merchant Marine, and Regulating Carriers by Water Engaged in the Foreign and Interstate Commerce of the United States.* 64th Cong., 1st sess., H. Rept. 659.

United States, Congress, House. *Causes of the Decadence of the Merchant Marine: Means for its Restoration and the Extension of Our Foreign Commerce.* 46th Cong., 3d sess., H. Rept. 342.

United States, Congress, House. *Causes of the Reduction of American Tonnage and the Decline of Navigation Interests.* 41st Cong., 2d sess., H. Rept. 28.

United States, Congress, House. *Foreign Commerce and Decadence of American Shipping.* 41st Cong., 2d sess., H. Exec. Doc. 111.

United States, Congress, House. *Government Ownership and Operation of Merchant Vessels in Foreign Trade of United States.* 63d Cong., 2d sess., Hearings before the House Committee on Merchant Marine and Fisheries on the Bill H.R. 18518. Washington, D.C., 1914.

United States, Congress, House. *Government Ownership and Operation of Merchant Vessels in the Foreign Trade of the United States.* 63d Cong., 2d sess., H. Rept. 1149.

United States, Congress, House. *Hearings before the Subcommittee on the Merchant Marine and Fisheries.* 66th Cong., 1st sess. Washington, D.C., 1920.

United States, Congress, House. *Report of the Committee on the Merchant Marine and Fisheries on Steamship Agreements and Affiliations in the American Foreign and Domestic Trade Under H. Res. 587.* 63d Cong., 2d sess., H. Doc. 805.

United States, Congress, House. *United States Shipping Board Operations.* 66th Cong., 2d and 3d sess., Hearings before Select Committee. Washington, D.C., 1920–21.

United States, Congress, House and Senate. *To Amend Merchant Marine Act of 1920.* 67th Cong., 2d sess., Joint Hearings before the Committee on Commerce and Committee on Merchant Marine and Fisheries. 2 vols. Washington, D.C., 1922.

United States, Congress, Senate. *Cooperation and Efficiency in Developing our Foreign Trade.* 64th Cong., 1st sess., S. Doc. 459.

United States, Congress, Senate. *The Establishment of an American Merchant Marine.* 66th Cong., 2d sess., Hearings before the Senate Committee on Commerce, Washington, D.C., 1920.

United States, Congress, Senate. *The Farmer and the Shipping Bill.* 64th Cong., 1st sess., S. Doc. 395.

United States, Congress, Senate. *Increased Ocean Transportation Rates.* 63d Cong., 3d sess., S. Doc. 673.

United States, Congress, Senate. *International High Commission.* 64th Cong., 1st sess., S. Doc. 438.

United States, Congress, Senate. *The Opposition and the Shipping Bill.* 63d Cong., 3d sess., S. Doc. 949.

United States, Congress, Senate. *Papers Relating to Imports in Vessels with American Register.* 63d Cong., 1st sess., S. Doc. 179.

United States, Congress, Senate. *The Republic of Chile.* 64th Cong., 1st sess., S. Doc. 437.

United States, Congress, Senate. *The Shipping Bill.* 63d Cong., 3d sess., S. Doc. 713.

United States, Congress, Senate. *Ties that Bind the Americas.* 64th Cong., 1st sess., S. Doc. 479.

United States, Congress, Senate. *United States Shipping Board Emergency Fleet Corporation.* 65th Cong., 2d sess., Hearings before the Senate Committee on Commerce. 2 vols. Washington, D.C., 1918.

United States, Federal Trade Commission. *Report on Cooperation in American Foreign Trade.* 2 vols. Washington, D.C., 1916.

United States, Federal Trade Commission. *Report on Trade and Tariffs in Brazil, Uruguay, Argentina, Chile, Bolivia, and Peru.* Washington, D.C., June 30, 1916.

United States, Industrial Commission. *Hearings and Reports* (1899–1902). 19 vols. Washington, D.C., 1900–1902.

United States, Merchant Marine Commission. *Report.* 3 vols. Washington, D.C., 1905.

United States, Shipping Board. *Annual Reports* (1918–22). Washington, D.C., 1919–23.

United States, Shipping Board. "How America Has Come Back Upon The Seas." Washington, D.C., January 31, 1919.

United States, State Department. *Papers Relating to the Foreign Relations of the United States* (1897–1926, including supplements). Washington, D.C., 1898–1941.

United States, State Department. *Papers Relating to the Foreign Relations of the United States: The Lansing Papers, 1914–1920.* 2 vols. Washington, D.C., 1939–40.

United States, Treasury Department. *Annual Reports on the Finances* (1914–18). Washington, D.C., 1915–19.

United States, War Trade Board. *Annual Reports* (1917–19). Washington, D.C., 1917–19.

Unterberger, Betty Miller. *America's Siberian Expedition, 1918–1920.* Durham, N.C.: Duke University Press, 1956.

Vanderlip, Frank A. *The American Commercial Invasion of Europe.* New York: Charles Scribner's Sons, 1902.

Webb, William Joe. "The United States Wooden Steamship Program during World War I." *American Neptune* 35(October 1975):275–88.

Weintraub, Hyman. *Andrew Furuseth: Emancipator of the Seamen.* Berkeley and Los Angeles: University of California Press, 1959.

Wells, David Ames. *The Question of Ships.* New York: G. P. Putnam's Sons, 1890.

Wells, H. G. "The Core of the Trouble: An Englishman to Americans." *The New Republic* 17(November 23, 1918):92–94.

Wiebe, Robert H. *Businessmen and Reform: A Study of the Progressive Movement.* Cambridge, Mass.: Harvard University Press, 1962.

White, Henry. "The Fourth International Conference of the American States." *Annals of the American Academy of Political and Social Science* 36(June 1911):585–93.

Williams, William A. *American–Russian Relations, 1781–1947.* New York: Rinehart, 1952.

Williams, William A. "The Frontier Thesis and American Foreign Policy." *Pacific Historical Review* 24(February 1955):379–95.

Williams, William A. "Rise of an American World Power Complex." In *Struggle Against History: U.S. Foreign Policy in an Age of Revolution,* edited by Neil D. Houghton, pp. 1–19. New York: Simon and Schuster, 1968.

Williams, William A. *The Roots of the Modern American Empire: A Study of the Growth and Shaping of Social Consciousness in a Marketplace Society.* New York: Random House, 1969.

Williams, William A. *The Tragedy of American Diplomacy.* Revised and enl. ed. New York: Dell Publishing Company, 1962.

Wilson, Woodrow. *A Cross Roads of Freedom: The 1912 Campaign Speeches of Woodrow Wilson.* Edited by John Wells Davidson. New Haven, Conn.: Yale University Press, 1956.

Wilson, Woodrow. "Democracy and Efficiency." *Atlantic Monthly* 87(March 1901):289–99.

Wilson, Woodrow. *A History of the American People.* 5 vols. New York: Harper & Brothers Publishers, 1902.

Wilson, Woodrow. "The Ideals of America." *Atlantic Monthly* 90(December 1902):721–34.

Wilson, Woodrow. *The Public Papers of Woodrow Wilson.* Edited by Ray Stannard Baker and William E. Dodd. 6 vols. New York and London: Harper & Brothers Publishers, 1925–27.

Wilson, Woodrow. *Selected Literary and Political Papers and Addresses of Woodrow Wilson.* 3 vols. New York: Grosset & Dunlap, 1926–27.

Wright, Carroll D. "The Commercial Ascendancy of the United States." *Century* 60(July 1900):422–27.

Yamasaki, Kakujiro, and Ogawa, Gotaro. *Effect of the War upon the Commerce and Industry of Japan.* New Haven, Conn.: Yale University Press, 1929.

Zeis, Paul Maxwell. *American Shipping Policy.* Princeton, N.J.: Princeton University Press, 1938.

Index